Programming the *dBase III Plus* User Interface

Programming the *dBase III Plus* User Interface

by

Malcolm C. Rubel

BANTAM BOOKS

TORONTO • NEW YORK • LONDON • SYDNEY • AUCKLAND

To Rachel

Programming the dBase III Plus User Interface
A Bantam Book / June 1987

ISBN 0-553-34408-0

Published simultaneously in the United States and Canada

Bantam Books are published by Bantam Books, Inc. Its trademark, consisting of the
words "Bantam Books" and the portrayal of a rooster, is Registered in U.S. Patent
and Trademark Office and in other countries. Marca Registrada. Bantam Books, Inc.,
666 Fifth Avenue, New York, New York 10103.

PRINTED IN THE UNITED STATES OF AMERICA

BH   0   9   8   7   6   5   4   3   1

Trademarks

dBase, dBase II, dBase III, and *dBase III Plus dBASE Tools for C*, are
trademarks of:

    Ashton-Tate, Inc.
    20101 Hamilton Ave.
    Torrence, CA 90502
    (213) 329-8000

SideKick is a trademark of:

    Borland International, Inc.
    4585 Scotts Valley Dr.
    Scotts Valley, CA 95066
    (408) 438-8696

R&R Relational Report Writer and *dB Report Writer* are trademarks of:

    Concentric Data Systems, Inc.
    18 Lyman St.
    Westborough, MA 01581
    (617) 366-1122

QUICKCODE, QUICKCODE Plus, dGRAPH for dBase and *QUICK-REPORT for dBase* are trademarks of:
Fox & Geller, Inc.
604 Market St.
Elmwood Park, NJ 07407
(201) 794-8883

IBM, IBM PC, IBM AT and *PC-DOS* are trademarks of:
International Business Machines Corp.
Boca Raton, FL 33432

Lotus and *Lotus 1-2-3* are trademarks of:
Lotus Development Corp.
161 First St.
Cambridge, MA 02142
(617) 492-7870

WordStar is a trademark of:
MicroPro International, Inc.
33 San Pablo Ave.
San Rafael, CA 94903
(415) 499-1200

MS-DOS is a trademark of:
Microsoft, Inc.
10700 Northup Way
Bellevue, WA 98004
(206) 828-8080

Clipper and *Nantucket* are trademarks of:
Nantucket Corp.
5995 South Sepulveda Blvd.
Cuver City, CA 90230
(213) 390-7923

dGENERATE is a trademark of:
Tom Rettig Associates
9300 Wilshire Boulevard, Suite 470
Beverly Hills, CA 90212
(213) 272-3784

SSYWHAT?! is a trademark of:
    The Research Group
    88 South Linden Ave.
    South San Francisco, CA 94080
    (415) 571-5019
    (800) HOTWARE (orders)

Flash Code, Flash-Up Windows, and *Speed Screen* are trademarks of:
    The Software Bottling Company of New York
    6600 Long Island Expressway
    Maspeth, NY 11378
    (718) 458-3700

ViewGen is a trademark of:
    Software Tools Development Corp.
    P.O. Box 3870
    Northridge, CA 91323
    (818) 885-0318

dFLOW, The Documentor and *UI Programmer* are trademarks of:
    WallSoft Systems, Inc.
    233 Broadway
    New York, NY 10279
    (212) 406-7026

dB III Compiler, dB Frame, dBXL and *Quicksilver* are trademarks of:
    WordTech Systems, Inc.
    P.O. Box 1747
    Orinda, CA 94563
    (415) 254-0900

XyWrite is a trademark of:
    XyQuest, Inc.
    P.O. Box 372
    Bedford, MA 01730
    (617) 275-4439

Preface

After working with *dBase* for a while and reading most of the good books on the product, I found, as I am sure you have also, that the subject of how to deal with the user interface was treated as a secondary topic by all the authors. This might be fine when the main thrust of the book is introducing people to the basic (and even some more advanced) topics of *dBase III Plus*, but it does the intermediate user no good to suffer through yet another description of the difference between data types when he or she has a very real problem in screen design. The result of this frustration is this book.

Programming The dBase III Plus *User Interface* is not an introductory book, even though it covers the basic commands and functions of the user interface. It is designed for the person that has at least a basic knowledge of *dBase III Plus* and it presupposes this knowledge. Basic *dBase* programming techniques such as arithmetic calculations, table definition, indexing, table linking through the SET RELATION TO command, and other mechanical aspects of getting *dBase III Plus* to work for you are assumed.

Programming The dBase III Plus *User Interface* deals with the programming techniques of the user interface. Before talking about the specifics of programming we will first deal with the basic rules of good screen design and how they impact the development of a specific user interface. Common sense tells you most of what is necessary for good design, but it is necessary to review the basics in this area. Second, we will discuss some of the *dBase* commands and functions that are particularly useful in screen design. Those with more experience with *dBase* might find this section to be repetitive, but you will probably find that the discussion, which is oriented towards the user interface, may bring out points that are not covered in the manual. Finally, we will discuss the nuts and bolts of programming the user interface. The areas that will be covered include the different types of menu design and the mechanics of menu programming, edit screen design and programming, data verification, common errors and how to trap them so that your application does not blow up in your face, how to develop help screens, and finally, how to view information, either on the screen or on paper. Throughout the book, tips will be given on specific programming techniques and program modules that can make the development of your application much easier and of more benefit to the user.

In the final chapter several development aids that are available will be evaluated for their abilities with screen design. The evaluations include the step-by-step creation of a simple data entry screen and an evaluation of the design process and the code that the program generates as a result. You may be surprised at the results of these evaluations.

Throughout this book I will mention differences in capabilities between *dBase III Plus* and two compilers that are available for *dBase* code. Where *Clipper* and *Quicksilver* differ greatly from *dBase* in their capabilities (and limitations) I will point them out.

It is the purpose of this book to identify and discuss the mechanics of the programming techniques that make the interface work. The programs are all stripped of excess "beautification." Color is discussed, but is not used in the programs, as it serves only to clutter up the code. Boxes and extended graphics are kept to a minimum simply because they tend to obscure the code.

The finished user interface is very personal thing. It should reflect not only the user and the environment, but also the developer. Different developers have different creative ideas, some better than others, but all intensely personal. *Programming The* dBase III Plus *User Interface* is designed to assist you in achieving your own design with a minimum of false starts and excess code.

Contents

CHAPTER 1

Basic Rules of
Program Design

Whether you are using *dBase,* Basic, Pascal, or COBOL makes little, if any, difference to the basic rules of good user interface design. Although the user interface is written in a specific program language, a good interface is independent of the language in which it is written. This book deals with *dBase*, but the rules are universal.

Over the past 20 years, a vast amount of work has been done on how humans process information. Surprisingly (or not surprisingly depending on how you think) much of this work was originally undertaken by the U.S. Department of Defense to improve combat pilots' ability to deal with the ever increasing data load being placed on them. Although few computer tasks reach this level of intensity, the findings generally hold true and have been distilled to apply to this environment as well.

Rule Number 1: Be Consistent in Presentation

Human beings are creatures of habit. When we wake up in the morning we expect to find the kitchen in the same place we left it last night. The coffee should still be in the same cupboard that we put it in yesterday so we can make our first cup without searching too much. When we drive a car, no matter which one it is, the accelerator pedal is on the right and the brake pedal is on the left. Although there may be minor differences to the way the car is laid out, we can get behind the wheel and drive it without having to go back and completely relearn the position of all the important controls.

The same should apply to the design of a computer program. Option menus should be designed so they look different enough for the operator to distinguish among them but similar enough to be familiar to the operator. If the main menu is a vertical series of options, then all menus should be a vertical series of options. If you choose an option from the main menu using a one character mnemonic without a carriage return, then all menu selections should be handled that way unless there is a specific reason you (the designer) want to stop the normal flow of the program.

The "geographic" location of information on the screen should be consistent. If you have a new customer data entry form and an existing customer data editing form, they should both have the same information in the same location on the screen. In programming, you may want to put different data checking routines behind the screens and do completely different things with the information once it is entered but, for the operator's benefit, the two screens should be similar if not the same (with different titles to distinguish where the operator is in the program). The reason for this is that people remember information *by location* as well as by labels. It is much easier for the operator if the customer identification number always appears in the same place when it is displayed and that the customer's name is always displayed last name first, first name next, and middle initial last.

The use of words within the interface must be internally consistent and externally obvious. What on one screen is marked SHOE SIZE should not be labeled FOOT SIZE on a different screen when it refers to the same piece of information.

The use of color should be consistent both within the program and with outside conventions as well. Color should be used sparingly but pleasingly. It should communicate something to the user along with the content of the message. A flashing red message, for instance, should mean "danger" and should be used only if the user is about to start a thermonuclear war (or its equivalent). Yellow usually means "caution," and green means "go." When you use color, use it to your advantage.

In fact, color is probably used more than it should be and, in most instances, is used badly. If it produces pleasing combinations on the screen it can enhance the effect of your program. If it is used to excess, however, it not only becomes tiresome quickly, but also can hide important messages and mistakes on the screen. A good rule of thumb is that it is hard to work with more than three colors on the screen at one time.

It is also important to be consistent in the location and color of user prompts and error messages. They should always show up in the same spot on the screen, in the same color from screen to screen.

Rule Number 2: Consider Fluidity of Program Operation

A good program is one in which the next move is not only logical, but follows intuitively from what has gone before. A fluid program does not "get in the way" of the user, but is designed to anticipate the most logical next move and present it. A fluid program does not require superfluous keystrokes from the oeprator, nor does it race ahead so that he or she gets lost.

Fluid program design is somewhat subjective and, to a great extent, depends on the level of expertise of the intended user. Nevertheless, there are many things that are constant, no matter what that level is. These basics include the following:

1. *Keep the operator's hands on the keyboard*. Wherever possible make the next action one that does not require the operator to reorient him- or herself on the keyboard. Although for some reason people love function keys (they are supposed to be easy to use) these keys require that the operator take his or her eyes away from the screen and move the left hand off the home keys to make the proper selection. In certain instances this may be good but, as a general rule, it takes time and interrupts the flow of the program.

2. *Keep the number of choices on a menu limited*. The greater the number of choices presented to an operator, the longer it will take to make a choice and the more difficulty the operator will have making it. As a general rule six or seven options is the

maximum for a normal menu. If more options are offered, they should be sorted into logical groups and be presented in two or more menu levels.

3. *The reverse of the point just made is that good, fluid programs do not require the user to go through multiple levels of menu choices to get to a desired action.* Whenever possible, menu paths should be kept short, requiring the operator to go through no more than two choices to get at most operations. When system complexity is such that this is not possible (given the constraint discussed in point number 1 above) you should design the menu structure so that *the most commonly used commands* are on short menu paths. Those commands that are seldom used can then be restructured onto longer menu paths.

Rule Number 3: Design a System for Its Intended Users _____

A good system is designed for its intended user and not every system design is aptly suited for all users. Work environments, the skill and computer experience of the system operators, the level of system usage, and, finally, the turnover of staff (and consequent training of new operators) all differ for different systems. These factors should be considered when designing your user interface.

Different work environments affect the way that the user interface should be designed. The two factors that influence interface design the most are the lighting and noise levels.

Lighting levels directly affect the use of intense colors. In low light too much high intensity tends to be fatiguing for the operator. In bright light and daylight, high intensity and the use of color becomes necessary if the operator is going to distinguish what is being presented on the screen. Design your program accordingly.

The noise level in the room where the program is going to be run makes a difference on how much you should use the beep to alert the operator to operating conditions. When the room is quiet, use the computer's beep less than you would if the room is noisy. The beep in a quiet room tends to be more annoying than it is in a room filled with noise.

The experience level of users can be defined as a continuum. At one end is the novice user, the person who may know how to put a diskette in a disk drive, but not much more. This person uses their computer only once a month and never can remember from one session to the next just what to do when he wants to run his *Family Budgeting in Five Minutes a Month* program. This person needs all the help and prompting he can get. At the other end of the continuum is the professional user. He or she spends six hours a day at the computer, using the same program to enter telephone orders from customers. The keyboard seems to be just an extension of his or her fingertips. This person does not need or want any prompting other than what is absolutely necessary.

As with the point made in the last paragraph, it makes a difference to the design of your application if the program is going to be used continuously by the operator or if it is going to be used only sporadically. One that is going to be used all the time should be designed for speed and fluidity. More attention will need to be given to informative prompts and safety precautions on programs that are only going to be used once a week for an hour or two.

Finally, operator turnover should be considered when designing your system. In a relatively stable environment, the ease with which a program can be learned does not need to be considered in front of some other design factors. In an environment where turnover is a factor, it will be necessary to take the ease with which your program can be learned into consideration when you design your interface.

The impact of these differing levels of user expertise on interface design is great. The challenge to the developer is to design a system that gives enough help to the lower limit of user experience while keeping user prompts and data security confirmations at a level that will not frustrate the more experienced user.

A corollary of this rule is to design computer programs to parallel the manual systems that they are intended to replace as closely as possible. This does not mean that you should simply mimic the manual systems, for this would mean that you would be giving up the possible advantages that a computerized system can give, but rather that the flow of the system should be familiar to the workers who will use it. Most cases of "failed" system implementations have not followed this rule and have paid for it.

Rule Number 4: Keep It Simple Stupid

After much heartache I have finally discovered that, without fail, the simplest way to do something is always the best. While this applies to life as well, when applied to programming it means that oversophistication increases development time by a factor of four and increases the chances for undetected errors by a factory of 16. (These statistics are fully documented in my own program rewrites.) When applied to the user interface, *keeping it simple* also applies to the operator as well. If you think that complex programming can make a program unusable, imagine when a careless operator can do if a poorly designed interface leaves him floundering.

Complexity in any form should be eliminated from the operator interface. The use of color should be kept to a minimum as too much or too many colors is confusing to the user. Any necessary prompts should be short, sequentially correct, and in the active voice. Never use a paragraph when a sentence will do and never leave any room for doubt in the operator's mind as to what has to be done next. Always give the prompt as a command. "Place the diskette in Drive A" is much clearer than "The diskette should be placed in Drive A." The same keys should be used for substantially the same purposes throughout the program. Critical information should always be verified, but once found correct, should not be passed before the operator for further checking. The list goes on. Use your head and, in the process of simulation, make sure that you do not get overly tired of the prompts and confirmations that the program puts in front of you. If you tire of them, chances are the user will also.

Rule Number 5: Give the Operator Feedback _____

I like user-friendly programs. I distinguish user-friendly programs from "chatty" ones that make me read what is being said before acting on a command. A user-friendly program tells the user what is going on as he is performing an operation. A single example will suffice here. When recreating an index (or when reindexing a large file) *dBase* sometimes takes several minutes to complete the task. Rather than have the screen go blank, or worse, "freeze up," it is a welcome relief to the user to know that *something* is going on and the computer did not "break down." All of us have ended up pounding different keys trying to bring the computer back to life. *dBase* clears the screen and puts up the message "Please wait. Indexing Database. Main Menu will appear when reindexing completed." on the screen while the computer is busy rather than leave the user unable to figure out what is going on. I know of several instances where people have turned off their computers and started again, thinking that something was wrong. The resulting corruption of the database is just the beginning of a user's problems.

Rule Number 6: Make the System "Crashproof"

Perhaps I should say that as the designer, you should make the system as crashproof as you can. There is nothing you can do to stop the user from turning off the computer in the middle of a session. You can, however, warn him or her at the beginning of the session that an interruption of power (the polite way to say "turning off the machine") while the program is in operation will result in serious problems with the database (here is also a good place to put in your telephone number so that they will know who to call if this happens).

Do not offer a user more than one way out of any program or subroutine. *Always* make "Quit" an option from the main menu and *always* inform the user to *leave the computer turned on until the DOS prompt appears on the screen*. The average user will type "Q" to quit and then immediately turn off the machine, assuming that everything is finished. Depending on how you have designed the system this can create minor damage or massive problems.

Always test everything. Even something as simple as a "yes/no" confirmation should not allow the user to enter a "T" or an "M."

Do not allow a user to "escape" directly out of trouble. Design the program to bring up a quit option menu that will allow you to clean up the damage that may have been done to a record.

Never allow the user to write directly to a field in a record unless you are looking for trouble. Always write to a memory variable and always run a complete validation routine on that memory variable *before* allowing its contents to be written into the file.

Storing information to memory variables has a second benefit: you can design your systems so that the data tables are only open to "load" the memory variables. The tables can then be closed (simply as a precaution against inadvertent power interruption and the resulting loss of the table header information). The data tables can then be reopened when the user has decided that his or her editing session on that record is over so that the modified memory variables can replace the contents of the data fields in the database.

As an extra precaution, use transaction files whenever you can and update the master files only at the end of the day. That way, if there are any problems, they can be edited out in the daily transaction files rather than in the primary databases. In addition, always keep sequential backups of your data. If the worst happens, you will not destroy everything.

There is much more that you can do to make your systems crashproof. We will be discussing some of these precautions in the following chapters.

dBase III Plus User Interface Structure and Commands

This chapter discusses the basic command verbs and functions that are available in *dBase III Plus* for the user interface, and discusses some of the programming applications in which they may be used. The command verbs are precisely that: the action verbs of the *dBase* language.Continuing with the grammatical syntax, the functions are the objects of the verbs and augment the *dBase* commands. The discussion is by no means complete. In certain instances, detailed programming can and should be used to control the user interface.

It is assumed that readers have a basic knowledge of *dBase*.

User Interface Commands

It is impossible to separate out particular commands of the *dBase III Plus* language and term them solely "user interface" commands. The following discussion is restricted to those commands that are generally used in building the user interface. The commands are broken down into these categories:

Operating Environment Commands: These commands deal with the operating environment of the program, and how *dBase III Plus* responds to the user.

Screen Presentation Commands: These commands deal with "painting" screens for the user, including both fixed text and data from data tables.

Data Acceptance Commands: This subset of commands allows the programmer to get information from the user and do something with it. It includes both data intended for the database and data used in program control.

Data Validation Commands: These commands fall into two different categories. The first set contains the simple data validation commands supplied by *dBase III Plus*. The second set is a bit more complicated as they are, in reality, programs themselves designed to test whether certain conditions are met by the data.

Operating Environment Commands _____

The operating environment command set includes the 50 SET commands contained in *dBase III Plus*. Each of them affects the way that the program operates. Not all, however, affect the user interface. We will only cover those commands that significantly affect how the user sees the application.

SET BELL on/off   Default for SET BELL in ON. When this environment command is enabled, the "bell" (usually a beep) sounds under certain conditions, such as when the operator completely fills a data field or when an error has been made in data entry.

When this command is enabled, it sometimes seems that the bell is sounding all the time. In certain situations it can become truly annoying and, like the boy who cried wolf, there is no difference between the bell that sounds when a field is full and the bell that sounds over a data entry error. My preference is to set the bell function OFF and alert the user to a data entry error by using the ON ERROR command. ON ERROR allows me to sound the bell as follows:

```
ON ERROR
   ?? CHR(7)
   DO ERROR
```

The "?? CHR(7)" "rings" the bell to alert the user that an error has been made. The "DO ERROR" transfers program control to an error program that allows me to customize the help that the user gets in dealing with the error.

Setting the bell off is not without its problems, however. If you use SET BELL OFF together with SET CONFIRM OFF you can run into data entry trouble when a fast typist is not paying attention to the screen. As there is no beep at the end of the field, data simply "flows" into the next field. For this reason I usually SET CONFIRM to ON.

SET CARRY on/off   Default for SET CARRY is OFF. The SET CARRY option only works with full-screen commands like APPEND and INSERT. When SET CARRY is ON, it carries the values from the last record into the next as starting values. The operator then has the option of accepting them, or changing them as necessary. Unfortunately *all* data is carried over, so you cannot select the fields you need. As this command works only in the full-screen *dBase* mode, it is not that useful. Instead, default values can be implemented conveniently be preloading memory variables with default values before GETting them to the screen.

SET CENTURY on/off   Default for SET CENTURY is OFF. When it is enabled all dates show a four-digit year.

A word of warning: the SET CENTURY ON and the date-to-character conversion function, DTOC(), are not completely compatible when the date is used as a part of an index. While the FIND and SEEK commands will work properly, the GOTO command will produce an error message stating that the record is not in the index.

SET COLOR on/off   SET COLOR is either ON with a color monitor or OFF with a monochrome monitor when *dBase* is loaded. When more than one monitor is used on a system this environment command allows you to select between the color display and the monochrome display.

SET COLOR TO [f1/b1] [,f2/b2] [,border]   The SET COLOR TO command accepts one basic parameter and two optional parameters.

Normal text (f1/b1) is the basic parameter. The two optional parameters are enhanced text (f2/b2) and the border color around the 25 x 80 screen area. The default values for normal text are white letters on a black background. The default for enhanced text (data fields, error messages, and other special text) is black letters on a white background (inverse video). The default for the screen border is black. Both foreground and background colors can be selected for normal and enhanced text. If you fail to specify a color, the last color you specified will be used. If none was specified earlier in the program, the color will be the default. The color options are:

Table 2.1. Set Color Selections

Color	Number Code	Letter Code
Black	0	N
Blue	1	B
Green	2	G
Cyan	3	BG
Red	4	R
Magenta	5	RB
Brown	6	GR
White	7	W
Blinking	*	
High Intensity	+	

Users of monochrome systems can also use SET COLOR TO. U will give you underlining. I gives inverse video. The + and the * parameters give you high intensity and blinking video as well. If you are careful when you select colors and intensities, they will work well on a monochrome system. One interesting note: low intensity blue shows up as underlining on a monochrome screen.

Remember, if you must have color, be sparing with its use. Your users will have to look at your color combinations for hours on end. Be careful not to set the foreground and the background to the same color. If you do, your text may be there, but you will not be able to see it.

SET CONFIRM on/off The default for SET CONFIRM is OFF. When SET CONFIRM is ON, the user must finish an entry into a field with a carriage return. When SET CONFIRM is OFF, the cursor automatically jumps to the next field when the current one is completely filled.

SET CONSOLE on/off The default for SET CONSOLE is ON. The SET CONSOLE OFF command inhibits the display of output and keyboard input to the screen. It does not have any effect on output routed to the printer. The SET CONSOLE OFF command is used primarily to suppress output to the screen while the SET PRINT command is ON and output is directed to the printer. The SET CONSOLE OFF command is also useful in password routines when the developer does not want the valid entry to be shown on the screen for security reasons.

Care must always be taken to couple a SET CONSOLE OFF command with a SET CONSOLE ON command, otherwise the screen display will remain off.

SET DATE American/ANSI/British/French/German/Italian The default date presentation is American. With SET CENTURY OFF the date presentation for the various options are:

Table 2.2. Date Presentation Options

American	mm/dd/yy
ANSI	yy.mm.dd
British	dd/mm/yy
French	dd/mm/yy
German	dd.mm.yy
Italian	dd-mm-yy

If you are looking for a difference between the British and the French date presentation, there is none. I suppose that the two are there because the British could not bear to have their dates set to the French format, and vice-versa.

The ANSI format makes sorting much easier as the date is arranged in the proper sort order.

SET DECIMALS TO n   The default for SET DECIMALS TO is 2. The SET DECIMALS TO command determines the minimum number of decimal places that will be displayed as a result of division, square root, exponent, and log operations.

The number of decimal places shown in a result is determined by the number of decimal places in the operators or the value of the SET DECIMALS TO command. With the default setting of 2 the results of the following calculations are:

```
   2 / 3       =    .67

   2 / 3.000   =    .667
```

This environment can be modified by the SET FIXED ON command to force only the number of decimal places specified in the SET-DECIMALS TO command to be shown.

SET DELETED on/off   The default value for SET DELETED is OFF. With the default value, records marked for deletion (but not yet deleted with a PACK command) are still shown as if they were part of the database.

SET DELIMITERS on/off, SET DELIMITERS TO   The default for SET DELIMITERS on/off is OFF. The default for SET DELIMITERS TO is a colon (:). The SET DELIMITERS command influences how field widths are shown in the full-screen mode. The field itself is shown in reverse video unless the SET INTENSITY OFF command is in effect. The default SET DELIMITERS setting of OFF gives the user nothing to mark the beginning and end of the field. The SET DELIMITERS ON command gives the user the default colon. If, for some reason, you wish to have the fields delimited with another character or characters, you can do this with the SET DELIMITERS TO command. Placing a single character in quotes after the command (SET DELIMITERS TO "*", for example) will mark both the beginning and the end of the field with an "*". If two characters are included between the quotes the first will mark the beginning of the field and the second will mark the end.

SET DEVICE TO screen/print   The default for SET DEVICE TO is SCREEN. In this mode the output from the @ SAY commands is directed to the screen. With SET DEVICE TO PRINT, the results of

@ SAY commands will be sent to the printer. The SET DEVICE TO PRINT command sends all information included in SAY commands to the printer. Do not try to send information to the printer using GETs: they are ignored.

A word of warning: when the SET DEVICE TO command is put to PRINT, care must be taken that no @ SAY command has a row number less than the one before. If this happens, the program will issue a form feed command before printing that row.

SET ESCAPE on/off   The default setting for SET ESCAPE is ON. With SET ESCAPE ON the user can interrupt the program while it is processing by pressing the **Escape** key. The user then has the option to cancel or suspend processing or ignore the interruption and continue with the program. If SET ESCAPE is OFF, you cannot interrupt the program while processing is being done.

SET ESCAPE also has an effect on the conditional command ON ESCAPE. SET ESCAPE must be ON in order for the program to recognize the ON ESCAPE commands.

If the user is in the middle of a READ he or she can terminate that READ by pressing the **Escape** key with SET ESCAPE either OFF or ON. There is no difference. If you are going to compile your application with *Clipper*, this is not the case. You must have SET ESCAPE ON in order to escape in this fashion in the middle of a READ.

Pressing the **Escape** key in the middle of a READ will end the READ, whether SET ESCAPE is ON or OFF.

SET EXACT on/off   The default for SET EXACT is OFF. This environment command influences how two character strings are compared. If SET EXACT is ON, the two character strings must match exactly for there to be a match. If SET EXACT is OFF, the comparison is true as long as the character string on the left of the operator starts out the same as the charcter string on the right of the operator. In other words, with SET EXACT OFF, "There" = "The" would return a TRUE, while "The" = "There" would return a FALSE.

This may sound trivial, but it is not. In the following example, whether SET EXACT is ON or OFF makes a world of difference.

```
List for Lastname = "T"
```

With SET EXACT ON only those people with last names of T will be listed. With SET EXACT OFF, all people with names beginning with T will be included.

SET FIELDS on/off, SET FIELDS TO <field list/all>   The default for SET FIELDS is OFF. The SET FIELDS TO command allows the developer to restrict the access to only the specified list of fields in the data tables. This listing is activated using the SET FIELDS ON command.

In order to reset the program to look at all fields you must either specify SET FIELDS OFF or reset SET FIELDS TO ALL, eliminating the previous field list.

SET FILTER TO fieldname/condition   There is no default value to this command. When a SET FILTER TO fieldname/condition is given only those records that satisfy the filter condition will be shown in all database operations. A SET FILTER TO salary > $25,000 will retrieve only those records that contain a salary figure greater than $25,000. Different SET FILTER TO conditions can be given for each open data table. This is a powerful tool in selecting data for viewing. To cancel the filter condition a SET FILTER TO without an argument must be issued.

SET FIXED on/off   The default for SET FIXED is OFF. In this state the SET DECIMALS TO command is not in effect and the number of decimal places is decided according to the rationale explained in the SET DECIMALS TO command explanation. When SET FIXED is ON, the number of decimal places defined in the SET DECIMALS TO <n> command will be displayed.

SET FORMAT TO <format filename>   There is no default value for this command. When SET FORMAT TO <filename> is given, the named format file is opened for data entry and editing. To close that format file, you must issue either a CLOSE FORMAT command or a SET FORMAT TO command without a filename.

SET FUNCTION n TO <expression>   For those of you who love function keys, this command allows you to reprogram all but the **F1** (help) function key to expressions of your choice. Strings can be either character or numeric and carriage returns can be represented by a semicolon (;). In the expression above, "n" represents the number of the function key. The maximum length of a string assigned to a function key is 254 characters. Much more can be done with the function keys using the INKEY( ) function. See the end of Chapter 3 for more information on the use of Function Keys.

SET HEADING on/off The default setting for SET HEADING is ON. SET HEADING ON displays the field names as a column title when a DISPLAY, LIST, SUM, or AVERAGE is performed. SET HEADING OFF suppresses this display.

SET INTENSITY on/off The default for SET INTENSITY is ON. With SET INTENSITY ON, fields are highlighted in reverse video. With SET INTENSITY OFF, fields are not so highlighted. When SET INTENSITY is OFF and you are using a color monitor, the enhanced video attributes of a SET COLOR TO command are inoperative.

SET MARGIN TO nn The SET MARGIN TO nn command does nothing to screen output but it acts as a left margin command when output is directed to the printer with a SET PRINTER ON or a SET DEVICE TO PRINT command. If you are contemplating using Nantucket's compiler, *Clipper*, care should be taken using this command as it does not work with the SET DEVICE TO PRINT command. The solution for this problem is to add a memory variable to the column location (cc + mvar) and start column positions at 00. By STOREing a numeric value to your memory variable, you can move all column locations to the right by that amount.

SET MEMOWIDTH TO nn The default value for SET MEMO-WIDTH TO is 50. The MEMOWIDTH controls the width of memo fields during output.

SET MESSAGE TO "character string" SET MESSAGE TO displays the specified character string on line 24 of the video display. The displayed message is erased by issuing a SET MESSAGE TO without a character string. The message is displayed only if SET STATUS is ON so the message displays below the status bar that occupies line 22. This makes the command less than totally useful. As this is not a compiler command, it should not be used if you are planning to compile your application. For these reasons the SET MESSAGE TO command is not of any real value. I SAY my messages and put them where I want them to go. I recommend that you do the same.

SET PRINT on/off The default value for SET PRINT is OFF. SET PRINT ON activates the printer and sends everything except full-screen displays using @ SAYs to the printer. To send @ SAYs you must use SET DEVICE TO PRINT. To send output to the printer that is not echoed on the screen use the SET CONSOLE OFF command.

When you have finished printing, be sure that you reset your environment with SET PRINT OFF and SET CONSOLE ON. If you do not, you will find yourself looking at your printer to find out what is happening with your program.

SET SAFETY on/off   The default value is ON. SET SAFETY provides confirmation prompts for potentially dangerous actions, such as overwriting files that already exist on disk and overwriting existing index files. While in the interactive mode these safety warnings are useful, but when you are writing application programs you do not want to have your user interrupted even when you are intentionally overwriting existing files. I recommend that SET SAFETY be turned OFF in most circumstances. When you want to get a confirmation from the user, write it yourself.

SET SCOREBOARD on/off   The default for SET SCOREBOARD is ON. With SET SCOREBOARD ON, *dBase III Plus* will tell you whether the record that you are working on has been marked for deletion and whether you are in insert or overwrite mode. The program will give you a prompt when input in a GET is not valid.
    SET SCOREBOARD works with SET STATUS. When SET STATUS is ON, the error information appears on the status line (22) of the screen. When SET STATUS is OFF, the information appears on line 0 of the screen. When SET SCOREBOARD is OFF, the error information is not shown. If SET BELL is also OFF, no tone will sound either.
    SET SCOREBOARD is a wonderful feature and, if you are not planning to compile your application, it can save you plenty of coding time as you get satisfactory feedback from features supplied by *dBase*. If you are planning to compile your application, the SCOREBOARD will not work, so you will have to code your error routine instead of relying on the one supplied by the program. As you can program greater error trapping than the program allows, you should do this anyway.

SET STATUS on/off   The default for SET STATUS is ON. SET STATUS ON gives you an inverse video bar across the screen at line 22. I have set it off in my CONFIG.DB file and find that I do not miss it at all.

Screen Presentation Commands

I like to differentiate between *dBase*'s screen presentation commands and data acceptance commands discussed in the next section. I find that it helps make the distinction between two completely different aspects of *dBase*. Screen presentation commands have to do with "painting" text and graphics on the screen. They do not influence data presentation and editing, but serve as the shell around the data presentation.

Screen presentation, although not directly linked to the capture, editing, and presentation of data, are vitally important to the ease with which a system can be used. Poorly presented screens are tiring, expose the system to data error, and are just not aesthetically pleasing. Last, but not least, the screen presentation is inextricably linked to how a system is perceived by the user. The best programming in the world is not visible to the user if the look of the screen stares him or her in the face all day long.

@ rr,cc This command positions the cursor at the appropriate spot on the screen and erases to the end of the specified row. The screen is 25 lines (rows) long and 80 columns wide. *dBase* starts at row 0 and goes through row 24 and starts at column 0 and goes to column 79.

@ rr,cc CLEAR This command will clear from the given cursor position to row 24, column 79. Everything beneath the cursor position will go. This command is useful in multiscreen entry formats where certain information is to remain on the screen. It will allow that information to occupy the upper portion of the screen while the lower portion is rewritten.

@ rr,cc CLEAR TO rr,cc This command is new to *dBase III Plus*. Unlike @ rr,cc CLEAR, which deletes from the given position to the end of the screen, CLEAR TO deletes all screen information in the box defined by the two sets of coordinates. The first set defines the upper left corner of the box, the second defines the lower right. Trying to define the upper right and lower left will not work.

CLEAR works on a single line with the first set of coordinates defining the starting point and the second set defining the end so this command can be used to blank the message line. The only problem is that *Clipper* does not recognize this command. Use @ rr,cc SAY space (nn) where "nn" is the number of spaces to be cleared.

@ rr,cc SAY <expression> [PICTURE] The SAY command displays characters on the screen starting at the specified coordinates. What you put on the screen can be either text or data. If it is text, it is enclosed in either single or double quotes. If it is data, the <expression> must be either a data field or a memory variable.

Data presented using a SAY command (as opposed to a GET command) cannot be edited. You can control data presentation by using the PICTURE functions and template symbols that will be discussed in Chapter 5.

Because *dBase III Plus* is an interpreter and reads each line of the program separately, screens paint faster if all @ SAYs for a single screen line are included in a single command rather than being broken up on to several different lines.

A command line that reads as follows:

```
@ 05,15 SAY "Title:                    Pay Grade: "
```

paints 25 percent faster than if the command were put on two lines like this:

```
@ 05,15 SAY "Title: "
@ 05,40 SAY "Pay Grade: "
```

In this example the actual time difference may not be appreciable, but in complicated screens it can make a significant difference.

Data that is to be sent to the printer must be presented with SAYs, not GETs. Any GETs that appear in a file that is being sent to the printer will be ignored. When sending data to the printer, the column coordinate maximum is 255, giving you the capability of printing on wide carriage printers and in compressed type. When sending data to a printer make sure that the row for each successive SAY is not less than the one that precedes it. If this happens, the program will issue a form feed before printing the new data. Make sure also that the column coordinates for successive SAYs on the same row have ascending values.

@ rr,cc TO rr,cc [DOUBLE]   This command will draw either a single line or double line (if the word DOUBLE is included after the coordinates) box on the screen with the upper left corner of the box placed at the first set of coordinates and the lower right corner placed at the second set of coordinates. As boxes seem to be all the rage in menu design and, as *dBase III* did not have a command that would allow you to construct a box easily, *dBase III Plus* includes this command. While the command makes basic box drawing much simpler than the old method, it is not supported by *Clipper*. *Clipper* has its own @ BOX function that allows you to define not only the coordinates for the two corners, but also the characters that are to be used for the four corners, the four sides, and to fill in the box. Unfortunately the two commands are not compatible, so you must use "@ SAYs" if you want to run your application in both interpreted and compiled forms or use the *Clipper* PUBLIC variable, which allows the user to identify specific commands that are to be used if the program is running under *dBase III Plus* and other commands that are to be used if the program is running as a compiled *Clipper* program.

    Quicksilver handles boxes in the same manner as *dBase III Plus*, but goes into a completely different realm with its SET WINDOW command. Boxes in *dBase* are just that: boxes on the screen. With *Quicksilver*, a box can also be a window that appears the same to the user, but is *completely* different as far as what the developer can do with it. A "window" (as opposed to a box) can be made in the active portion of the screen and allows the developer to use that part to run different programs. The possibilities are immense but, unfortunately, are completely outside the capabilities of *dBase III Plus*. They are **not** outside the capabilities of WordTech System's *dBase III Plus* work-alike *dBXL:* the full set of window functions are included in this product, which makes development and debugging for *Quicksilver* possible while running an interpreter. The *Quicksilver* W.SET WINDOW also includes the capability of "naming" the background fill character so that, if you wished (keep in mind screen simplicity and ease of viewing) you could have "$"s as a background fill character for a window (box) that deals with financial matters.

CLEAR   CLEAR does what its name implies. It clears the screen of all information and presents you with a blank screen with the cursor positioned at 00,00. Without issuing a CLEAR command before presenting new data, the old information will stay on the screen. This can get confusing quickly. Make a habit of issuing a CLEAR at the beginning of a program, within it as necessary, and again at the end of the program. This may seem excessive, but you will be amazed at the number of times during development that one screen writes on top of another.

TEXT <text...> ENDTEXT   TEXT and ENDTEXT are two separate commands. TEXT starts the block of characters and ENDTEXT (on a separate line) ends the block. The text will be placed on the screen (or to the printer) exactly as it is typed. The command in effect suspends the interpreter and allows whatever is written to be put to the screen or the printer.

With larger blocks of text that will be occupying the screen without any interaction with the user, the TEXT-ENDTEXT function allows the developer to get away from using @ rr,cc SAYs. In certain circumstances, it can save some typing.

Data Acceptance Commands

Once a structure for viewing and editing information has been painted on the screen, the user must have some way of communicating with the program to influence the course of action that it takes and to enter and edit data in the system. The data acceptance commands provide these ways.

@ rr,cc GET <expression> [PICTURE <picture clause>] [RANGE <lower, upper limit>]   The GET displays the contents of either the field name or the named memory variable (if there are any contents) and allows the user to either enter new data or change the existing data contained within that expression. The GET must be followed by a READ statement to confirm those changes.

Like the @ SAY statement, the GET can be formatted using the PICTURE function. The PICTURE function, however, is materially different when used with an @ GET statement. Not only will it format the input field, it will also not allow data outside the specification of the PICTURE clause to be placed in the field. Numbers, for instance, can be excluded from a character field (even though a character field by itself will accept them) simply by attaching the appropriate PICTURE clause to the GET. RANGEs can also be specified for numeric characters using the RANGE function. Details on these functions are included in Chapter 5, which covers data validation and error checking.

ACCEPT [<prompt>] TO <mvar>   ACCEPT TO allows the user to type in a character string of up to 254 characters and have that string placed into memory as the specified memory variable. Data entry is terminated by a carriage return. The optional prompt must be delimited by either single or double quotes, or brackets.

INPUT [<prompt>] TO <mvar>   INPUT TO is the same as but different from ACCEPT TO. While ACCEPT TO will only allow the input of a character string, INPUT TO will accept any legal data type or expression and initialize the memory variable to that data type. Data entry is terminated when the user hits the carriage return.

INPUT TO is also different from ACCEPT TO in that if the user simply hits the carriage return (as if to create a null string) either the memory variable will not be created (if it does not already exist) or the contents of it will remain unchanged (if it already exists).

READ [save]   A READ must be issued to activate the series of GETs that precedes it. GETs without a READ mean nothing. When a READ is issued all the GETs issued since the last READ will be activated. The cursor will be placed in the entry field for the first GET issued. A maximum of 128 GETs can be activated by a single READ command.

It all sounds so simple, but it is not. The READ statement is one of the major user interface commands that *dBase* offers the programmer to control the action on the screen with the user. Used with other commands, it behaves differently.

A simple READ statement carries with it an implicit CLEAR GETS. This means that the GETS that are associated with the command are cleared and deactivated *except* when using a multipage FORMAT (.FMT) file. Here READ not only activates the GETs, it serves as a page break point for each data screen. When either the last GET before the READ is filled and a carriage return is issued or the user presses **PgDn**, *dBase* will go on to the second data screen. To go back to the first screen, the user must press **PgUp**. What the manual does not say is that, unless you place the format file within a data acceptance loop (see Chapter 4) when the final field of the final screen is filled or when **PgDn** is pressed while on the final screen, *dBase* terminates the READ and saves the values to the appropriate data tables.

The problem with using the multiscreen format file approach to multiple screen data entry procedures is that the *dBase III Plus* improvements do not work on either of the two compilers. There are other, less elegant, procedures that can provide you with the same features and will work not only with *dBase III Plus*, but also with *dBase III* and the compilers.

If you do not want your GETs to be cleared, you must use the READ SAVE command. The save option deactivates the implicit CLEAR GETS command of the READ statement. The contents of all activated GETs remain in place until an explicit CLEAR GETS command is issued. A simple CLEAR command also has the effect of clearing the GETs.

WAIT [<prompt>] TO <mvar>   WAIT without a prompt string and without a TO clause will issue a "Press any key to continue..."

statement at column 0 of the line that the cursor is on and will suspend execution of the program until any key on the keyboard is pressed.

WAIT with a prompt string (even if the prompt string is the null string " ") will suppress the "Press any key to continue..." string and will substitute the prompt string, starting at column 0 of the line that the cursor is on and will wait for a key press before continuing the execution of the program.

WAIT TO <mvar> will store a one-character string to the named memory variable and will continue execution of the program after that single character is accepted. The program does not wait for a carriage return. The data type is always "character."

Keyboard Interpretation Commands_____

dBase III Plus includes several very valuable improvements over its predecessors in its ability to deal with direct interpretation of key presses. The INKEY( ) and READKEY( ) functions and the ON KEY, ON ESCAPE, and ON ERROR commands that serve to branch the program to a separate processing routine when the proper condition is met.

INKEY( )   The INKEY( ) function returns the ASCII value of the current key press. It does *not* continually test for a certain condition, but rather works only at the specific point in the program where it is located. INKEY( ) allows the developer to design programs that make use of the nonalphanumeric keys on the IBM PC keyboard. A good example of the use of the INKEY( ) function is in the "bounce bar" menu program in the Menu Design chapter (Listing 3.5).

INKEY( ) returns ASCII values for the cursor keypad keys as shown in the Table 2.3.

The simple program as shown in Listing 2.1 will give you the ASCII value on any key press.

It is important to note that this little program contains a DO WHILE loop to determine the value of the INKEY( ) function. This is necessary as INKEY( ) evaluates the "current" key press, not the last key pressed. When waiting for a key press in a menu program, you must stop the program to wait for a key press in this manner, or INKEY( ) will not work properly.

READKEY( )   READKEY( ) returns a numeric value of the key pressed to exit a full-screen *dBase III Plus* operation such as APPEND,

Table 2.3.   INKEY( ) Return Values

KEY	ASCII VALUE
Up Arrow	5
Down Arrow	24
Left Arrow	19
Right Arrow	4
PgUp	18
PgDn	3
Home	29
End	23
Insert	22
Delete	7

Listing 2.1.   INKEY( ) Value Program

```
CLEAR
STORE 0 TO I
@ 5,10 SAY "PRESS A KEY"

DO WHILE I = 0
  I = INKEY()
ENDDO

@ 10,30 SAY "KEY VALUE OF KEYPRESS IS " I
```

INSERT, BROWSE, or EDIT. Interrogating this value in a DO CASE construct gives the programmer a versatile tool to use in determining what action to take. The value of READKEY( ) is incremented by 256 if any of the displayed data has been updated. Thus "terminate with save" (either **Control W** or **Control <End>**), which returns a value of 14 from READKEY( ) when no data has been changed, returns a value of 270 when data has been modified.

If you are going to use the full-screen edit functions of *dBase III Plus*, the READKEY( ) function can be a powerful and very flexible tool. Unfortunately, the function has no direct equivalent with any of the compilers, which do not support the full-screen operations of *dBase*.

Clipper has a function called LASTKEY( ), which is similar to READKEY( ) in that it stores the value of the last key pressed. It is different from READKEY( ) in that it stores the value for all situations and operates more like INKEY( ) without the need to work within a loop.

ON KEY   ON KEY is a *dBase* command while INKEY( ) is a *dBase* function. ON KEY will execute the action described following the command whenever a key is pressed. Unlike just a simple INKEY( ) function, the ON KEY command will stop processing after the command that was being processed is finished. ON KEY will not, for example, stop an index procedure in the middle. *dBase III Plus* will process the ON KEY commands after the line of code that caused the indexing. Listing 2.2 shows the use of ON KEY to allow a user to interrupt printing.

The routine allows printing until the end of the file is reached unless a key press suspends operation. Several points must be made about the use of ON KEY. First, make sure that you reset the command after it is no longer needed using the ON KEY <cr> command as is shown in Listing 2.2. If you do not do this you may find some unintended actions taking place in your program. Second, be sure to clear out the memory variable (in the this case "key") after the ON KEY sub-program has used it, otherwise the action will continue to be repeated.

ON ERROR   The ON ERROR command branches processing to the specified routine (or program) when an error is detected. It can be extremely useful in recovering from serious errors on the part of the user. When used with the ERROR( ) function (which returns a numeric value of the error) the ON ERROR command can handle any number of problems through a single procedure file containing the proper CASE statements relating to the value of the ERROR( ) function.

ON ERROR responds only to *dBase III Plus* errors. The command is not functional with operating system errors.

ON ESCAPE   ON ESCAPE offers the developer the option of allowing the user to interrupt the program and perform conditional processing at any time by pressing the **Escape** key. ON ESCAPE works only when SET ESCAPE is ON. ON ESCAPE takes precedence over ON KEY and, unless there is a specific reason to use ON KEY (such as a need to keep SET ESCAPE OFF), it is usually a better choice than ON KEY for program control.

Listing 2.2.   Stop Print Routine

```
@ 23,10 SAY "Press A to abort or P to pause printing"

<Start Printing Routine>

STORE "" TO key
ON KEY WAIT TO key

DO WHILE .NOT. EOF()

  DO CASE
    CASE UPPER(key) = "A"
      DO abort
    CASE UPPER(key) = "P"
      @ 23,00 CLEAR
      @ 23,10 SAY "Press any key to start printing again"
      WAIT ""
    OTHERWISE
      <do processing>
  ENDCASE

  STORE "" TO key

ENDDO

ON KEY
```

Data Validation Commands

The data acceptance and validation commands that are included in *dBase III Plus* can only be described as limited in nature. There are several things that make the program's capabilities in this area less than you would desire. Probably the most unfortunate factor is *dBase III Plus*'s inability to do anything in the middle of a READ. Because of this, you will be limited by *dBase* in the data validation that you can do during a READ to the simple PICTURE and RANGE clause validations that can be added to a GET statement. More sophisticated data checking routines must be performed after a READ is finished on data that has already been accepted into memory variables.

PICTURE   The *dBase III Plus* programming language includes an extensive sub-language for controlling data acceptance. The PICTURE functions and template symbols make up a large part of this language. The template functions allow the developer to specify what types of data will be acceptable for a specific GET and how that data will be shown to the user later in other GETs or SAYs. The template symbols can be used either separately or with the template functions to limit the types and lengths of data in specific GETs.

A PICTURE statement typically is made up of a single function (only one is allowed) followed by a space and then followed by a set of template symbols. The total statement is termed the PICTURE clause and, depending on what is included in the clause, it will regulate what is allowed into a field and how that data will be shown. A PICTURE clause takes the following form:

@ rr,cc GET <variable> PICTURE "@(function) (symbols)"

PICTURE functions all are preceeded by an "@" sign. There are five PICTURE functions used for working with numeric data, two functions for working with the date data type, and three for working with character data.

The numeric PICTURE functions and their uses are:

@C   for displaying a positive number with a "CR"
@X   for displaying a negative number with a "DB"
@(for displaying a negative number in parentheses
@Z   for suppressing zeros in null or blank fields
@B   for displaying numbers left justified

The character PICTURE functions and their uses are:

@A   for restricting input to alpha characters only
@!   for converting all alpha data to uppercase
@R   for removing literal symbols from the stored data

The date PICTURE functions and their uses are:

@D   for displaying a date in the mm/dd/yy format
@E   for displaying a date in the dd/mm/yy format

There is one other picture function, @S<n> which is different from the others discussed. If you have a very long field and cannot (or do not want to) display the entire field on the screen at once, you can use this command to open a "window" <n> spaces long for your data. As you type in the contents of the field the window "scrolls" to the left. You can go back and edit the data by scrolling back the other way as well.

PICTURE symbols control the length and the formatting of the GET. As with the functions, some of the symbols deal with numbers, some with character data, and one with logical data.

The PICTURE symbols associated with numbers and their uses are:

9   allows only digits to be entered
allows digits, blanks, and signs to be entered
.   specifies the position of the decimal point
,   shows a comma if one is needed there
$ fills in leading zeros with dollar signs
*   fills in leading zeros with asterisks

The PICTURE symbols associated with character data and their uses are:

A   allows only letters to be entered
N   allows letters and digits to be entered
X   allows any character to be entered
!   converts alpha character to uppercase
L   allows only logical data (T,t,F,f,Y,y,N,n) to be entered

The PICTURE symbol "L" is *not* used with logical data fields. It is used only to restrict data entry in a character field. The PICTURE symbol associated with the logical data type is the "Y" symbol, which converts a "T" for and "F" entry (and the contents of the field) to a "Y" or a "N" in the display.

Beyond these PICTURE symbols the developer has the freedom to include other text in the PICTURE clause as "literal" text. The most common example of this is with telephone numbers, where the parentheses and the dash used in the number (215) 543-6578 can be put in the PICTURE clause. A PICTURE clause to format this telephone number would look like this:

@ rr,cc GET telno PICTURE "(999) 999-9999"

This PICTURE clause will display *and save* the literal text as part of the character field so the characters (and spaces) must be considered when planning the size of the field. If you did not want to include the literal text as a part of the field, you would have to use the "@R" PICTURE function to remove the literal text from the field.

RANGE   *dBase III Plus* has a second data validation function that the developer can use to restrict entry in numeric fields. It is the RANGE statement. RANGE requires two arguments: a lower limit value and an upper limit value. When data is entered that falls outside of the range, *dBase III Plus* will beep (if SET BELL is ON) and notify the user in the upper right hand corner of the screen (if SET SCOREBOARD is ON) of the proper range for entry. If SET BELL is OFF and SET SCOREBOARD is OFF, the user will receive no indication that there is a problem except that the number that he or she is trying to enter will just not stick.

    dBase III Plus's data validation capabilities are not the most extensive. They are, in fact, pretty basic. If you want to do anything more sophisticated, you will have to program your own validation routines that take place after the READ. We will be talking at much greater length about this in the chapter on data validation.

CHAPTER 3

Program Menu Designs
and Considerations

A user interacts with a program through keyboard responses to options that the program presents. Exactly *how* these options are presented and how a user can react to them is the subject of this chapter.

Before starting it is worthwhile to review at least one of the basic design principles discussed in Chapter 1. That principle is "Keep it Simple Stupid" (rule number four). There is no question that a programmer can design "sexy" menus that jump out and entertain the user but there is also no question that this approach to menu design does nothing but confuse and tire the user. All studies have shown that, over time, the user is not interested in pyrotechnics, funny comments, or an invasion of options. Users in such an environment quickly get annoyed and then angry with a program that intrudes unnecessarily into their equilibrium.

The best rule of thumb for menu design is that if there is any doubt about the usefulness of a specific piece of information on a menu, it is better left out. The rule also implies that the number of option choices should be limited and that multiple menu levels should be implemented when necessary.

Many alternatives are open to the programmer when developing the user interface. The developer's choices depend on the levels of expertise of the user and the operating environment in which the program will be used. We will discuss the various types of menu designs that are available and the environments where they best apply.

Before discussing menu design it is necessary to talk about designing menus. More specifically, we need to discuss the IBM PC's extended character set, otherwise known as the PC graphics character set.

The IBM PC (and most clones) use an extended character set that is mostly graphic characters. This extended set is unlike the USASCII and the Roman 8 extensions that most printers (and print wheels) come with. Attempting to print these characters on an output device that does not support them will give you interesting results. The graphic characters that you see in the tables in this book were printed on a Hewlett-Packard LaserJet using a special PC Graphic Symbol set.

Similarly, you may not be able to see these characters on the screen inside of some word processors and text editing programs because access to these characters is restricted in some manner. For example, *WordStar* in the document mode uses the extended character set to do hyphenation and any attempt to view them will fail. You must use the nondocument mode to get at these characters. *SideKick* has a graphics mode that must be invoked to view these graphic characters.

Using the graphic characters can significantly improve the way your screens look but, at the same time, you should pay attention to rule number four on simplicity as stated in Chapter 1. You can do many silly things with graphics, and all of them detract from the final application. Keeping it clean and simple will make what you do look better and will assist the user in interpreting your screens.

The primary use for the graphics character set is boxes. *dBase III Plus* has a command (@ rr,cc TO aa,bb [DOUBLE]) that draws simple boxes on screen defined from the upper left corner (rr,cc) to the lower right corner (aa,bb). I do not use this command in my work for a number of reasons, some of which will be explained later. Instead, I choose to paint the boxes when I develop screens.

If you decide to paint your boxes or if you need complicated boxes, you must use the appropriate ASCII numbers for the box characters. IBM, in its infinite wisdom, managed to put them all in a sequence whose logic escapes mortal men.

Table 3.1.   ASCII Numbers for Box Characters

Single Line Box		Double Line Box	
Dec. Number	Char.	Dec. Number	Char.
218	┌	201	╔
191	┐	187	╗
192	└	200	╚
217	┘	188	╝
179	│	186	║
196	─	205	═
197	┼	206	╬
195	├	204	╠
180	┤	185	╣
194	┬	203	╦
193	┴	202	╩

There are more characters available that can, in certain circumstances, help you make your point when you are designing screens. You will find a chart of the extended ASCII table in several places. The complete 256 character set is included in an appendix to the IBM BASIC manual. The *dBase III Plus* manual gives you only the lower 128 characters.

Now that we have discussed the extended character set, how do you get the characters into your program files? There are three ways: the *dBase* way, the ASCII way, and the easy way.

The *dBase* way uses the *dBase* function CHR(n), where "n" is an ASCII value from 000 to 255. You can put in not only graphic characters, but letters, numbers, punctuation, or other characters included in the set this way. In some situations (such as ringing the bell (CHR(7))) this is the best approach. Drawing boxes using the *dBase* way, even with the REPLICATE( ) function, is to ask for frustration.

The ASCII method, just a bit easier than the first, is to use your program editor or word processing program to dump extended characters into the middle of a text file. Some programs will allow this, others will not. The method works well when there are only a few characters that need to be placed on the screen. If you are going to draw boxes, this method is not much better than the *dBase* way.

The third way is the easy way. Use a screen development program that allows you to paint with a single character (or set of characters) and to select from the extended character set at will. More will be said in Chapter 10 where we discuss development tools. All that needs to be said here is "try painting a screen without one of these programs and you will go out and get one."

The Command Menu

By far the most direct way for the operator to initiate program execution is through the command menu. The operator simply types in the name of the desired program and the application executes it. From a programming standpoint this type of interface is simple. The program is short and requires few lines of code. It allows the expert user to skip whatever menu levels are nested in some of the program calls and it increases the speed at which the user can use the program.

A simple command interface program looks like Listing 3.1.

This menu will work if the .PRG files are named so that their filenames are two characters and are the same as "vchoice" in Listing 3.1. It is simple, and it works. It also is an unsatisfactory program in that it does not provide any information about what choices are available to the user for execution or any error trapping for nonvalid choices or for bad typing. These shortcomings can be taken care of by expanding the text to include prompts on what the valid options are, and an AT( ) verification that includes all the valid options in the string.

Listing 3.1.   Command Entry Program

```
CLEAR
SET TALK OFF
SET ESCAPE OFF
vchoice = SPACE(2)
TEXT

             MAIN COMMAND MENU

ENDTEXT
ACCEPT "ENTER PROGRAM COMMAND HERE:   " TO vchoice
DO vchoice

*** End Command Entry Program
```

Many users working in a full-time production environment prefer the above menu type. It is quick and, if carefully planned, can circumvent tiring and repetitive menu choices. As most micro software is not designed for or targeted at this type of user, one does not often see this design. While there are definite advantages to this type of menu, the overriding disadvantage is that it takes too much time to become comfortable in a system that provides so little prompting for the user. It works best in systems where the user is constantly exposed to system operation so that he or she can remember all the commands that are available.

Menu Choice Programs

Everyone loves a menu. It usually provides so much information that you cannot be confused about what to do next. It is probably the best way to communicate with the user but, despite all of its advantages, there are hidden problems as well.

The best way to illustrate one of the most serious problems that exists with menu programs is to talk about a menu. Not a computer menu, but a restaurant menu. Everyone has been to a restaurant where the menu goes on for eight *pages*. Do you remember all those wonderful dishes that were described in minute detail? While these menus make fascinating reading, it is impossible to choose from one of them. Why? Data overload. There is simply too much there to pick from. Each choice has more information than can possibly be absorbed and so, in the end, one is tempted to leave the restaurant, go down to the corner McDonalds, and get a Big Mac. Why? It is easier to make up one's mind from a limited and familiar menu.

The same analogy holds true for computers. Menus should be kept short; descriptions (if any) should be short and to the point. The number of options on any single menu should also be limited: no more than seven or eight if you can help it. The time and keystrokes necessary to select any single option should also be kept to a minimum. *Everything* should be streamlined.

There are many different types of menus, ranging from the simple to the complex and, depending on the circumstances, different types are better or worse suited. As a menu becomes more complex, there are trade-offs that come into play. The first trade-off is in development time. The more complex the menu, the longer it will take to develop. The longer it takes to develop, the less time there will be for other aspects of the program. The larger the menu program, the slower it will run. If the user's actions in the menu are subjected to continuous interpretation by the menu program, the program can noticeably slow down.

There are two basic types of menu structures: horizontal and vertical. Horizontal menus use the least space, while vertical menus are the easiest to interpret.

We will also develop both vertical and horizontal bounce bar menus. While they are simply vertical and horizontal menus with a different method of choice selection, their programming is materially different from the normal menu structure that they must be discussed separately. Finally, we will discuss both pull-down and function key menus.

Horizontal Menu

Horizontal menus are best suited to being "dropped" on top of work in progress. They can take up as little as one line (usually at either the top or the bottom of the screen) and they do not necessarily interfere with the work on the screen. The menu choices are laid out on the same line and the user is asked for a choice. A simple single-line horizontal menu program looks like Listing 3.2.

Listing 3.2. Simple Horizontal Menu

```
STORE " " TO vchoice
STORE "SDENPQ" TO valchoice

DO WHILE .NOT. vchoice $ valchoice
  @ 24,00 CLEAR
  @ 24,00 Say "Save    Delete    Edit    Next    Previous    Quit    Choice?    "
  @ 24,62 GET vchoice
  READ

  IF .NOT. vchoice $ valchoice
    @ 24,00 CLEAR
    WAIT "CHOICE MADE NOT A VALID CHOICE.   PRESS ANY KEY TO TRY AGAIN."
  ENDIF

ENDDO

DO CASE
  CASE UPPER(vchoice) = 'S'
    DO save
  CASE UPPER(vchoice) = 'D'
    DO delete
  CASE UPPER(vchoice) = 'E'
    DO edit
  CASE UPPER(vchoice) = 'N'
    SKIP 1
    DO show
  CASE UPPER(vchoice) = 'P'
    SKIP -1
    DO show
  CASE UPPER(vchoice) = 'Q'
    RETURN
ENDCASE

*** End Simple Horizontal Menu Program
```

This menu, when used in a full-screen editing program, looks like Figure 3.1 on the screen.

This sample menu is displayed on the bottom row of the screen. In order to make it readable, it should be displayed either in an intense color or in inverse video. This makes it easier to read and also makes it possible to differentiate the menu from the screen.

In the example, invalid entries are handled by a simple error trapping device that continues to cycle the user through the VCHOICE loop until a proper selection is made. An error line is included in the loop that overwrites the menu and tells the user to try again. The loop is controlled

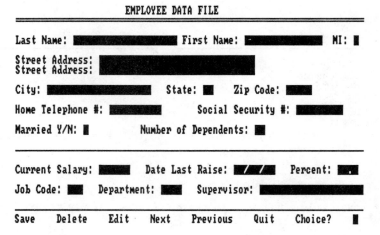

Figure 3.1. Editing Screen with Horizontal Menu at Bottom

by a logical relationship between the memory variable "vchoice" and the list of valid answers included in the memory variable "VALCHOICE". If the value entered in vchoice is not part of the string valchoice the error message is displayed and the operator is prompted to enter a new choice. The loop continues until the relationship becomes true (that is, until a valid choice has been made).

One important operation to notice in this example is the use of the UPPER( ) function in the DO CASE command. As discussed earlier, the UPPER( ) function converts all alpha characters to uppercase for the comparison. This ensures that entries made in lowercase (which will often be the case) will match the options that are entered in uppercase. Here we have an example of a case where a little extra effort in programming makes a big difference in the usability of the program. This operation could also have been done by including a PICTURE "!" statement with the GET but I prefer using the UPPER command as it explicitly indicates the programmer's desires and works with the WAIT command, while the PICTURE clause does not.

It is quite normal for a horizontal menu to take up two lines. It will if you include a prompt line along with the menu as we will see later in this chapter. If this is the case, you will want to be able to rewrite the contents of the lines that you used for your menu. If your menu is at the bottom of the screen you can issue an "@ 23,00 CLEAR" command and clear the last two lines before reissuing your "@ SAY"s and "@GET"s for the two affected lines. The "@ CLEAR" command clears out the last two lines of the screen. The SAYs and GETs are then rewritten on a cleared screen.

If the horizontal menu appears anywhere else other than the bottom of the screen, care must be taken when first writing the horizontal menu and then rewriting the overwritten lines. The best practice is to make sure that the menu occupies the entire width of the screen (all 80 columns) so that all text is covered over. When the "@ SAY"s and "@ GET"s are rewritten, you must either make sure that they take up the entire 80 columns or else CLEAR the lines, otherwise a remnant of the horizontal menu will still be visible until the next CLEAR statement is issued in the program.

Vertical Menu

The vertical, or list, menu is the one that is most commonly thought of as a "menu." It usually takes over the entire screen, has a banner headline that announces what the menu is and what it is used for. It shows a list of all the possible selections open to the operator, and a place for the operator to make a selection. It can also have "embellishments" to satisfy the artistic ego of the programmer. Programmers with restraint limit these embellishments to simple boxes and lines to aid the user in distinguishing separate areas of the menu. Other designers involve themselves in a visual smorgasbord that neither makes the program better nor makes the program execute faster. A simple, well designed main menu would look like Figure 3.2.

The menu is clean, easy on the eyes, and gives the user enough information to make a choice about which areas of the program he should invoke to perform the desired operation.

The program that supports this main menu is as shown in Listing 3.3.

The basic logic of this menu program is similar to that of the horizontal menu program discussed previously but the orientation and use of this type of menu is different. Where the horizontal menu is easily dropped underneath an active screen, the vertical menu does not lend itself to this type of presentation. It usually takes the entire screen and is therefore used more often as a choice menu to initiate different activities.

What could be done to make this program more attractive? Notice that the menu is presented in one color: low intensity white. As discussed earlier, studies have shown that this is easiest on the eyes of the

```
┌─────────────────────────────────┐
│  USER INTERFACE IN dBASE III     │
│                                  │
│     DEMONSTRATION MAIN MENU      │
└─────────────────────────────────┘
```

A   ADD A NEW RECORD

E   EDIT AN EXISTING RECORD

D   DELETE AN OLD RECORD

P   PRINT REPORTS

B   BACKUP DATABASE

       X   EXIT FROM SYSTEM

Figure 3.2.   Typical Main Menu

Listing 3.3.   Main Menu Program

```
CLEAR
@ 01,23 SAY "                                    "
@ 02,23 SAY "                                    "
@ 03,23 SAY "    USER INTERFACE IN dBASE III     "
@ 04,23 SAY "                                    "
@ 05,23 SAY "     DEMONSTRATION MAIN MENU        "
@ 06,23 SAY "                                    "
@ 07,23 SAY "                                    "
@ 11,24 SAY "A    ADD A NEW RECORD"
@ 13,24 SAY "E    EDIT AN EXISTING RECORD"
@ 15,24 SAY "D    DELETE AN OLD RECORD"
@ 17,24 SAY "P    PRINT REPORTS"
@ 19,24 SAY "B    BACKUP DATABASE"
@ 22,32 SAY "X    EXIT FROM SYSTEM"

STORE "AEDPBX" TO valchoice
WAIT "" TO vchoice

DO WHILE .NOT. vchoice $ valchoice
   @ 24,00 CLEAR
   WAIT "CHOICE MADE NOT A VALID CHOICE.  TRY AGAIN " TO vchoice
ENDDO
```

```
DO CASE
   CASE UPPER(vchoice) = 'A'
      DO add
   CASE UPPER(vchoice) = 'E'
      DO edit
   CASE UPPER(vchoice) = 'D'
      DO delete
   CASE UPPER(vchoice) = 'P'
      DO print
   CASE UPPER(vchoice) = 'B'
      DO backup
   CASE UPPER(vchoice) = 'X'
      DO exit
ENDCASE

***  End Main Menu Program
```

user. I would not recommend changing it. An invalid key press can be brought to the attention of the user and highlighted. To do this the error trapping portion of the program would be changed as in Listing 3.4.

The addition of the "SET COLOR TO GR+" command changes the prompt line to bright yellow on a color monitor (high intensity white on a monochrome monitor). Note that the SET COLOR TO command is immediately reverted to SET COLOR TO W After the prompt is issued. This is good programming practice and keeps you from being surprised too often by funny color combinations on the screen. The program line ?? CHR(7) will ring the bell, further notifying the user of the mistake.

Bounce Bar Main Menu

The rage in programming is the so-called "bounce bar" or "light bar" menu. This type of vertical menu allows not only for a choice to be made by pressing the associated trigger key, but also for selection by highlighting (lighting) the desired choice in inverse video using the cursor keys to move (bounce) the highlighted choice (bar) to the appropriate line of the menu and making the selection by hitting the carriage return.

Listing 3.4.   Menu Choice Error Trapping Routine

```
DO WHILE .NOT. vchoice $ valchoice
  SET COLOR TO GR+
  ?? CHR(7)
  @ 24,00 CLEAR
  WAIT "CHOICE MADE NOT A VALID CHOICE.  TRY AGAIN " TO vchoice
  SET COLOR TO W
ENDDO

*** End Error Trapping Routine
```

This type of programming, while visually pleasing, has its price. The programming necessary to develop this type of menu is substantially greater than the programming necessary for a simple choice menu. This does two things: it increases the size of your application and, in operation, reduces the speed of menu operation. The bounce bar menu has so much programming associated with it that it cannot be recommended for interpreted operation on anything less than an IBM PC AT. On a standard PC or an XT the response time between hitting the cursor keys and seeing the results on the screen is simply too long. The program puts on the appearance of one that is slow in operation. Even on the AT, this type of menu program is slower than it should be. If you are going to use *Clipper* or *Quicksilver* to compile your application, you will notice a substantial improvement in the menu "bounce" speed. I do not use them unless I am going to compile the application.

This menu shows up like Figure 3.3 on the screen.

This program is over 3,000 bytes in size and 86 lines of code. The simple main menu program is only 1,300 bytes and 34 lines of code. Are the extra features worth the extra weight? Try both of them and decide for yourself.

If you decide that the bounce bar menu is for you it is important that you understand the mechanics of the program. The menu is divided into six parts and each should be discussed separately.

As with the simple main menu program, the first part sets up the environment that the application will be running under. The second part

Listing 3.5. Bounce Bar Main Menu Program

```
<set environment>

CLEAR
@ 00,23 SAY "┌─────────────────────────────┐"
@ 01,23 SAY "│                             │"
@ 02,23 SAY "│   USER INTERFACE IN dBASE III│"
@ 03,23 SAY "│                             │"
@ 04,23 SAY "│    BOUNCE BAR DEMO MENU     │"
@ 05,23 SAY "│                             │"
@ 06,23 SAY "└─────────────────────────────┘"
@ 10,24 SAY " A    ADD A NEW RECORD "
@ 12,24 SAY " E    EDIT AN EXISTING RECORD "
@ 14,24 SAY " D    DELETE AN OLD RECORD "
@ 16,24 SAY " P    PRINT REPORTS "
@ 18,24 SAY " B    BACKUP DATABASE "
@ 21,32 SAY " X    EXIT FROM SYSTEM "

DO WHILE .T.
  valchoice = "AEDPBX"
  vchoice = 6
  key = 24

  DO WHILE key <> 13
    SET COLOR TO W/

    DO CASE
      CASE vchoice = 1
        @ 10,24 SAY " A    ADD A NEW RECORD "
      CASE vchoice = 2
        @ 12,24 SAY " E    EDIT AN EXISTING RECORD "
      CASE vchoice = 3
        @ 14,24 SAY " D    DELETE AN OLD RECORD "
      CASE vchoice = 4
        @ 16,24 SAY " P    PRINT REPORTS "
      CASE vchoice = 5
        @ 18,24 SAY " B    BACKUP DATABASE "
      CASE vchoice = 6
        @ 21,32 SAY " X    EXIT FROM SYSTEM "
    ENDCASE
```

```
DO CASE
  CASE AT(UPPER(CHR(key)),valchoice) > 0
    vchoice = AT(UPPER(CHR(key)),valchoice)
    EXIT
  CASE key = 24 .OR. key = 4 .OR. CHR(key) = ' '
    IF vchoice = 6
      vchoice = 1
    ELSE
      vchoice = vchoice + 1
      ENDIF
    CASE key = 5 .OR. key = 19
      IF vchoice = 1
        vchoice = 6
      ELSE
        vchoice = vchoice - 1
      ENDIF
ENDCASE

SET COLOR TO +W/B

DO CASE
  CASE vchoice = 1
    @ 10,24 SAY " A    ADD A NEW RECORD "
  CASE vchoice = 2
    @ 12,24 SAY " E    EDIT AN EXISTING RECORD "
  CASE vchoice = 3
    @ 14,24 SAY " D    DELETE AN OLD RECORD "
  CASE vchoice = 4
    @ 16,24 SAY " P    PRINT REPORTS "
  CASE vchoice = 5
    @ 18,24 SAY " B    BACKUP DATABASE "
  CASE vchoice = 6
    @ 21,32 SAY " X    EXIT FROM SYSTEM "
ENDCASE

STORE INKEY() TO key

DO WHILE key = 0
  key = INKEY()
ENDDO

ENDDO

SET COLOR TO W
```

```
ENDDO

DO CASE
   CASE vchoice = 1
      DO add
   CASE vchoice = 2
      DO edit
   CASE vchoice = 3
      DO delete
   CASE vchoice = 4
      DO print
   CASE vchoice = 5
      DO backup
   CASE vchoice = 6
      DO exit
ENDCASE
```

---

of the program is the fixed text and, if it looks just like the simple main menu program, it does because it is. What happens to it from this point, however, is different.

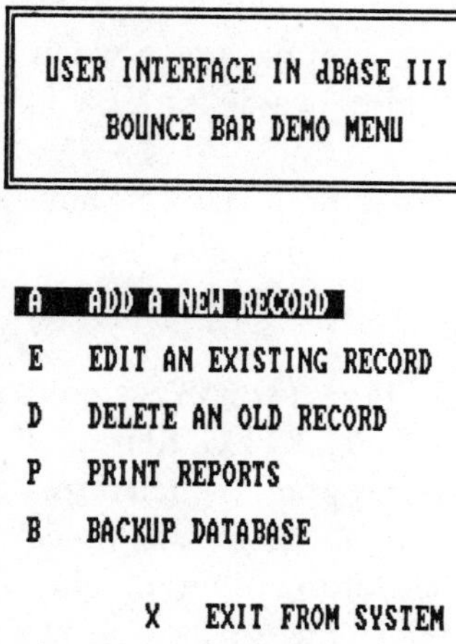

```
┌─────────────────────────────────┐
│  USER INTERFACE IN dBASE III     │
│     BOUNCE BAR DEMO MENU         │
└─────────────────────────────────┘
```

```
█ A    ADD A NEW RECORD █

  E    EDIT AN EXISTING RECORD

  D    DELETE AN OLD RECORD

  P    PRINT REPORTS

  B    BACKUP DATABASE

          X    EXIT FROM SYSTEM
```

Figure 3.3.   Screen Shot of Vertical Bounce Bar Menu

The bounce bar menu program then goes into a continuous loop. The only way out of the "DO WHILE .T." statement is through the EXIT routine that is invoked by the "X" menu selection. The valid choice and the number of menu choices are declared as is the starting value for the key press (down).

The fourth part of the program is the bounce loop. Every time a navigation key is pressed a part of the screen is repainted so that the previously highlighted option is returned to its original state and the next option is highlighted. As can be seen, the loop ends when the key press is a carriage return. This termination freezes VCHOICE at a given value and moves processing on to the last section of the program.

The fourth part contains four separate sections. The first section is the initial DO CASE command. It resets the prior menu choice to the original color, which, in this case, is low white. When the loop is entered for the first time the value for VCHOICE is 6 so the first thing that happens is that the initial highlighted choice (number 6) is returned to white.

The second section is the first CASE of the second DO CASE command. It deals with the user pressing an activator key, just as if the "bounce" portion of the program was not there. Translated into English the CASE states "if the uppercase of the pressed key exists within the string VALCHOICE then VCHOICE is equal to the numerical position within the string that the pressed key occupies. If this condition is met, exit from this section of the program and go on to the next section."

The next two CASES of the DO CASE structure comprise the third subsection of this part of the program. They either increment or decrement the value of VCHOICE by 1 and loop back to a value of 1 when VCHOICE is 6 and cursor DOWN is pressed or loop back to 6 when VCHOICE is 1 and cursor UP is pressed. As the initial value for KEY is 24 (DOWN), option 1 is now highlighted.

The last subsection is the next DO CASE structure. It takes the new value of VCHOICE and points that choice with the highlighted colors. The program then goes into the INKEY()N loop waiting for the next key press.

If the key press is a carriage return, the ASCII value of 13 is stored to KEY. As the termination condition for the outside DO LOOP is now met, control is passed on to the last portion of the program, which resets the color to the original choice and executes the final DO CASE. Since value of VCHOICE is now frozen, the sixth part of the program takes the VCHOICE value and branches the program to one of the various execution subprograms or menus.

The fifth part of the program is contained within DO WHILE key <> 13 DO LOOP and is the heart of a bounce bar menu program. The part is the four lines of code shown in Listing 3.6.

This section of code is important because it captures the key presses in the menu program. STORE INKEY( ) TO key sets KEY to 0 as no key is being pressed. Control then passes to the DO LOOP, which continues looping until a key is pressed. The value of that key is then stored to KEY, the loop ends, and the program then loops back to the start of the DO WHILE key <> 13 loop. The menu status changes to reflect the new value of KEY. It is important to note that the only way to capture the value of the key press is within the short loop above. INKEY( ) tests for a current key press. If that information is to be captured the loop must be used to establish the "wait" necessary to allow the operator to press a key and store the value to a memory variable.

As mentioned earlier, both *Clipper* and *Quicksilver* will compile this type of menu and execute it with considerably greater speed than *dBase III Plus* will. The latest release of *Clipper* features a simpler bounce menu structure that allows the developer to create this type of menu with many fewer steps. In its simplest form the menu program looks like Listing 3.7.

The user has the option of either typing the first letter of the PROMPT to activate the command or positioning the highlight bar over the proper choice and pressing the carriage return to trigger the appropriate action.

The screen that is generated by this code looks like Figure 3.4 on page 49.

Listing 3.6.   INKEY( ) Loop

```
STORE INKEY() TO key

DO WHILE key = 0
   key = INKEY()
ENDDO

*** End INKEY() Loop
```

Listing 3.7.   Clipper Bounce Bar Menu Program

```
CLEAR
SET MESSAGE TO 20
@ 08,25 SAY "TEST MENU FOR CLIPPER"
@ 11,15 PROMPT " Add "  MESSAGE "Use to add a new customer"
@ 13,15 PROMPT " Edit " MESSAGE "Use to edit an existing customer"
@ 15,15 PROMPT " Print " MESSAGE "Use to print reports"
MENU TO vchoice

DO CASE
   CASE vchoice = 1
     DO add
   CASE vchoice = 2
     DO edit
   CASE vchoice = 3
     DO print
ENDCASE

*** End Clipper Bounce Bar Menu
```

The size of the code necessary to create a bounce bar menu using the *Clipper* code is much less than it is using *dBase III Plus* code. Beyond this, there are other advantages to this *Clipper* enhancement to *dBase*. The *Clipper* version of the **F1** help key is in effect while this menu is on the screen, so context-sensitive help is directly available. The message function allows for the developer to give up to 80 characters of information about the highlighted PROMPT on the same line as the prompt.

The menu shown above is a "bare bones" menu that can be improved substantially. The PROMPT can be reduced to a single character, with the rest of the line given as a SAY. This will reduce the highlighting to only that single character, but will allow the developer to use a letter trigger that is not necessarily the first character of the prompt. The code for these two lines would look like this:

```
@ 10,10 PROMPT "A" MESSAGE "Use to add new customer"
@ 10,13 SAY "Add"
```

If desired, the rest of the PROMPT line can then be set off in a different color and intensity to further improve the look of the menu. If you decide to do this, you will have to put the SAYS for the *remainders* of the PROMPT lines *before* the PROMPT lines, as color changes inside of the PROMPTS do not work.

There are some things that *Clipper*'s manufacturer, Nantucket, did not do with this enhancement that would have made it more interesting to the developer. First, the menu choice bounces up and down (or right and left: this structure works just as well horizontally) using the cursor keys but, once you have reached the last selection, you cannot get back to the first option by pressing the down cursor key again. The *Clipper* menu does not "roll over" as does the *dBase III Plus* menu shown in Figure 3.4. Second, there is no way of centering (or even indenting) the MESSAGEs other than typing in the spaces inside the quotes of each message. Third, the prompt highlight is displayed in the enhanced color combination set and the message associated with the prompt is set in the regular color (which is also the color of the unselected options on the menu). There is no flexibility to do anything different if it is needed.

Horizontal Bounce Bar Menu

There are only two cases where a horizontal bounce bar menu might justify its programming cost. The first is where the menu must give information about the impact of the choice being selected. The second is where the choice of an option must bring up a submenu for the user to choose from. The Lotus *1-2-3* menu structure is an excellent example of these cases. Its menus provide a tremendous amount of information and offer many selections in a small space.

```
            TEST MENU FOR CLIPPER


        Add
        Edit
        Print




Use to add a new customer
```

Figure 3.4.   Screen Shot of *Clipper* Bounce Bar Menu

A horizontal bounce bar version of the standard horizontal menu with an information line below it is shown in Listing 3.8.

Listing 3.8.   Horizontal Bounce Bar Menu with Information Line

```
@ 23,00 CLEAR
@ 23,02 SAY " S ave    D elete    E dit    N ext    P revious    Q uit
Choice?"

DO WHILE .T.
  valchoice = "SDENPQ"
  vchoice = 6
  key = 4
  DO WHILE key <> 13
    SET COLOR TO W/
    DO CASE
      CASE vchoice = 1
        @ 23,02 SAY " S "
      CASE vchoice = 2
        @ 23,11 SAY " D "
      CASE vchoice = 3
        @ 23,22 SAY " E "
      CASE vchoice = 4
        @ 23,31 SAY " N "
      CASE vchoice = 5
        @ 23,40 SAY " P "
      CASE vchoice = 6
        @ 23,53 SAY " Q "
    ENDCASE

    DO CASE
      CASE AT(UPPER(CHR(key)), valchoice) > 0
        vchoice = AT(UPPER(CHR(key)), valchoice)
        EXIT
      CASE key = 24 .OR. key = 4 .OR. CHR(key) = ' '
        IF vchoice = 6
          vchoice = 1
        ELSE
          vchoice = vchoice + 1
        ENDIF
      CASE key = 5 .OR. key = 19
        IF vchoice = 1
          vchoice = 6
        ELSE
          vchoice = vchoice - 1
        ENDIF
    ENDCASE

    DO CASE
      CASE vchoice = 1
        SET COLOR TO +W/B
        @ 23,03 SAY "S"
        SET COLOR TO W
        @ 24,03 SAY "Save currently displayed record              "
```

```
      CASE vchoice = 2
        SET COLOR TO +W/B
        @ 23,12 SAY "D"
        SET COLOR TO W
        @ 24,03 SAY "Delete current record from database           "
      CASE vchoice = 3
        SET COLOR TO +W/B
        @ 23,23 SAY "E"
        SET COLOR TO W
        @ 24,03 SAY "Edit currently displayed record              "
      CASE vchoice = 4
        SET COLOR TO +W/B
        @ 23,32 SAY "N"
        SET COLOR TO W
        @ 24,03 SAY "Go to the next record in the database         "
      CASE vchoice = 5
        SET COLOR TO +W/B
        @ 23,41 SAY "P"
        SET COLOR TO W
        @ 24,03 SAY "Move to the previous record in the database"
      CASE vchoice = 6
        SET COLOR TO +W/B
        @ 23,54 SAY "Q"
        SET COLOR TO W
        @ 24,03 SAY "Quit this session and leave the program       "
    ENDCASE

    key = INKEY()

    DO WHILE key = 0
      key = INKEY()
    ENDDO

  ENDDO

  DO CASE
    CASE vchoice = 1
      DO save
    CASE vchoice = 2
      DO delete
    CASE vchoice = 3
      DO edit
    CASE vchoice = 4
      SKIP 1
    CASE vchoice = 5
      SKIP -1
    CASE vchoice = 6
      EXIT
  ENDCASE

ENDDO

**  End Horizontal Bounce Bar Menu With Prompts ***
```

The basic structure of the menu in Listing 3.8 is the same as the previous one but it appears on only the last two screen lines instead of occupying the entire screen. The prompt line (line 24) changes with each selection. The extra spaces that you see after some of the prompts are to ensure that the entire line is repainted with each change in the highlighted selection. One other difference that you can see in this menu is that the highlight is on only the first character of the word, not on the whole word.

The horizontal menu with prompts on line 24 looks like Figure 3.5.

There is one annoying anomaly that exists with *dBase III Plus*. INKEY( ), while nearly flawless in its ability to capture the currently pressed key, fails to do very well with the left arrow key. It captures only one out of roughly every ten presses. If you hold the key down for a second, it will usually work but this is hardly a good solution to the situation. This problem seems to occur only when SET ESCAPE is ON. If SET ESCAPE is OFF, INKEY( ) seems to work well. I have heard that later versions of *dBase III Plus* have "fixed" this problem: INKEY( ) now does *not* capture the left arrow key even when SET ESCAPE is OFF. So much for progress. If this bug exists in your copy of the program, I suggest that you add an INKEY condition for using the **Home** or **End** key (with INKEY( ) values of 1 and 6 respectively) to supplement the left arrow key in your program. If you compile using either *Clipper* or *Quicksilver*, the problem goes away.

Pull-Down/Pop-Up Menu

The introduction of the Apple Macintosh computer brought us into the age of the pull-down (or pop-up) menu for the masses. The tool is a good one when working with a mouse, but it is not as functional when dealing with the traditional cursor controls that are the primary means of navigation around a *dBase III Plus* screen. You *can* develop pull-down menus with *dBase* but you will face a massive coding job. A second problem is running the resulting code using the *dBase* interpreter. As the program is really nothing more than several bounce bar menus strung together, the speed at which the menu system executes is affected in a similar manner. As with the bounce bar menu, I recommend that you plan to run

```
S ave    D elete   E dit   N ext    P revious    Q uit        Choice?
Save currently displayed record
```

Figure 3.5. Horizontal Bounce Bar Menu with Prompt Line

the program on a PC AT if you are going to use interpreted code, or run compiled code to get satisfactory performance.

Before the programming for pull-down menus is detailed, one thing must be made clear. The program that follows makes no consideration for any text that may be on the screen underneath the menus. With *dBase III Plus*, it will be necessry to repaint the entire screen with each change in horizontal menu choice. With *Clipper*, you can SAVE SCREEN and RESTORE SCREEN to get around this problem without any difficulty. This method is much quicker than the *dBase* repaint.

Listing 3.9. Pull-Down Menu Program

```
*** Main Control Program for Pull Down Menu **
CLEAR
PUBLIC key
mchoice = 5
KEY = 4

DO WHILE .T.

 DO CASE
    CASE key = 4 .OR. CHR(key) = ' '

      IF mchoice = 5
        mchoice = 1
      ELSE
        mchoice = mchoice + 1
      ENDIF
    CASE key = 19

      IF mchoice = 1
        mchoice = 5
      ELSE
        mchoice = mchoice - 1
      ENDIF

    ENDCASE

    DO CASE
      CASE mchoice = 1
        DO add
      CASE mchoice = 2
        DO edit
      CASE mchoice = 3
        DO delete
      CASE mchoice = 4
        DO reports
      CASE mchoice = 5
        DO quit
    ENDCASE
```

```
ENDDO

*** End main control program

*** Add Module for Pull Down Menu Program ***

DO WHILE .T.
  SET COLOR TO W/
  CLEAR
  @ 00,00 SAY " ┌───────────┐ "
  @ 01,00 SAY;
  "│ Add    │     Edit        Delete           Reports          Quit"
  @ 02,00 SAY "│                           "
  @ 03,00 SAY "│  Add to Customer File   │ "
  @ 04,00 SAY "│                         │ "
  @ 05,00 SAY "│  Add to Inventory File  │ "
  @ 06,00 SAY "│                         │ "
  @ 07,00 SAY "│  Add to Employee File   │ "
  @ 08,00 SAY "│                         │ "
  @ 09,00 SAY "│  Add to Tax File        │ "
  @ 10,00 SAY "│                         │ "
  @ 11,00 SAY "└─────────────────────────┘ "

  vchoice = 4
  key = 24

  DO WHILE key <> 13
    SET COLOR TO W

    DO CASE
      CASE vchoice = 1
        @ 03,01 SAY " Add to Customer File  "
      CASE vchoice = 2
        @ 05,01 SAY " Add to Inventory File "
      CASE vchoice = 3
        @ 07,01 SAY " Add to Employee File  "
      CASE vchoice = 4
        @ 09,01 SAY " Add to Tax File       "
    ENDCASE

    DO CASE
      CASE key = 24 .OR. CHR(key) = ' '

        IF vchoice = 4
          vchoice = 1
        ELSE
          vchoice = vchoice + 1
        ENDIF

      CASE key = 5

        IF vchoice = 1
          vchoice = 4
        ELSE
          vchoice = vchoice - 1
        ENDIF

    ENDCASE
```

```
    SET COLOR TO +W/B

      DO CASE
        CASE vchoice = 1
          @ 03,01 SAY " Add to Customer File  "
        CASE vchoice = 2
          @ 05,01 SAY " Add to Inventory File "
        CASE vchoice = 3
          @ 07,01 SAY " Add to Employee File  "
        CASE vchoice = 4
          @ 09,01 SAY " Add to Tax File       "
      ENDCASE

      key = INKEY()

      DO WHILE key = 0
        key = INKEY()
      ENDDO

      IF key = 4 .OR. key = 19
        RELEASE ALL LIKE V*
        RETURN
      ENDIF

    ENDDO

    DO CASE
      CASE vchoice = 1
        DO custadd
      CASE vchoice = 2
        DO invadd
      CASE vchoice = 3
        DO empadd
      CASE vchoice = 4
        DO taxadd
    ENDCASE

ENDDO

*** End Add module of Pull-Down Menu Program ***

*** Edit Module of Pull-Down Menu Program ***

DO WHILE .T.
  SET COLOR TO W/
  CLEAR
  @ 00,14 SAY " ┌─────────┐ "
  @ 01,02 SAY;
  "Add        Edit     │    Delete          Reports          Quit"
  @ 02,14 SAY " │         │         "
  @ 03,14 SAY " │ Edit Customer File │ "
  @ 04,14 SAY " │                    │ "
  @ 05,14 SAY " │ Edit Inventory File │ "
  @ 06,14 SAY " │                    │ "
  @ 07,14 SAY " │ Edit Employee File │ "
  @ 08,14 SAY " │                    │ "
  @ 09,14 SAY " │ Edit Tax File      │ "
  @ 10,14 SAY " │                    │ "
  @ 11,14 SAY " └────────────────────┘ "
```

```
vchoice = 4
key = 24

DO WHILE key <> 13
  SET COLOR TO W/

  DO CASE
    CASE vchoice = 1
      @ 03,15 SAY " Edit Customer File  "
    CASE vchoice = 2
      @ 05,15 SAY " Edit Inventory File "
    CASE vchoice = 3
      @ 07,15 SAY " Edit Employee File  "
    CASE vchoice = 4
      @ 09,15 SAY " Edit Tax File       "
  ENDCASE

  DO CASE
    CASE key = 24 .OR. CHR(key) = ' '

      IF vchoice = 4
        vchoice = 1
      ELSE
        vchoice = vchoice + 1
      ENDIF

    CASE key = 5

      IF vchoice = 1
        vchoice = 4
      ELSE
        vchoice = vchoice - 1
      ENDIF

  ENDCASE

  SET COLOR TO +W/B

  DO CASE
    CASE vchoice = 1
      @ 03,15 SAY " Edit Customer File  "
    CASE vchoice = 2
      @ 05,15 SAY " Edit Inventory File "
    CASE vchoice = 3
      @ 07,15 SAY " Edit Employee File  "
    CASE vchoice = 4
      @ 09,15 SAY " Edit Tax File       "
  ENDCASE

  key = INKEY()

  DO WHILE key = 0
    key = INKEY()
  ENDDO
```

```
   IF key = 4 .OR. key = 19
     RELEASE ALL LIKE V*
     RETURN
   ENDIF

ENDDO

DO CASE
   CASE vchoice = 1
     DO custedit
   CASE vchoice = 2
     DO invedit
   CASE vchoice = 3
     DO empedit
   CASE vchoice = 4
     DO taxedit
ENDCASE

ENDDO

*** End Edit Module of Pull-Down Menu Program ***

*** Delete Module of Pull-Down Menu Program ***

DO WHILE .T.
   SET COLOR TO W
   CLEAR
   @ 00,32 SAY " ┌─────────┐ "
   @ 01,02 SAY;
   "Add          Edit        │ Delete  │          Reports          Quit"
   @ 02,28 SAY " ┘         └ "
   @ 03,28 SAY " │ Delete customer record   │ "
   @ 04,28 SAY " │                          │ "
   @ 05,28 SAY " │ Delete inventory record  │ "
   @ 06,28 SAY " │                          │ "
   @ 07,28 SAY " │ Delete employee record   │ "
   @ 08,28 SAY " │                          │ "
   @ 09,28 SAY " │ Delete tax record        │ "
   @ 10,28 SAY " │                          │ "
   @ 11,28 SAY " └──────────────────────────┘ "

   vchoice = 4
   key = 24

   DO WHILE key <> 13
      SET COLOR TO W/

      DO CASE
         CASE vchoice = 1
           @ 03,29 SAY " Delete customer record   "
         CASE vchoice = 2
           @ 05,29 SAY " Delete inventory record "
         CASE vchoice = 3
           @ 07,29 SAY " Delete employee record   "
         CASE vchoice = 4
           @ 09,29 SAY " Delete tax record         "
```

```
ENDCASE

DO CASE
  CASE key = 24 .OR. CHR(key) = ' '

    IF vchoice = 4
      vchoice = 1
    ELSE
      vchoice = vchoice + 1
    ENDIF

  CASE key = 5

    IF vchoice = 1
      vchoice = 4
    ELSE
      vchoice = vchoice - 1
    ENDIF

ENDCASE

SET COLOR TO +W/B

DO CASE
  CASE vchoice = 1
    @ 03,29 SAY " Delete customer record   "
  CASE vchoice = 2
    @ 05,29 SAY " Delete inventory record "
  CASE vchoice = 3
    @ 07,29 SAY " Delete employee record   "
  CASE vchoice = 4
    @ 09,29 SAY " Delete tax record        "
ENDCASE

key = INKEY()
DO WHILE key = 0
  key = INKEY()
ENDDO

IF key = 4 .OR. key = 19
  RELEASE ALL LIKE V*
  RETURN
ENDIF

ENDDO

SET COLOR TO W

DO CASE
  CASE vchoice = 1
    DO delcust
  CASE vchoice = 2
    DO delinv
  CASE vchoice = 3
```

```
      DO delemp
    CASE vchoice = 4
      DO deltax
  ENDCASE

ENDDO

*** End Delete module of Pull-Down Menu Program ***

*** Reports module of Pull-Down Menu Program ***

DO WHILE .T.
  SET COLOR TO W
  CLEAR
  @ 00,50 SAY "┌──────────┐ "
  @ 01,02 SAY;
  "Add         Edit            Delete      | Reports |         Quit"
  @ 02,33 SAY "└──────────────┘                 "
  @ 03,33 SAY "│ Print customer log             "
  @ 04,33 SAY "│                                 "
  @ 05,33 SAY "│ Print current order list        "
  @ 06,33 SAY "│                                 "
  @ 07,33 SAY "│ Print current inventory status  "
  @ 08,33 SAY "│                                 "
  @ 09,33 SAY "│ Print inventory order status    "
  @ 10,33 SAY "│                                 "
  @ 11,33 SAY "│ Print employee data file        "
  @ 12,33 SAY "│                                 "
  @ 13,33 SAY "│ Print employee salary list      "
  @ 14,33 SAY "│                                 "
  @ 15,33 SAY "│ Print quarterly tax deposit list "
  @ 16,33 SAY "│                                 "
  @ 17,33 SAY "└─────────────────────────────────┘ "

  vchoice = 7
  key = 24

  DO WHILE key <> 13
    SET COLOR TO W/

    DO CASE
      CASE vchoice = 1
        @ 03,34 SAY " Print customer log              "
      CASE vchoice = 2
        @ 05,34 SAY " Print current order list        "
      CASE vchoice = 3
        @ 07,34 SAY " Print current inventory status  "
      CASE vchoice = 4
        @ 09,34 SAY " Print inventory order status    "
      CASE vchoice = 5
        @ 11,34 SAY " Print employee data file        "
      CASE vchoice = 6
        @ 13,34 SAY " Print employee salary list       "
      CASE vchoice = 7
        @ 15,34 SAY " Print quarterly tax deposit list "
    ENDCASE
```

```
DO CASE
  CASE key = 24 .OR. CHR(key) = ' '

    IF vchoice = 7
      vchoice = 1
    ELSE
      vchoice = vchoice + 1
    ENDIF

  CASE key = 5

    IF vchoice = 1
      vchoice = 7
    ELSE
      vchoice = vchoice - 1
    ENDIF

ENDCASE

SET COLOR TO +W/B

DO CASE
  CASE vchoice = 1
    @ 03,34 SAY " Print customer log               "
  CASE vchoice = 2
    @ 05,34 SAY " Print current order list         "
  CASE vchoice = 3
    @ 07,34 SAY " Print current inventory status   "
  CASE vchoice = 4
    @ 09,34 SAY " Print inventory order status     "
  CASE vchoice = 5
    @ 11,34 SAY " Print employee data file         "
  CASE vchoice = 6
    @ 13,34 SAY " Print employee salary list        "
  CASE vchoice = 7
    @ 15,34 SAY " Print quarterly tax deposit list "
ENDCASE

key = INKEY()

DO WHILE key = 0
  key = INKEY()
ENDDO

IF key = 4 .OR. key = 19
  RELEASE ALL LIKE V*
  RETURN
ENDIF

ENDDO

DO CASE
  CASE vchoice = 1
```

```
       DO custlog
    CASE vchoice = 2
       DO orders
    CASE vchoice = 3
       DO invent
    CASE vchoice = 4
       DO instat
    CASE vchoice = 5
       DO empdat
    CASE vchoice = 6
       DO empsal
    CASE vchoice = 7
       DO quartax
    ENDCASE

ENDDO

***  End Reports module of Pull-Down Menu Program **

*** Quit module of Pull-Down Menu Program ***

SET COLOR TO W/
CLEAR
@ 00,67 SAY " ┌─────────┐ "
@ 01,02 SAY;
"Add           Edit           Delete           Reports        |    Quit │"
@ 02,59 SAY " ┌─────────┘            "
@ 03,59 SAY " │ Quit the system │ "
@ 04,59 SAY " │                 │ "
@ 05,59 SAY " └─────────────────┘ "

DO WHILE key <> 13
  SET COLOR TO W+/B
  @ 03,60 SAY " Quit the system "
  SET COLSOR TO W
  key = INKEY()

  DO WHILE key = 0
     key = INKEY()
  ENDDO

  IF key = 4 .OR. key = 19
    RETURN
  ENDIF

ENDDO
QUIT

*** End Quit module of Pull-Down Menu Program ***
```

The pull-down menu is nothing more than the two halves of the regular bounce bar menu. The horizontal control is given to the master program that invokes each of the program modules. Each program module is actually the vertical and choice routines of the complete bounce bar menu. The only thing that has been added is the IF structure to identify the trigger keys for moving the pull-down portion of the menu to the left or the right. If you code this program you will find that the left arrow/ INKEY( ) problem can really become annoying. I suggest that you follow my earlier advice and SET ESCAPE OFF at the start of the menu and set it back on at the end if you are using that setting.

The pull-down menus look like this on the screen:

As one can readily see, even a simple pull-down menu is a massive coding job and, whether or not it is compiled, it will give the appearance of slowing down the execution of the program. To be certain, almost 12,000 bytes and 360 lines of code for a pull-down menu is a factor to be

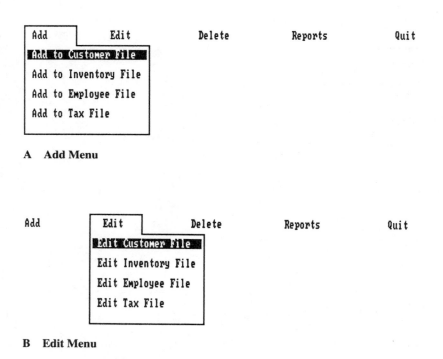

A   Add Menu

B   Edit Menu

Figure 3-6.   Screen Shots of Pull-Down Menus

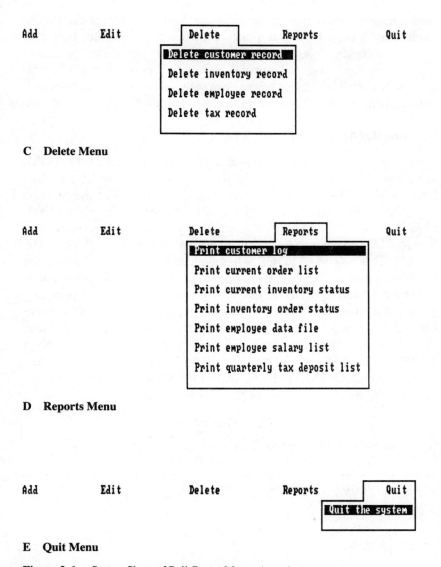

C   Delete Menu

D   Reports Menu

E   Quit Menu

Figure 3.6.   Screen Shots of Pull-Down Menus (cont.)

considered especially when there are more efficient alternatives that can
be coded more quickly and with fewer lines.

If you use the pull-down menu logic, a whole different world of user interface programming can open up. Nothing requires each set of choices to be pulled down at a different place on the screen. It is quite possible to construct the menu program so that the "pull-down" portion of the menu occupies a set column at the left or right of the screen. The contents of this column and the choices open to the user would change depending on where the user was in the application. The possibilities are endless.

Function Key Menu Actuation

There are two different ways to look at the 10 (or 12) function keys that are a part of the standard keyboard. The first is through the SET FUNCTION command where the text string assigned to each of the function keys (except **F1**) can be changed. We will not worry too much about this view now. The second view of function keys is what interests us here. The INKEY( ) values of function key presses can be easily picked up by our little INKEY( ) DO LOOP. These values can be used directly in the navigation loop of the program instead of the test for an alpha key press. If your application needs to use function keys to branch processing, simply insert CASE KEY = "n" statements for each of the needed function keys. Unlike the SET FUNCTION option, **F1** is fully available to the programmer this way. The INKEY( ) value for **F1** is 28. The values for **F2** through **F10** are − 1 through − 9 respectively.

The complete INKEY ( ) values of the function keys in the normal, shifted, control, and alternate states is as shown in Table 3.2.

Table 3.2.   INKEY( ) Return Values for Function Keys

	Normal	Shifted	Control	Alternate
F1	28	84	94	104
F2	− 1	85	95	105
F3	− 2	86	96	106
F4	− 3	87	97	107
F5	− 4	88	98	108
F6	− 5	89	99	109
F7	− 6	90	100	110
F8	− 7	91	101	111
F9	− 8	92	102	112
F10	− 9	93	103	113

The navigation section of the bounce bar menu looks as shown in Listing 3.10.

Obviously, you need the INKEY( ) DO loop to pick up the key values. You can create a nonbouncing menu using function keys just as easily. You simply use the individual CASE key = statements to branch the programming directly instead of using them to exit the navigation

Listing 3.10. Navigation Section of Function Key Actuated Bounce Bar Menu

```
DO CASE
  CASE key = 28
    vchoice = 1
    EXIT
  CASE key = -1
    vchoice = 2
    EXIT
  CASE key = -2
    vchoice = 3
  CASE key = 24 .OR. key = 4 .OR. CHR(key) = ' '

    IF vchoice = 6
      vchoice = 1
    ELSE
      vchoice = vchoice + 1
    ENDIF

  CASE key = 5 .OR. key = 19

    IF vchoice = 1
      vchoice = 6
    ELSE
      vchoice = vchoice - 1
    ENDIF

ENDCASE

*** End Function Key Navigation Module
```

loop and do the branching routine. One oddity that exists is that the values of **F2** to **F10** are negative numbers. You will find it necessary to put your CASE statements for these keys in *before* CASE statements including a CHR( ) function to convert the value of KEY to a character. CHR( ) only works on positive numbers and will give you an execution error if it confronts a negative number.

CHAPTER 4

Edit Screen Design

There are two basic file types that the developer can use to create a screen interface in *dBase III Plus*. The first is the program file (.PRG extension) and the second is the format file (.FMT extension). A format file is actually a special type of program file, containing only the screen format descriptions and the GETs for data and possibly a READ statement to activate the GETs.

Format Files

The programmer is severely restricted in the type of programming that can be included in a format file. Only SAYs, GETs, and READs are allowed.

When a specific screen is called more than once in a program, it is efficient to call that screen from a format file using the SET FORMAT TO <filename> command. This ensures that the same screen form is shown in each instance. Using format files also allows a change to be made only once (in the .FMT file) when a general format change in the screen is made.

dBase III Plus allows multiple-page screen forms to be created with format files. This is a new feature to the product: with *dBase II* and *III*, screen entry forms were limited to one page. The format file can now be separated into up to 32 pages with individual READ statements acting as page breaks. When the program encounters a READ in the file, it clears the screen and shows the next group of SAYs and GETs, and their own READ. The operator can move back and forth between pages with the **PgUp** and the **PgDn** keys. Unfortunately there is no built-in prompt to show that this is the case, so, when programming, it is important to include at least one line at the bottom of the screen to inform the user that this is an option.

A second limitation to this multiple-page format is that the pages of the format must occupy the full screen. You cannot keep information on the top half while you present the user with new information on the bottom half. You can get around this by repeating the same formatting instructions for the top half of the screen on both pages, but this is inefficient programming and, if you do this too much, the advantages of the multiple-page entry screen decrease when compared with the size of your code.

Format files also suffer from *dBase*'s inability to work with more than two data tables at once. The *dBase* SET RELATION TO command can link only two data tables. While this is also true if you are working with a program file, there are ways around this limitation in such a case.

A format file is required if you are planning to include memo fields in your database. *dBase III Plus* does not allow you to access this feature in a program file. Format files are also needed if you wish to design screens to use with the *dBase* full-screen commands APPEND, CHANGE, EDIT, and INSERT. If you use these in your applications, format files become a necessity. However, *dBase* full-screen commands leave you little flexibility to do your own data validation and error trapping routines. These commands are not supported by the compilers.

Finally, you cannot selectively carry over information in specific fields using a format file. With SET CARRY ON, all information is written over to the next record. With SET CARRY OFF, no information is carried over. If you want only certain information to carry over to the next record when adding data, you must use a program file.

Except for the multiple-page screen format, the format file is a static device. By itself, it allows you to SAY text and GET information only once. The advantage to the program file is that you can make the user interface dynamic. In reality, you can easily fold a complete format file into a program file and build up commands around it.

Program Files

Unless it is absolutely necessary, stay away from format files. They have too many limitations. Work with program files instead. The flexibility that you gain will more than compensate for the small amount of incremental work that is necessary to code program files.

If you look at a basic screen editing program file, you will see that there are not too many differences between it and a similar format file. You can take a format file, rename it with a .PRG extension, and slap on a READ statement at the end of the GETs (if the format file did not have one included in it), and you will have a perfectly good screen editing program file. You will not be able to use the .PRG file with the full-screen editing functions supplied by *dBase* but, if you are writing your own programs, this is not a problem.

When you work with .PRG files, the main thing you lose for which there is no solution is access to memo fields. In most business applications the memo field is not that useful as it is difficult to control the types of data that get stored there and even more difficult to control the output of this field type. In some applications, however, the memo field is an excellent tool and its loss would severely compromise the system. In these cases, your only option is to go with a .FMT file so that you will have access to this field type. You will also lose the ability to get multiple-screen data entry forms directly but that, too, can be worked around in a program file.

As you will see, what you pick up by going to .PRG files will more than compensate for any shortcomings that they may have.

In this and the next two chapters, we will be dealing with data entry screens, data validation, and error trapping. Wherever possible we will stick to a single example so that you can compare the similarities and differences among alternate methods of getting a job done. The example is not too complicated, but represents many of the problems that a developer will encounter in designing and coding a system.

Our system is a simple employee database, consisting (for the moment) of one data table containing the fields shown in Listing 4.1.

If you add up the lengths of all the fields you will find that they total 190 bytes. The extra byte is for the delete flag that *dBase* automatically attaches to each record.

Listing 4.1.   Employee Data Table

Field	Field Name	Field Type	Width	Decimals
1	LNAME	Character	20	
2	FNAME	Character	15	
3	MI	Character	1	
4	STADD1	Character	30	
5	STADD2	Character	30	
6	CITY	Character	20	
7	STATE	Character	2	
8	ZIP	Character	5	
9	HTEL	Character	10	
10	SSN	Character	9	
11	MARRIED	Logical	1	
12	DEPENDS	Numeric	2	0
13	CURSAL	Numeric	6	0
14	RAISEDAT	Date	8	
15	RAISEPCT	Numeric	4	1
16	JCODE	Character	3	
17	DEPART	Character	4	
18	SUPERV	Character	20	
		Total	191	

Everything in the data table above should be self-explanatory with one exception. In almost every case in which there are numbers the fields have been defined as character fields. As a rule, it is much better to define your fields as character and then limit input to numbers by using a PICTURE clause than it is to define a field as a numeric value. The only fields that should be defined as numeric are those with which some arithmetic calculations will be done. There are several reasons for this, but probably the biggest is that if indexing is to be done on a multiple-field key expression that includes a character field, all numeric and date fields included in the key expression must first be changed to character. While this is not a problem, it does require that you remain aware of it so, unless you intend to do arithmetic on a field, you should define it as a character field.

Design Considerations

When developing data entry screens, the KISS (Keep It Simple Stupid) rule and the rule of good taste should prevail in the layout of the screen. As mentioned earlier, keep the use of color to a minimum, and keep the screens clean and open. Too much text on the screen will "hide" the data being worked on and make the operator's job much more difficult than it should be. If there is a lot of data, think very hard about splitting the data entry process into two or even more separate screens, containing only those items that are logically related. Over the course of a day, the operator's life will be made much easier if he or she can mentally "group" the entries into different categories and go to a specific portion of the screen (or to a specific screen) to find that information. It makes no sense to have an employee's Social Security number field located next to an employee's supervisor's name field. Place it where it logically belongs and, when possible, place it with other fields that will require number entry so that the operator's trips back and forth to the numeric keypad are reduced.

If you have a complicated system, make sure that good help is available where it is needed, and load your help with specific examples of valid entries so that new operators will have a model to refer to. However, do not overload the system with help, as it is very distracting if it is not necessary. Remember your operator and how tired he or she will be at the end of the day if excess messages are continually flashed across the screen. Where possible, put in default values for the operators so they will not have to type in material that is either repetitive or available from elsewhere within the system.

Data Entry Screens

Let us start our discussion of data entry screens by discussing format (.FMT) files.

The simplest data entry screen that we will be generating will look like Figure 4.1.

The format file that generated this code looks like Listing 4.2.

There are many alternate coding methods that produce precisely the same screen output. Some are easier; some are faster. It is important to discuss the differences between at least two different methods. But first, is the second format program to generate the screen shown in Figure 4.1.

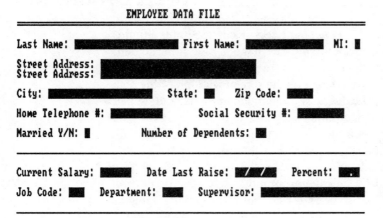

Figure 4.1.   Data Entry Screen

The main difference between the two files is the way the SAY and GET commands are configured. In Listing 4.2, each data field has a single @ nn,nn SAY "<text>" GET <field> statement. The location of the GET is determined by the starting position of the SAY command and the length of the text used in the SAY portion of the command. Changing the starting column position for the statement changes the position of both the text and the GET associated with it. In Listing 4.3, all the fixed text is put into a series of SAY statements and all the GET statements are grouped together. The positions of the SAYs and the GETs are independent — changing one will not affect the other. When changing a SAY line, however, the positioning of all the text on that line for each of the text blocks is changed. Finally, the first file contains 22 lines of code while the second contains 30 lines so the first format file "paints" 10 percent faster than the second.

The advantage of the second type of programming is that it is more readable than the first type. The fixed text portion of the screen is shown in the file as it will appear on the screen and it is easier to "fill in" the fields from the list of GETs below than to try to construct the screen from the row and column positions given in the first example. When final programming, modifying, and debugging time is calculated, less time is spent with the second type of file. In addition, nonprogrammers better understand system documentation that uses the second technique. This book, therefore, uses the less efficient, but more readable approach.

Listing 4.2.   Data Screen Format File

```
@ 02,26 SAY "EMPLOYEE DATA FILE"
@ 03,05 SAY
"════════════════════════════════════════════════════════"
@ 05,05 SAY "Last Name:" GET lname
@ 05,37 SAY "First Name:" GET fname
@ 05,66 SAY "MI:" GET mi
@ 07,05 SAY "Street Address:" GET staddl
@ 08,05 SAY "Street Address:" GET stadd2
@ 10,05 SAY "city:" GET city
@ 10,34 SAY "state:"GET state
@ 10,47 SAY "zip Code:" GET zip
@ 12,05 SAY "Home Telephone #:" GET htel
@ 12,40 SAY "Social Security #:" GET ssn
@ 14,05 SAY "married Y/N:" GET married
@ 14,29 SAY "Number of Dependents:" GET depends
@ 16,05 SAY
"_____"
@ 18,05 SAY "Current Salary:" GET cursal
@ 18,30 SAY "Date Last Raise:" GET raisedat
@ 18,58 SAY "Percent:" GET raisepct
@ 20,05 SAY "Job Code:" GET jcode
@ 20,21 SAY "department:" GET depart
@ 20,40 SAY "supervisor:" GET superv
@ 22,05 SAY
"_____"

*** End Data Screen Format File
```

What is there to say about the format file shown above? You will note that there is no READ statement included in the file. If one was included in the format file, you would automatically drop out of the format when the last field was filled and (if SET CONFIRM is ON) the carriage return was pressed. As there are very few instances where you would want to let data go into your database so easily, I recommend that you put your READ in your program file, so that you can have some control over how data from a data entry session is disposed of after editing has ended.

You will also note that the file is a "bare" file: no data checking of any sort is being performed. The only limitations on data entry are in the current salary and raise percent fields, where data input is limited to

Listing 4.3.   Alternate Code for Data Screen Format File

```
@ 02,26 SAY "EMPLOYEE DATA FILE"
@ 03,05 SAY;
"═══════════════════════════════════════════════════════════"
@ 05,05 SAY "Last Name:                    First Name:                MI:"
@ 07,05 SAY "Street Address:"
@ 08,05 SAY "Street Address:"
@ 10,05 SAY "city:                     state:       zip Code:"
@ 12,05 SAY "Home Telephone #:                 Social Security #:"
@ 14,05 SAY "married Y/N:              Number of Dependents:"
@ 16,05 SAY;
"═══════════════════════════════════════════════════════════"
@ 18,05 SAY "Current Salary:          Date Last Raise:          Percent:"
@ 20,05 SAY "Job Code:       department:        supervisor:"
@ 22,05 SAY;
"═══════════════════════════════════════════════════════════"

@ 05,16 GET lname
@ 05,50 GET fname
@ 05,71 GET mi
@ 07,21 GET staddl
@ 08,21 GET stadd2
@ 10,11 GET city
@ 10,42 GET state
@ 10,58 GET zip
@ 12,23 GET htel
@ 12,59 GET ssn
@ 14,18 GET married
@ 14,51 GET depends
@ 18,21 GET cursal
@ 18,47 GET raisedat
@ 18,67 GET raisepct
@ 20,15 GET jcode
@ 20,33 GET depart
@ 20,52 GET superv

*** End Alternate Data Entry Screen Format File
```

---

numeric values, and in the raise date field, where data input is limited to valid dates. This is nowhere near enough data checking for this type of system. Data validation is discussed in detail in Chapter 5.

It is important to note that the format file (and the program files that follow) do not make use of line 0 or lines 23 and 24. It is a good programming practice to leave these three lines blank if possible. You should leave line 0 open because *dBase* uses it for messages when SET STATUS (the reverse video line across the screen at line 22) is OFF. *Clipper* also uses this line for its runtime error messages. If you are going to compile your system or if you intend to let *dBase* give you a hand with its error messages, it is much better to leave this line blank. I leave lines 23 and 24 blank for my prompts and error messages whenever possible.

The format file shown above is nothing by itself. It must be invoked from within a program file with the SET FORMAT TO command. The simplest program that allows you to enter new customers into the data table is shown in Listing 4.4.

There is not much to the file, nor is there much that you can do with it. The program does nothing to position the record pointer within the data table, or to do anything but accept the data that the operator puts in and READ it into the current record of the data table. It is not good for anything by itself, but it does serve to demonstrate the basis upon which more complicated (and more useful) programs are built.

Let us now take this small example and expand it into a useful data entry program (Listing 4.5) that adds records to an existing data table.

The guts of this program is the READ loop, which allows the user to enter as many new records as desired and the decision loop, which gives the user the choice of terminating the data entry session. As you can see, the program makes use of the space left in lines 23 and 24 for the prompts.

You can easily get rid of the format file if you so wish by simply getting rid of the SET FORMAT TO <filename> command and folding in the entire format file just above the READ command. If I were to use

Listing 4.4.   Simplest Data Entry Program

```
USE <tablename>
SET FORMAT TO <filename>
APPEND BLANK
READ
```

```
*** End Simplest Data Entry Program
```

Listing 4.5.   Simple Data Entry Program

```
USE <tablename>
SET FORMAT TO <filename>
GO BOTTOM
STORE .T. TO loop

DO WHILE loop
  APPEND BLANK
  READ
  STORE .T. TO loop1

  DO WHILE loop1
    @ 22,00
    WAIT "     Add Another Record?  (Y/N) :" TO vchoice

    DO CASE
      CASE UPPER(vchoice) = "Y"
        STORE .F. TO loop1
      CASE UPPER(vchoice) = "N"
        STORE .F. TO loop1
        STORE .F. TO loop
      OTHERWISE
        @ 24,00 say "     Not A Valid Choice -- Try Again"
    ENDCASE

  ENDDO

ENDDO
EXIT

***  End Simple Data Entry Program
```

---

this example in an application, I would most probably have a very small program to position the record pointer at the bottom of the file, and then invoke a more generic edit program that could be used either to add records inside the Add program shell, or edit records in a different shell (calling) program.

Now let's move up in complexity and look at an edit program that will introduce several new concepts.

First, we will do precisely what was just suggested above: build an edit program shell that takes control of the basic edit housekeeping routines. The shell will find the proper record for us, access the edit program, and determine whether the user wants to edit another record.

Second, we will move away from working directly on the data table. We will, instead, store the contents of the selected record into memory variables and display these memory variables on the screen instead of the contents of the data record. This change moves us further away from *dBase* and its built-in capabilities, but the departure is worth the cost. I have never regretted the incremental time that it takes to work with memory variables. The cost is measured both in programming time and in the time that it takes the application to execute. There is no question that these applications take longer to code and run slightly slower than they would if I worked directly on the data within the file. There is also no question that there is more flexibility in programming options and less vulnerability to data corruption in these applications than there is in many other applications built with different programming techniques.

Before starting, it is necessary to step to one side and say that the programming approach that is being used to show edit screen design and control is only one of a great many different approaches that are open to the *dBase* developer. I would hope that the reader study this and all programs in this book to understand the principles of creating *dBase* applications rather than to simply copy the programs line by line. For instructional purposes I have kept the actual programming as simple and open as possible. Understanding the logic behind the programming structures shown may open many new avenues that will satisfy your programming needs; simply adopting these programs will not give you that. For this reason, we will be spending some time discussing the *whys* behind some of the code as well as its function.

First, look at the edit program calling shell shown in Listing 4.6 (see page 79). This program is responsible for getting the user's choice for editing, verifying that the choice is the right one or moving the record pointer through the file until the correct record is found and then accessing the actual editing program.

Note first that except for the opening CLEAR and the closing EXIT statement, the entire calling program is nested within a DO LOOP. Unless you are absolutely certain that the specific task will always involve only one iteration, you should adopt this program structure. It takes in a few more lines of code, but the finished program will be much easier to use. Here the loop control is positioned at the end of the program in its own DO LOOP and asks the user if he or she wants to edit another record.

The loop control module of this program brings up a second program structure that should be used whenever possible. The control module is itself a loop, requiring a correct answer before giving control back to the main loop. As the possible correct answers are only "Y" and "N," the loop may seem to be a bit much for so simple a task. It might be in this example, but when the number of possible choices increases, the chance for a bad key press goes up exponentially, so an error trapping routine such as this becomes more important. As any good application should trap even the most harmless of bad key presses, we employ the device here even though it is not essential. Note that the same loop controls the movement of the record pointer within the file and transfers control to the editing program. There are four choices in this control loop, and the need for the control of the key press is commensurately greater.

Both of these loop control modules convert the key presses to uppercase by using the UPPER( ) function to allow for a lowercase key press to match an uppercase CASE. The same thing can be achieved by using the CASE statement CASE vchoice = "y" .OR. vchoice = "Y" but this alternative requires more typing and more processing time because logical comparisons take longer to process than data transformations.

You should have seen by now that the vast majority of the dialogue between the operator and the application takes place on lines 23 and 24. If you were to run this program and the edit program that it calls, you would see that, with the exception of a "Not Found" condition, all dialogue is on these two lines. This allows us to keep the edit screen (once it has been painted for the first time) on the screen. The two bottom lines provide the choices for actions, accept input from the operator, and tell the user when a mistake has been made.

Now let's go back to the actual operation of the calling program. The data table is indexed on the employee's last name and the program accepts input from the operator into the memory variable MLNAME. The first check that should be done is to see whether a record that matches the search criteria exists in the data table. If you have SET EXACT ON, you are going to be looking for an exact match. If SET EXACT is OFF (as it probably should be in a case like this) you will get a match against the first record that *starts* with the search string. If there

Listing 4.6.   Edit Calling Program

```
CLEAR
STORE .T. TO loop

DO WHILE loop
  USE <tablename>
  INDEX ON lname TO lname
  STORE "" TO mlanem
  @ 23,00 CLEAR
  @ 23,10 SAY "Last Name of Employee Record You Wish to Edit? "
  ACCEPT "            Name: " TO mlname
  SEEK mlname

  IF EOF()
    CLEAR
    @ 16,10 SAY "Employee  '" + "&mlname" + "'  Not in Data File"
    STORE "" TO vchoice
    ?
    STORE .T. TO loop1

    DO WHILE loop1
      WAIT "        Do You Wish to Try Again? (Y/N) " TO vchoice

      DO CASE
        CASE UPPER(vchoice) = "Y"
          CLEAR
          EXIT
        CASE UPPER(vchoice) = "N"
          STORE .F. TO loop1
          STORE .F. TO loop
        OTHERWISE
          @ 20,10 SAY "Not A Valid Choice -- Try Again"
      ENDCASE

    ENDDO
    LOOP

  ELSE
    STORE .T. TO loop1

    DO WHILE loop1
      @ 23,10 SAY SPACE(50)
      @ 23,10 SAY TRIM(LNAME) + ", " + TRIM(FNAME) + "   " + mi
      WAIT "          Edit This Record (Y-Yes   N-Next   P-Previous   A-Abort) "
TO vchoice

      DO CASE
        CASE UPPER(vchoice) = "Y"
          DO EDIT1
          STORE .F. TO loop1
        CASE UPPER(vchoice) = "N"
          @ 24,00 CLEAR
```

```
        SKIP 1
      CASE UPPER(vchoice) = "P"
        @ 24,00 CLEAR
        SKIP -1
      CASE UPPER(vchoice) = "A"
        EXIT
      OTHERWISE
        @ 24,10 SAY " Not A Valid Choice -- Try Again"
    ENDCASE

    IF BOF()
      @ 24,00 CLEAR
      ?? CHR(7)
      @ 23,00
      WAIT "            First Record In File. Do Not Go Further"
      SKIP 1
    ENDIF

    IF EOF()
      @ 24,00 CLEAR
      ?? CHR(7)
      @ 23,00
      WAIT "            Last Record In File. Do Not Go Further"
      SKIP -1
    ENDIF

  ENDDO

ENDIF
STORE .T. TO loop1

DO WHILE loop1
  @ 23,00 SAY "            Edit Another Record? (Y/N) "
  WAIT "                                    " TO vchoice

  DO CASE
    CASE UPPER(vchoice) = "Y"
      STORE .F. TO loop1
    CASE UPPER(vchoice) = "N"
      STORE .F. TO loop
      EXIT
    OTHERWISE
      @ 24,10 SAY " Not A Valid Choice -- Try Again"
  ENDCASE

ENDDO

ENDDO
EXIT

*** End Edit Calling Program
```

is no record in the table that matches the search criteria, *dBase* will search until it reaches the end of the file. If this happens, then the *dBase* function EOF( ) will be true and the IF EOF( ) conditional processing module will be activated.

If there is no match for the specified search criteria you will want to get the operator's attention. I do this by making a big statement on the screen. This is done by CLEARing the screen and announcing outside of the normal dialogue box that the record has not been found. Notice also that the *exact* search string is put up on the screen for the operator's inspection (the "&MLNAME" portion of the announcement) so that he or she can see if there was a mistake when the search string was entered. This type of feedback is essential to any program, as the operator *must* be given cues about what is happening when there is even the slightest possibility of a problem.

Assume that *dBase* has gone through the data table and found a match. The most direct approach to editing would be to dump the user directly into the editing screen. This might be fine in situations where the search string will always be unique to a single record, but it is not suitable in this case. We are searching on the last name only and, as last names are not unique, it is quite probable that there will be two or more people in the file with the same last name. The least that you should do to give the operator a chance to decline before dumping him into the editing screen is to offer more information about the specific record selected and ask for edit confirmation.

In our example we have gone a bit farther than the minimum. We have given the operator a chance to look at the employee's complete name, presented without the excess spaces that exist in records with data less than the allotted width (the TRIM( ) on both lname and fname) and to move both forward and backward through the file before making a final commitment to either edit the currently selected record or abort the operation. Given the nature of the search string used and the type of file being dealt with, this approach is necessary if you are going to program an application that will be well received by users.

The method used to move the record pointer is, as you can see, quite simple. Pressing **N** for the next record simply moves the record pointer forward one record (SKIP 1). Pressing **P** for the previous record simply moves the record pointer back one record (SKIP − 1). The only complication that this type of programming causes is that, by repeatedly pressing **N** or **P** the user can arrive at the end or the beginning of the file, causing *dBase* to have a nervous breakdown when you command the program to move the pointer outside the file. The two conditional processing modules IF EOF( ) and IF BOF( ) handle this situation by alerting the user both audibly (the ?? CHR(7) causes the computer to beep) and visually (the prompt) that they have reached either the beginning or the end of the file. Suicidal maniacs are also taken into consideration in these two conditional processing modules: when the IF BOF( ) processing module is activated, the record pointer is repositioned one record forward into the file (SKIP 1). When the IF EOF( ) processing module is activated, the record pointer is moved back one record (SKIP − 1). The maniac can sit there all day long trying to bust out, but he will not be able to.

The record selection process could be "slicked" up a bit by changing the **Y N P A** menu structure to keypad control. This change is quite simple and can be done with an INKEY( ) loop and by assigning the **PgUp** and **PgDn** keys to move the record pointer forward and backward, the carriage return to activate the edit on the selected record, and **Escape** to abort the process. We will use this in a later program.

As you can see, a **Y** response to the "Edit This Record" prompt turns processing control to the edit program. That program as shown in Listing 4.7.

The first thing to notice in this edit program is the many STORE <fieldname> TO <mvarname> statements in the beginning of the program and the REPLACE <fieldname> WITH <mvarname> statements at the end of the program. These two sections of the program load the contents of the selected data record into memory variables at the beginning of the edit and, if desired, store the contents of the memory variables back into the data record at the end of the edit session. Clearly, many lines of code are needed to accomplish this transfer. As the number of field goes up, the time spent programming this operation will also increase. However, if you are using a good word processor with complete search and replace and block copying capability, the process will not take too much time.

Notice also that the memory variables created are simply the field names with a "V" added to the beginning of the field name to signify to the programmer that these are memory variables. I use "V" but it is not an absolute necessity. If you are going to use *Quicksilver*, using the "M − >" prefix will speed up your application as it tells the compiler to skip looking for a field variable of that name first.

The practice of differentiating your memory variables using some type of consistent naming system makes it much easier to see what you are doing. It also helps you control the release of different classes of memory variables. There is also a second memory variable called

Listing 4.7. Edit Program

```
CLEAR
STORE lname TO vlname
STORE fname TO vfname
STORE mi TO vmi
STORE stadd1 TO vstadd1
STORE stadd2 TO vstadd2
STORE city TO vcity
STORE state TO vstate
STORE zip TO vzip
STORE htel TO vhtel
STORE ssn TO vssn
STORE married TO vmarried
STORE depends TO vdepends
STORE cursal TO vcursal
STORE raisedat TO vraisedat
STORE raisepct TO vraisepct
STORE jcode TO vjcode
STORE depart TO vdepart
STORE superv TO vsuperv
CLOSE DATABASES
STORE .T. TO loop2

DO WHILE loop2
  @ 02,26 SAY "EMPLOYEE DATA FILE"
  @ 03,05 SAY;
"═════════════════════════════════════════════════════"
  @ 05,05 SAY "Last Name:            First Name:
MI:"
  @ 07,05 SAY "Street Address:"
  @ 08,05 SAY "Street Address:"
  @ 10,05 SAY "city:                    state:      zip Code:"
  @ 12,05 SAY "Home Telephone #:           Social Security #:"
  @ 14,05 SAY "married Y/N:        Number of Dependents:"
  @ 16,05 SAY;
"_____"
  @ 18,05 SAY "Current Salary:      Date Last Raise:         Percent:"
  @ 20,05 SAY "Job Code:      department:        supervisor:"
  @ 22,05 SAY;
"_____"

  @ 05,16 GET vlNAME
  @ 05,50 GET vfNAME
  @ 05,71 GET vmi
  @ 07,21 GET vstadd1
  @ 08,21 GET vstadd2
  @ 10,11 GET vcity
  @ 10,42 GET vstate
  @ 10,58 GET vzip
  @ 12,23 GET vhtel
  @ 12,59 GET vssn
  @ 14,18 GET vmarried
```

```
@ 14,51 GET vdepends picture "99"
@ 18,21 GET vcursal picture "999999"
@ 18,47 GET vraisedat
@ 18,67 GET vraisepct picture "99.9"
@ 20,15 GET vjcode
@ 20,33 GET vdepart
@ 20,52 GET vsuperv
READ SAVE

ON ESCAPE
  STORE .T. TO loop3

  DO WHILE loop3
    @ 23,00 SAY "        A - Abort Edit    R - Re-Edit Record    S - Save Edits

    WAIT "" TO vchoice

  DO CASE
    CASE UPPER(vchoice) = "A"
      @ 23,00 CLEAR
      STORE .F. TO loop2
      RELEASE ALL LIKE V*
      EXIT
    CASE UPPER(vchoice) = "R"
      @ 24,00 CLEAR
      EXIT
    CASE UPPER(vchoice) = "S"
      @ 24,00 CLEAR
      USE UI INDEX lname
      SEEK mlname
      REPLACE lname WITH vlNAME
      REPLACE fname WITH vfNAME
      REPLACE mi WITH vmi
      REPLACE stadd1 WITH vstadd1
      REPLACE stadd2 WITH vstadd2
      REPLACE city WITH vcity
      REPLACE state WITH vstate
      REPLACE zip WITH vzip
      REPLACE htel WITH vhtel
      REPLACE ssn WITH vssn
      REPLACE married WITH vmarried
      REPLACE depends WITH vdepends
      REPLACE cursal WITH vcursal
      REPLACE raisedat WITH vraisedat
      REPLACE raisepct WITH vraisepct
      REPLACE jcode WITH vjcode
      REPLACE depart WITH vdepart
      REPLACE superv WITH vsuperv
      STORE .F. TO loop3
      STORE .F. TO loop2

      IF mlname <> vlNAME
        REINDEX
      ENDIF

     RELEASE ALL LIKE V*
     RELEASE mlname
```

```
        @ 23,00 CLEAR
     OTHERWISE
        @ 24,00 CLEAR
        @ 24,10 SAY " Not A Valid Choice -- Try Again"
     ENDCASE

  ENDDO

ENDDO
RETURN

***  End Edit Program
```

MLNAME created in the edit calling program in Listing 4.7. It starts off with the same value of VLNAME but, if the employee's last name changes during the edit (as it might be for an employee who just got married), the MLNAME (unchanged) allows us to find the record again to store the information. Note also that a reindexing routine is included to maintain our index if this happens.

Editing memory variables instead of field data also allows us to close the active data tables while the edit is in progress. (Note the CLOSE DATABASES command immediately after the memory variables are loaded from the proper record in the data table.) While this practice means that the table may have to be accessed twice for each record edited, this method of handling tables provides much better data safety for the application. As the data tables are only open for a brief instant at the beginning and the end of the edit operation, the tables are less vulnerable to power interruptions caused by blackouts and angry or unthinking flips of the computer's power switch. As a result of this, the incidence of corrupted table headers and loss of edit data is greatly reduced.

WordTech's compiler will work with these memory variables, but the system runs faster if the variables are marked as memory variables by putting an "M − >" in front of the variable name. If this is done, the program will not search for a field name first, thereby improving the execution speed.

Editing memory variables will also give you the capability to do things with the edit process that you would not be able to do if you were editing the data tables directly. Notice the main editing loop that allows the user to go back over the data as many times as necessary before finally making a choice about the final disposition of the record. This allows the user to get out of a bad edit without changing the contents of the database.

Card Entry System

In this chapter, we have so far been looking at simple data entry screens and simple programs using the Employee Data File as a basis of discussion. Let's look at the same system, but implemented in a different and more useful fashion.

The long program that follows uses the same information and the same database that we have been working with previously but presents the user with a "Rolodex" view of the file. The screen looks like Figure 4.2.

In this system, the user gets more information about the file he or she is working with than he would get in a flat view of only one record. The system will allow the user to scroll forward and backward, seeing not only the current record but also the four records either in front of the current record (if scrolling backward) or behind the current record (if scrolling forward).

When you examine the program in Listing 4.8 you will find that it is not that complicated at all. All the programming is straightforward, but manages to get the job done. There are only a couple of points to consider.

The first point has to do with the INKEY( ) loop at the end of the main program. You will notice that there are more than a few choices for the program to go through each time a key is pressed. In order to minimize the amount of unnecessary processing that the program goes through, the DO WHILE loop is a bit different from the simple one that we saw in Chapter 3, Listing 3.5). Instead of going through and processing every key press as a valid command, the INKEY( ) loop keeps processing until a valid response is given. It speeds up processing response. The validation consists of first changing the value of KEY from numeric to character and then seeing if the value is included in the validation string of the AT( ) function. If the value of KEY is not in the string, the value of AT( ) is zero and the INKEY( ) DO LOOP continues. The spaces between the valid entries are there so that values such as "83" or "31" are not interpreted as valid responses.

The second thing to note in the program is that certain characters in the screen (most notably the up and down arrows) are specified by CHR( ) and their ASCII value. Although *dBase* can handle ASCII characters below 32 (the space bar) easily, most printers will choke in

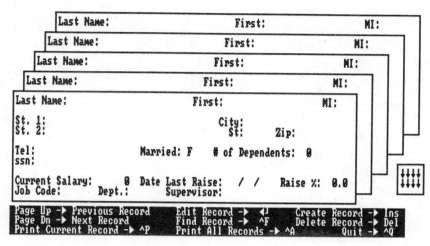

Figure 4.2.   Screen Shot of Rolodex System

Listing 4.8.   Rolodex Program

```
*** MAIN PROGRAM

SET TALK OFF
SET STATUS OFF
SET SCOREBOARD OFF
SET ESCAPE OFF
SET SAFETY OFF
SET EXACT OFF

USE <data table name>
INDEX ON lname TO name

SET COLOR TO W+
CLEAR
@ 02,08 SAY;
     " _____ "
@ 03,08 SAY;
     "|Last Name:                    First:              MI:       |"
@ 04,06 SAY;
     " _____ |"
@ 05,06 SAY;
     "|Last Name:                    First:              MI:       |  |"
@ 06,04 SAY;
     " _____ |  |"
@ 07,04 SAY;
```

```
     "|Last Name:                    First:                MI:    |   |   |"
@ 08,02 SAY;
     "┌─────────────────────────────────────────────────────────┐   |   |   |"
@ 09,02 SAY;
     "|Last Name:                    First:                MI:   |   |   |   |"
@ 10,00 SAY;
     "┌──┴──────────────────────────────────────────────────────┐   |   |   |"+;
     "   |  |"
@ 11,00 SAY "|Last Name:                     "+;
            "First:                MI:   |   |   |   |   |"
@ 12,00 SAY "|                               "+;
            "                            |   |   |   |   |"
@ 13,00 SAY "|St. 1:                         "+;
            "     City:                  |   |   |   |   |"
@ 14,00 SAY "|St. 2:                         "+;
            "         St:     Zip:        |   |   | ┌───┘ "
@ 15,00 SAY "|                               "+;
            "                            |   |   |   |"
@ 16,00 SAY "|Tel:                    Married: "+;
            "       # of Dependents:     |   | ┌───┘ "
@ 17,00 SAY "|ssn:                           "+;
            "                            |   |   |"
@ 18,00 SAY "|                               "+;
            "                            |   └───┘ "
@ 19,00 SAY "|Current Salary:         Date Last "+;
            "Raise:          Raise %:    |   |"
@ 20,00 SAY "|Job Code:        Dept.:        "+;
            "Supervisor:                   └───┘ "
@ 21,00 SAY;
     "└──────────────────────────────────────────────────────────┘ "
SET COLOR TO N/W
@ 22,00 CLEAR TO 24,75
@ 22,01 SAY "Page Up -"+CHR(16)+" Previous Record      Edit Record -"+CHR(16)+;
            " "+CHR(17)+"┘     Create Record -"+CHR(16)+" Ins"
@ 23,01 SAY "Page Dn -"+CHR(16)+" Next Record         Find Record -"+CHR(16)+;
            "  ^F     Delete Record -"+CHR(16)+" Del"
@ 24,01 SAY "Print Current Record -"+CHR(16)+" ^P     Print All Records -"+;
            CHR(16)+" ^A         Quit -"+CHR(16)+" ^Q"

SET COLOR TO W
GO TOP
STORE .T. TO loop
STORE 3 TO key
STORE .T. TO start

DO WHILE loop

  DO CASE
    CASE key = 18
       @ 17,74 SAY " ┌───┐ "
       @ 18,74 SAY " |"+CHR(24)+""+CHR(24)+""+CHR(24)+""+CHR(24)+"| "
       @ 19,74 SAY " |"+CHR(24)+""+CHR(24)+""+CHR(24)+""+CHR(24)+"| "
       @ 20,74 SAY " └───┘ "
       STORE .T. TO loop1

       DO WHILE loop1
         SKIP -1
```

```
      IF BOF()
        ?? CHR(7)
        @ 11,12 SAY "END OF FILE          "
        @ 11,42 SAY "                  "
        @ 11,64 SAY " "
        EXIT
      ELSE
        DO paint
      ENDIF

      SKIP -1

      IF BOF()
        @ 09,14 SAY "END OF FILE          "
        @ 09,44 SAY "                  "
        @ 09,66 SAY " "
        EXIT
      ELSE
         @ 09,14 SAY lname
         @ 09,44 SAY fname
         @ 09,66 SAY mi
      ENDIF

      SKIP -1

      IF BOF()
         @ 07,16 SAY "END OF FILE          "
         @ 07,46 SAY "                  "
         @ 07,68 SAY " "
         SKIP 1
         EXIT
      ELSE
         @ 07,16 SAY lname
         @ 07,46 SAY fname
         @ 07,68 SAY mi
      ENDIF

      SKIP -1

      IF BOF()
         @ 05,18 SAY "END OF FILE          "
         @ 05,48 SAY "                  "
         @ 05,70 SAY " "
         SKIP 2
         EXIT
      ELSE
         @ 05,18 SAY lname
         @ 05,48 SAY fname
         @ 05,70 SAY mi
      ENDIF

      SKIP -1

      IF BOF()
         @ 03,20 SAY "END OF FILE          "
         @ 03,50 SAY "                  "
```

```
                     @ 03,72 SAY " "
                     SKIP 3
                     EXIT
                  ELSE
                     @ 03,20 SAY lname
                     @ 03,50 SAY fname
                     @ 03,72 SAY mi
                     SKIP 4
                     EXIT
                  ENDIF

            ENDDO
      CASE key = 3
         DO down
      CASE key = 13
         DO edit
      CASE key = 6
         STORE .T. TO loop1

         DO WHILE loop1
            @ 22,00 CLEAR
            @ 23,10 SAY "Enter Last Name for Search.  Press <Return> When Done."
            STORE "                  " TO vlname
            @ 11,12 GET vlname
            READ
            SEEK vlname
            @ 22,00 CLEAR

            IF EOF()
               STORE .T. TO loop2

               DO WHILE loop2
                  @ 23,10 SAY "Record Is Not in File.  Try Again? (Y/N)"
                  WAIT "                      " TO vchoice

                  DO CASE
                     CASE UPPER(vchoice) = "Y"
                        STORE .F. TO loop2
                     CASE UPPER(vchoice) = "N"
                        STORE .F. TO loop2
                        STORE .F. TO loop1
                     OTHERWISE
                        @ 22,00 CLEAR
                        @ 23,10 SAY "Not a Valid Choice.  Try Again? (Y/N)
                        WAIT "                    " TO vchoice
                  ENDCASE

               ENDDO
            ELSE
               STORE .F. TO loop1

            ENDIF

         ENDDO
```

```
      IF .NOT. EOF()
        DO down
      ENDIF

    CASE key = 22
      APPEND BLANK
      DO edit
    CASE key = 7
      @ 22,00 CLEAR
      SET COLOR TO W+
      @ 23,10 SAY "Current Record Will Be Deleted.  Press "Y" To Confirm."
      WAIT "                          " TO vchoice
      SET COLOR TO W

      IF UPPER(vchoice) = "Y"
        DELETE
        PACK
      ENDIF

    CASE key = 16
      DO printone
    CASE key = 1
      DO printall
    CASE key = 17
      @ 22,00 CLEAR
      @ 23,10 SAY "Exit the System? (Y/N)"
      WAIT "                  " TO vchoice

      IF UPPER(vchoice) = "Y"
        CLOSE DATABASES
        CLEAR
        EXIT

      ENDIF

  ENDCASE
  CLEAR GETS
  SET COLOR TO N/W
  @ 22,00 CLEAR TO 24,75
  @ 22,01 SAY "Page Up -"+CHR(16)+" Previous Record     Edit Record -"+CHR(16)+;
          " "+CHR(17)+"⌐    Create Record -"+CHR(16)+" Ins"
  @ 23,01 SAY "Page Dn -"+CHR(16)+" Next Record        Find Record -"+CHR(16)+;
          " ^F     Delete Record -"+CHR(16)+" Del"
  @ 24,01 SAY "Print Current Record -"+CHR(16)+" ^P     Print All Records -"+;
          CHR(16)+" ^A        Quit -"+CHR(16)+" ^Q"
  SET COLOR TO W
  STORE 0 TO key

  DO WHILE AT(STR(key,2),"18 3 13 6 16 1 22 7 17") = 0
    STORE INKEY() TO key
  ENDDO

ENDDO

***   END MAIN.PRG
```

```
***  PAINT.PRG

@ 11,12 SAY lname
@ 11,42 SAY fname
@ 11,64 SAY mi
@ 13,08 SAY stadd1
@ 14,08 SAY stadd2
@ 13,46 SAY city
@ 14,46 SAY state
@ 14,56 SAY zip
@ 16,06 SAY htel
@ 17,06 SAY ssn
@ 16,34 SAY married
@ 16,56 SAY depends
@ 19,17 SAY cursal
@ 19,42 SAY raisedat
@ 19,61 SAY raisepct
@ 20,11 SAY jcode
@ 20,24 SAY depart
@ 20,42 SAY superv
RETURN

** END PAINT.PRG

***  DOWN.PRG

@ 17,74 SAY " ┌─────┐ "
@ 18,74 SAY " │"+CHR(25)+""+CHR(25)+""+CHR(25)+""+CHR(25)+"│ "
@ 19,74 SAY " │"+CHR(25)+""+CHR(25)+""+CHR(25)+""+CHR(25)+"│ "
@ 20,74 SAY " └─────┘ "
STORE .T. TO loop1

DO WHILE loop1

  IF .NOT. start
    SKIP 1
  ENDIF

  STORE .F. TO start

  IF EOF()
    ?? CHR(7)
    @ 11,12 SAY "END OF FILE        "
    EXIT
  ELSE
    DO paint
  ENDIF

  SKIP 1

  IF EOF()
    @ 09,14 SAY "END OF FILE        "
    @ 09,44 SAY "                "
    @ 09,66 SAY " "
    SKIP -1
    EXIT
```

```
ELSE
  @ 09,14 SAY lname
  @ 09,44 SAY fname
  @ 09,66 SAY mi
ENDIF

SKIP 1

IF EOF()
  @ 07,16 SAY "END OF FILE         "
  @ 07,46 SAY "                  "
  @ 07,68 SAY " "
  SKIP -2
  EXIT
ELSE
  @ 07,16 SAY lname
  @ 07,46 SAY fname
  @ 07,68 SAY mi
ENDIF

SKIP 1

IF EOF()
  @ 05,18 SAY "END OF FILE         "
  @ 05,48 SAY "                  "
  @ 05,70 SAY " "
  SKIP -3
  EXIT
ELSE
  @ 05,18 SAY lname
  @ 05,48 SAY fname
  @ 05,70 SAY mi
ENDIF

SKIP 1

IF EOF()
  @ 03,20 SAY "END OF FILE          "
  @ 03,50 SAY "                  "
  @ 03,72 SAY " "
  SKIP -4
  EXIT
ELSE
  @ 03,20 SAY lname
  @ 03,50 SAY fname
  @ 03,72 SAY mi
  SKIP -4
  EXIT
ENDIF

ENDDO
RETURN

*** END DOWN.PRG
```

```
*** EDIT.PRG

STORE lname TO vlname
STORE fname TO vfname
STORE mi TO vmi
STORE stadd1 TO vstadd1
STORE stadd2 TO vstadd2
STORE city TO vcity
STORE state TO vstate
STORE zip TO vzip
STORE htel TO vhtel
STORE married TO vmarried
STORE depends TO vdepends
STORE ssn TO vssn
STORE cursal TO vcursal
STORE raisedat TO vraisedat
STORE raisepct TO vraisepct
STORE jcode TO vjcode
STORE depart TO vdepart
STORE superv TO vsuperv
STORE .T. TO loop1

DO WHILE loop1
   @ 22,00 CLEAR
   @ 11,12 GET vlname
   @ 11,42 GET vfNAME
   @ 11,64 GET vmi
   @ 13,08 GET vstadd1
   @ 14,08 GET vstadd2
   @ 13,46 GET vcity
   @ 14,46 GET vstate
   @ 14,56 GET vzip
   @ 16,06 GET vhtel
   @ 17,06 GET vssn
   @ 16,34 GET vmarried
   @ 16,56 GET vdepends PICTURE "99"
   @ 19,17 GET vcursal PICTURE "999999"
   @ 19,42 GET vraisedat
   @ 19,61 GET vraisepct PICTURE "99.9"
   @ 20,11 GET vjcode
   @ 20,24 GET vdepart
   @ 20,42 GET vsuperv
   @ 23,10 SAY "Press <Escape> To End Edit"
   READ SAVE
   STORE "" TO vchoice
   @ 22,00 CLEAR
   SET COLOR TO W+
   WAIT " (Q) Quit Edits - No save   (R) Re-edit table  (S) Save edits ";
        to vchoice
   SET COLOR TO W

   DO CASE
      CASE UPPER(vchoice) = "Q"
        STORE .F. TO loop1
      CASE UPPER(vchoice) = "R"
        STORE .T. TO loop1
      CASE UPPER(vchoice) = "S"
```

```
      REPLACE lname WITH vlname
      REPLACE fname WITH vfname
      REPLACE mi WITH vmi
      REPLACE stadd1 WITH vstadd1
      REPLACE stadd2 WITH vstadd2
      REPLACE city WITH vcity
      REPLACE state WITH vstate
      REPLACE zip WITH vzip
      REPLACE htel WITH vhtel
      REPLACE ssn WITH vssn
      REPLACE married WITH vmarried
      REPLACE depends WITH vdepends
      REPLACE cursal WITH vcursal
      REPLACE raisedat WITH vraisedat
      REPLACE raisepct WITH vraisepct
      REPLACE jcode WITH vjcode
      REPLACE depart WITH vdepart
      REPLACE superv WITH vsuperv
      RELEASE ALL LIKE V*
      STORE .F. TO loop1
   OTHERWISE
      @ 22,00 CLEAR
      @ 23,10 SAY "Not a Valid Choice.  Press <Escape> to Try Again.
      STORE .T. TO loop1
   ENDCASE

ENDDO
RETURN

*** END EDIT.PRG

*** END CARD FILE PROGRAM ***
```

their own unique and bizarre ways on these characters. It is therefore best if they are represented in your program files as CHR( ) values. Printers will work with this and, although documentation will be less exciting, it will be readable.

It is important to note the way the program handles EOF( ) and BOF( ). Any program must be able to handle this type of situation, or it cannot be considered a valid application. If you allow a user to try and press beyond the beginning or end of the file, *dBase III Plus* will issue a notice that end (beginning) of file has been reached, and then cease to function properly.

Also, when SAYing, "END OF FILE" spaces are also used at the end of the expression to ensure that the entire field space is blanked. The space that is normally occupied by the first name and the middle initial is also blanked so that data from the previous record is erased. This takes a bit of extra time, but it is worth it to make the screen look cleaner.

In order to offset the extra time that is needed to do some of the screen painting, most of the screen (not the data) is painted only once. The only part of the screen that is repainted is the up and down (direction) box on the right side and the command area (the bottom three lines) of the screen. This allows us to avoid rewriting the entire screen each time a new command is issued.

Now that we've discussed the Rolodex system, let's look at the next subject, screen saves.

Saving the Screen

One of the most frustrating things about *dBase III Plus* is that the program is slow when it paints screens. Depending on how you write a file, a complicated screen with several different colors can take as long as five or six seconds to paint. When the screen has to be painted and repainted often, this time can become a real drawback to the program. If, for example, you use pop-up boxes, you have to repaint every time you erase a box. There are, however, ways to circumvent this problem using *Clipper*, *Quicksilver*, and some of the add-on products. Unfortunately, *dBase III Plus* scores a minus: the only way that I know of to handle this problem is to repaint, repaint, and repaint.

Clipper provides probably the easiest method of solving the problem of screen painting. The program allows you to save the screen *at any time* to a memory variable using the SAVE SCREEN (TO <memvar>) and the RESTORE SCREEN (FROM <memvar>) commands. Note that a single screen can be saved and restored at any time without the memory variable designation, or any number of different screens can be saved using memory variables and recalled in whatever order you desire, using the RESTORE SCREEN command with the appropriate memory variable. Either the screen outline (without data) or a complete screen (including the current data) can be saved and restored, making pop-up help and menus much easier to program. As the screens are saved in memory variables, which are RAM-resident, the screens paint quickly. The only drawback to the *Clipper* solution is that *each* of the created memory variables is 4 kilobytes in size, so memory will be eaten up with astonishing speed if you are not careful. The second problem with the SAVE SCREEN command is that it is not compatible with *dBase III Plus*, so you must use the IF CLIPPER statement when you use it. This is not a problem, but programming the *dBase* code necessary to perform the same function is usually so different from the *Clipper* code that the two types of programs are virtually incompatible.

Quicksilver handles saving and restoring screens as part of its WINDOW command set. *Quicksilver* does true windows. As a developer you can have as many as 99 active windows on the screen at any one time, with any number of them overlapping and covering up other windows. What is important here is that if you use windows, you do not have to SAVE the main screen; it can be overwritten using the WINDOW commands and, when the later windows are CLOSEd, the main screen (window 0) will still be there. You can, if you want, SAVE the window to a named disk file, or move it off the screen temporarily and return to it later. The capabilities are truly mind expanding. The only problem with the set of WINDOW commands is that there is nothing like it at all in *dBase* so, if you decide to use them to any extent, you will move so far away from *dBase III Plus* that your programs will no longer run on the *dBase* interpreter.

At least three companies dealing in *dBase* add-on products have options for fast screens. Both work with save the screen formats (not the fields) in RAM and both will paint screens so much faster than *dBase* that comparisons are not meaningful. The first of thse products is *SpeedScreen*, from the Software Bottling Company of New York. *SpeedScreen* takes up to 36 different screen files (.SCR) created with its own products, *Screen Sculptor* and *Flash Code*, and compresses them into a single file that is loaded into RAM when the application is invoked. These screens can be data format files, help screens, menus, or whatever you wish. They are called by the SPEEDSCR module with a single command and are "dropped" onto the screen in a flash. Although you must include the SPEEDSCR module with all your applications, The Software Bottling Company of New York does not require any license fees or royalties when you use the product. The cost is only $35 so, if you are already using *Flash Code* or *Screen Sculptor*, it is a bargain. *SpeedScreen*, however, does not work with either *Clipper* or *Quicksilver*.

Wallsoft includes a memory resident display program with its screen generating program *UI*. The program is called *MRD* (Memory Resident Display) and is more flexible than *SpeedScreen*. The *MRD* module must be present during program execution and screens must be generated using *UI* and become a special type of file (.SIF). You can specify the size of the screen buffer that you want (up to 63K). It can be CALLed from within *dBase* and new .SIF files can be loaded and unloaded at will. The .SIF files can be either full-screen or pop-up, and screen coordinates can be given at execution time to place the boxes on the screen. *MRD* also has the SAVE and RESTORE commands so that screens that are going to be overwritten can be restored without being repainted. This gives you almost complete control over your screens. *MRD* object code is also provided with the program so that the module can be linked into a final application when the *Clipper* .EXE file is created.

Saywhat?!, from The Research Group, has a memory resident utility called VIDPOP that will display one of its screens using a single command in a *dBase* file. It does not save screens but will redisplay them when they are "popped" again. If you are using memory variables for your GETs, the current values will be shown so you have the same effect.

In summary, if you are going to be going heavily into boxes, windows, and pop-ups, I suggest that you use something more than *dBase III Plus*. While *dBase III Plus* will execute these features, it may take you more time to program and debug than it's worth.

Default Values

In production-oriented applications, saving keystrokes in data entry is important for two reasons. First, it saves time and, if you are paying data entry operators, time is money. Second, default values usually improve the accuracy of data entry. Improved accuracy means less time spent correcting errors and . . . time is money. This section will deal with different ways that you can program time savers into your applications.

The easiest default value routine simply puts a specified value into a field before it is put to the screen. In our employee example it would be a simple matter to change the "STORE state TO vstate" statement to "STORE 'CA' TO vstate" when a new record is created (but not when an existing record is edited). If our company is located in Los Angeles, it is most likely that almost all our employees will live in California. If one employee does not, the operator can simply change the default value to the proper data for that person before going on with the editing. The same thing can be done with the telephone number field by saying "STORE (213) " TO vhtel". While this does not fill in the entire entry, it suggests the most likely area code for the operator to either accept or type over.

The next type of default value is the carry-over value. This represents the value of the field from the last record added. If, for example, we are adding six new employees to the accounting department, we can make the value of the last record entered show up as the default by changing it in such a way that it does not get erased in the RELEASE ALL LIKE V* command. I usually use an M prefix for memory variables that I do not want to have erased at the end of a READ. These memory variables must be initialized before going into the "Add" section of your program so that they will not be reinitialized for each new record as the others will be. Once this is done, it is a simple matter to exclude these variables from the initialization process. The carry-over value will still be there and can be accepted or changed at the operator's will, read into the proper field in the new record, and then carried over to the next record.

The last type of default value we will discuss is system clock information. Any MS-DOS computer will give you the calendar date and the time. It is up to the computer operator to ensure that they are accurate (up to a point: we will discuss a very simple way to keep the operator honest in Chapter 6) but *dBase* can make good use of this information as default values. STORE DATE( ) to VDATE will store the system date to the memory variable VDATE. STORE DATE( ) + 2 TO VSHIPDATE will suggest a shipping date to the operator that is two days hence. The same can be done with the time or the day of the week if it is necessary.

Automatic date and time stamping, so necessary in a transaction file for security and data integrity, are placed in the file by this simple method.

Data Entry Verification

The oldest computer expression in the world is "GIGO" or "Garbage In, Garbage Out." One of the most important jobs of the program developer is to ensure that the data the operator is entering in to the system has been checked for careless errors.

   dBase III Plus offers little in the way of data validation functions but the program is designed so that you can write your own routines to check data. We will start this chapter by discussing what *dBase* does offer the user, and then proceed to develop several data verification routines using some of *dBase*'s programming capabilities. We will then go beyond *dBase* and look at what the compilers offer.

PICTURE Templates

dBase III Plus has a series of PICTURE templates that can be used to verify data entry when using GETs. The PICTURE templates also serve a second, very important, purpose — they help format screen (and printer) output for the developer. We will discuss both uses here.

PICTURE formatting is a powerful sublanguage of *dBase III Plus*. I constantly find new and more useful ways to use the language and suggest that the best way to learn it is to experiment with it yourself. You should consider the following to be only a brief introduction to the capabilities of PICTURE templates.

All PICTURE templates are issued right after the SAY or GET and take the form PICTURE "<clause>." The opening and closing quote marks are necessary so that *dBase* can determine exactly what the length of the PICTURE clause is. The template language is broken into two distinct sets: the template symbol set and the function set.

Template Functions

Template functions define how certain types of data are displayed. Most of them are used to format numbers. The functions are all identified by the "@" symbol that precedes them. You must leave a space between the template function and template symbols. The list of functions and what they do is as follows:

1. @C   *Displays a positive number with a "CR" after it.*

2. @X   *Displays a negative number with a "DB" after it.*

These two PICTURE functions are a boon to those of you with financial applications. The value "123" (numeric, not character value) using the PICTURE "@C" function is displayed "123 CR". The value "−234" is displayed "234 DB" when the PICTURE "@X" template function is used. These two functions are independent of each other but can be used together. The PICTURE "@CX" statement will put "CR" after a positive number and "DB" after a negative one.

3. @(*Displays negative numbers inside parentheses.*

If you did not like using debits and credits in the preceding examples, you can always use the parentheses around negative numbers. The example of "−234" could be shown as "(234)" using this template function. You will notice that I say "could" and not "would" or "will." This is because *dBase III Plus* is showing some of its character to us with this function. Some discussion on this point is needed.

If you were to write the following program:

```
STORE -234 TO vnum
@ 10,10 SAY vnum PICTURE "@("
```

and run it, you would get the following output at screen position 10,10:

```
(        234)
```

This is because *dBase* automatically initializes any numeric memory variable to 10 spaces. There is nothing that you can do about this. You must control the length of the output by using template symbols. Here either the "#" or the "9" symbol will work. If we want the parentheses to surround the number, we should be able to simply expand the PICTURE clause to "@(999" to get that result. If you tried this, you would get the following output:

```
(***)
```

Not quite what was expected. The asterisks signify that the number is too big to fit in the space provided for it. *dBase* stores the minus sign that accompanies a negative number as part of the value of that number. Even though you have instructed the program to replace that minus sign with the parentheses, as far as *dBase* is concerned, it is still there. The best that you can do directly is use the PICTURE "@(9999" statement, which will give you this output:

```
( 234)
```

If it is *absolutely* essential that the brackets be around the number and that there be no spaces, you will have to convert it to a character string and SAY it as in Listing 5.1.

This will finally give you your "(234)" but you must remember that the variable is now a character string, and is useless in its current form for any further arithmetic calculations. Working from the inside out, the STR( ) function converts VNUM to a character string 10 characters long that looks like this: "   −234". This will allow for most large negative numbers. The LTRIM( ) function gets rid of all spaces on the left

Listing 5.1.   Space Trim on Negative Number Parentheses

```
STORE "("+SUBSTR(LTRIM(STR(vnum),10)),2)+")" TO vchar
@ 10,10 SAY vchar

*** End Trim Module
```

---

hand side of the expression and leaves us with "-234" as our expression. The SUBSTR( ) function gives us a string starting at the second position, thereby getting rid of the minus sign. The requisite parentheses are then added to the beginning and the end of our string as literal text.

If you are dealing with numbers in a column that must line up, a second, more complicated, approach is required. This is the *dBase* workaround for this problem:

Listing 5.2.   Column Alignment of Negative Numbers in Parentheses

---

```
STORE STR(vnum, nn, n) TO vchar
STORE AT("-", vchar) TO vposition
@ 10,10 SAY SPACE(vposition-1)+"("+SUBSTR(vchar,vposition+1)+")"

*** End Alignment Module
```

The values "nn" and "n" in the first expression are the total length of the character string and decimal values respectively. The first value should be large enough to handle any number (including the decimal point and the numbers to the right of the decimal point) that you could reasonably expect. If anything, it should be a few characters larger as the extra spaces will be trimmed off later. The second statement determines the location of the minus sign and is important both in positioning the resulting string and in determining where to start the cut. The third statement positions the resulting field correctly (using the SPACE command and padding in the correct number of spaces) and then SAYs the number as a substring starting after the minus sign of the original string and surrounded by the literal "(" and ")".

4. @Z   *Displays a null field (or field with value of zero) as a blank.*

dBase III Plus displays a blank number field with a "0" in it unless specifically told to suppress the zero. Be careful how you use this function because, in use, it is impossible to differentiate between a blank field and one with a zero in it as a valid data point.

5. @B   *Displays numbers left justified.*

Unless this template function is used, all numeric data is shown right justified. When you use the @B function, all leading zeros are trimmed and the first digit of the number starts at the designate row/column coordinate. The only problem with this function is that numbers of differing lengths have a ragged right edge.

There are two template functions for dates:

6. @D   *Displays a date in the mm/dd/yy format*

7. @E   *Displays a date in the dd/mm/yy format*

Character strings can be controlled by three different functions:

8. @A   *This function will restrict input to alphabetic characters only, no blanks or numbers or signs will be accepted.*

9. @!   *This function converts all characters entered to uppercase, but will allow input of blanks, numbers and signs.*

The @A and @! template functions are mutually exclusive. If you wish to restrict entry to alpha characters and have them all converted to uppercase, you will have to do it using the PICTURE "@A !!!!!!!!!!!..." combination of the @A template function plus the ! template symbol. This may sound confusing, but remember that the "@!" function does not do the same thing as the "!" symbol, which works only on the one space in the field where it is located.

10. @R   *Literal text in the PICTURE template that follows this function will not be stored with the values entered.*

The @R function is a useful command for entering formatted numbers on which no math will be done. Although we are getting slightly ahead of ourselves, it is instructive to see how this function works. Our example will be a telephone number field. Telephone numbers are normally numeric (except for those holdovers from the old days like "SUssex 2 3456" instead of "782-3456"). I have never heard of an application where any math was done on a telephone number so there is no reason to have a telephone number labeled a numeric field. It should be made a character field. If you need to select all telephone numbers with the 913 area code, for example, you can SET FILTER to take care of this criteria.

A basic telephone number is 10 digits long, but it is usually configured with literal text so that it looks like this:

```
(213) 789-4455
```

The open and close parentheses, the space after the close parentheses, and the minus sign between the third and fourth digits of the main part of the telephone number are conventions that everyone in the United States recognizes. *dBase* allows us to create a PICTURE template that contains these literals as part of the template. The actual PICTURE statement is:

```
PICTURE "(999) 999-9999"
```

Without using the @R function the character field to hold this data point must be 14 characters long and numbers in the file will appear just as they do on the screen, with all the literal text included. If, however, you use the @R template function, the field need only be 10 characters long. Only the numbers themselves will be stored but, when displayed, will show properly in the template. In this particular case, you have saved four bytes for each record in the system. If there are many formatted fields like this, the savings can mount up rapidly.

11. *@S<n>   Displays a "window" 'n' characters long and scrolls text through that window.*

The @S function is essential when you have a field that is wider than the screen. By specifying a width (<n>) you specify the window size into that field. When you fill it up, the text starts to scroll across the window. This can also be useful if you have a crowded data entry screen and one or more uncomfortably long fields.

Template Symbols

The second part of the template language deals with the language's symbols. In theory, these are easy to understand and use but, in practice, nothing is as it seems. Let us first say what the symbols are used for, and then discuss what they are and how they are used.

The template functions tell *dBase* what to do with data but they tell the program nothing about how big the data point is or how it is to be formatted internally. The symbols do that. The symbols act differently depending on whether the data point is numeric or character and whether the data point is a field or memory variable.

As with the template functions, the template symbols can be divided into those dealing with numerical values, those dealing with character fields, and those dealing with logical values. There are no template symbols for data type fields.

Numbers provide the most complexity, so let's start there. If the number that you GET or SAY is either a field value or a memory variable that was initialized with a field value, the space provided (and the number of decimal places) conforms to that of that field. If you have a numeric field with a length of six and two decimal places, the SAY or GET will give you three places to the left of the decimal point, a decimal point, and then two places to the right of the decimal place. If, on the other hand, you have a memory variable that was simply initialized as a numeric variable (either by using a "STORE 0 to vnum" or by getting a number from an ACCEPT or WAIT command) the displayed field will be 10 spaces long. This can wreck your formatting when you have calculated fields, so something must be done to bring these memory variables back under control. Template symbols do this.

If the numeric memory variable also has decimal places, you will have to do something about that as well. You can set the number of places when you initialize the variable by specifying the correct number like this:

```
STORE 0.000 TO vnum
```

but this does nothing about the 10 places to the left of the decimal point and the number of decimal places is also subject to being overridden by a different value that is read into the variable at some later point in the program. The template symbols will take care of this also.

Template symbols limit the length of the field, how the field will be formatted, and the type of data that will be accepted to that field. The length of the field is determined by the number of data symbols that are included, the formatting is controlled by the literal text that is included in the PICTURE clause, and the type of data that will be accepted in the field in a GET is determined by the type of symbol(s) used.

Depending on how you look at it, there are two, four, or six numerical template symbols. The two about which there are no arguments are the "#" and "9" symbols. The pound sign will limit input to digits, blanks, and arithmetic signs. The number "9" in the template will limit data input to only digits and signs. When dealing with numbers you also have the use of the second pair for formatting symbols, the decimal point, and commas. PICTURE "999,999.99" is a valid template statement that should give you a GET field 10 characters long to accept a number anywhere from $-99,999.99$ to $999,999.99$ (remember that the minus sign must be counted as a character in the field). Please note the use of the word "should" in the last sentence. How the field is displayed, what it will accept, and what is stored in the variable or field depends on whether the variable or field is charcter or numeric. The following three examples show some of the differences:

```
Example A:   Numeric field  PICTURE "999,999.99"
             Empty GET looks like:  [      0.00]
             Full GET looks like:   [123,456.78]
             Stored value is:        123456.78

Example B:   Character field  PICTURE "999,999.99"
             Empty GET looks like:  [   ,    .   ]
             Full GET looks like:   [123,456.73]
             Stored value is:        123,456.78

Example C:   Character field  PICTURE "@R 999,999.99"
             Empty GET looks like:  [   ,    .   ]
             Full GET looks like:   [123,456.73]
             Stored value is:        12345678
```

The only field that you can directly use for numeric calculations is the first. The numeric field is also the only one that behaves as numbers should. When you put in the number 6 as the value of the field and press the carriage return to go on to the next entry the results are completely different with the numeric and character fields:

```
Numeric field:    [      6.00]
Character field: [6    ,    ,    ]
```

The same is true of the decimal point. With the numeric field, pressing the period moved data entry to the right of the decimal point. With the character field, pressing the period is not a valid entry and the operator will get a beep from the computer.

Note that the length of the two character fields is different in examples B and C: the comma and period must be considered in the first.

We can now turn our attention to the third set of numeric symbols, the * and the $ signs. Both these symbols act in the same manner in numeric fields: poorly. The template PICTURE "$999,999.99" (or "*999,999.99") will fill in *all* leading zeros with either dollar signs or stars. Notice that I say "all" leading zeros. To continue with our example, the value of 6.00 will be displayed as follows:

```
[$$$$$6.00]
```

I cannot think of too many applicatoins where this is a desired function. The single dollar sign should either be displayed in a fixed position or should be placed directly preceding the first digit of the number. If you want the dollar sign to be in a fixed position, a simple set of SAYs will work. In order to avoid a data type mismatch error you must use two SAYs like this:

```
@ 10,10 SAY "$"
@ 10,11 SAY vnum PICTURE "999,999.99"
```

The workaround to get *dBase* to display a "floating" dollar sign in front of the number is not too difficult:

```
STORE 1234.56 TO vnum
SAY "$" + LTRIM(STR(vnum,12,2))
```

unless you want the numbers to be lined up properly in a column. If this is necessary, the procedure becomes a bit more complicated.

Listing 5.3.   Workaround for Aligned Floating Dollar Sign

```
STORE 1234.56 TO vnum
vchar = STR(vnum,12,2)
STORE 1 TO vcount
STORE .T. TO loop

DO WHILE loop

  IF AT(" ",vchar) <> 0
    vcount = vcount + 1
    vchar = SUBSTR(vchar,2,12)
  ELSE
    STORE .F. TO loop
  ENDIF

ENDDO

@ 10,10 SAY SPACE (vcount-1) + "$" + vchar

*** End Dollar Sign Module
```

Processing time on this program can be reduced by reducing the size of the original string conversion. The screen location of the resulting character string will also be influenced by any PICTURE clauses that you wish to use.

If you need not only a dollar sign, but also want commas, you can still use the above program, but with a few modifications. First, the original conversion process from numeric to character string must take place in two parts. You must make the conversion from numeric to character, ensuring that you convert to a character string that has either three, six, or nine (or more) places to the left of the decimal point. You then "insert" the commas by breaking up the string and concatenating it back together with commas in the appropriate location. If we use the nine places to the left of the decimal point we would break apart "vchar" and put it back together like this:

```
vchar1 = SUBSTR(vchar,1,3)+"," + SUBSTR(vchar,4,3):
        + ","+SUBSTR(vchar,7,6)
```

Note that the decimal point and the two places to the right of it are included in the last substring segment.

Second, we must now change our IF statement in the DO LOOP to include the possibility of encountering a leading comma as well as a leading zero. The IF statement should look like this:

```
IF AT(" ",vchar1) <> 0 ,OR, AT(",",vchar1) = 1
```

The SUBSTR( ) trim that follows the IF statement will take care of trimming off these leading commas.

All this is necessary for the leading dollar sign. I hope that it is worth it. I also hope that Ashton-Tate is thinking seriously about doing something about this problem.

The next set of template symbols deals with alpha characters. Fortunately, they do not complicate the programmer's life the way the numeric symbols do. The A symbol in a PICTURE template will limit the input values to letters only. The N symbol limits input to letters and numbers only, and the X symbol will accept any input from the keyboard. The only benefit to the X symbol is that it limits the size of the input field. Last, the ! symbol converts and stores alpha key presses to uppercase. For example, a PICTURE "!AAAAAAAAAAAAAA" will give you a 15 character data field that will accept only alpha characters and will convert the first letter. A city or a name field might have use for such a template.

A few words of caution about alpha symbols. The A symbol will only accept alpha characters. Spaces are not acceptable and neither are dashes (-) that you would use in hyphenated names (Ashton-Tate?). The ! symbol will convert the first character *if that character is alpha*. If it happens that the operator inadvertently strikes something else, it will be accepted as valid input. It would ruin your alphabetical index if someone's name turned out to be " + smith" instead of "Smith."

The last template symbol for the character data type is the L symbol, which will limit data to only logical values (T,f,F,f,Y,y,N,n) and will convert the key press to uppercase and store any of the four values (T,F,Y,N) to the field or the variable. As the logical data type will only accept these values, the template symbol is not needed. The actual value of the logical field is also only T or F: Y and N are not legal data values although these two letters can be substituted using the @Y template function. It therefore follows that the L template symbol should be used only with character fields where you wish to have any of the four possible alpha values shown.

dBase III Plus has a template symbol that works with the logical data type. It is the Y symbol. In *dBase III Plus* logical values are stored as either a T (for true) or F (for false). When the value of the field is shown on the screen, it is shown as either a T or as an F which, to most users in most situations is less meaningful than a Y (for yes) or N (for no). *dBase III Plus* will accept the Y or N in either upper- or lowercase, but will store it and show it from that point on as either a T or an F unless you use the PICTURE Y template symbol. If you use this, the value in the field is shown as either a Y or an N, which is much more to most users' liking.

In summary, Ashton-Tate's PICTURE language serves two purposes. It helps the programmer format screens, and it restricts input to certain types of data. By itself, it provides a bare minimum of data security, but it is by no means enough to ensure that bad data does not get into a system. We need more.

RANGE

The next piece of data validation is also provided by Ashton-Tate. RANGE clauses can be included in the GETs and they will restrict data to the specified range of values. The clause is constructed as follows:

```
RANGE nn ,mm
```

where "nn" is the lower limit of the range and "mm" is the upper limit. The RANGE clause will work only on number and date data types. RANGE works with or without the PICTURE clause. While it is possible to leave out either the lower or upper limit of the RANGE statement, it is advisable to put a value in, even if it will never be reached: *dBase* will work, but the error message value for the missing number is "none." It does not make any sense to have a statement "RANGE is from 500 to none" pop up on the screen. The RANGE error message appears in the scoreboard area (line 0, right side) when SET SCOREBOARD in ON and SET STATUS is OFF. When SET STATUS is ON it appears below the status bar.

One thing that is not clear from the *dBase* manual is that, when using the RANGE clause with dates, the RANGE must be defined using the CTOD( ) function to convert dates to character strings. The correct syntax is as follows:

```
RANGE CTOD("mm/dd/yy"),CTOD("mm,dd,yy")
```

Trying to do range checks without making this conversion will only result in an error message.

A word of caution about RANGE. The RANGE check takes place only on data entered from the keyboard. If you have an application in which you get information outside of keyboard input (either system date or time or data APPENDed from another file) the RANGE check will not take place. Care should be taken to ensure that data entered through these means is checked using some other validation process.

VALID

VALID is not a *dBase* function, but it should be. It belongs to Nantucket's *Clipper* and provides a way to greatly expand an application's data verification capabilities. In this next section we will discuss some of the methods that you can include in your programs to improve data checking. While they all work well, they all execute *after* the READ for the GETs. As a consequence, you will have to program your validation routines inside a DO LOOP in order to have them work properly. As you will see, this can lead to a substantial increase in code size. *Clipper*'s VALID function does not work in the same way. It acts on the specific data field while it is being filled out, so the feedback is immediate. The VALID function also provides the developer with a much broader range of options for data entry validation than does the *dBase* PICTURE and RANGE statements (both of which are also supported by *Clipper* and can be used with a VALID clause as well.)

VALID takes the following structure:

```
@ rr,cc GET <variable> VALID <expression>
```

where <expression> can be any valid *dBase* expression. This means that the VALID operator will do the following:

- It will define a RANGE for alpha entries (VALID vchar > "N" .AND. vchar < "Q" (to limit entries to only those words beginning with "O" and "P").

- It will do lookups while entering data (VALID (vchar $ "NY-NJ-CT") (limits vchar to those three state abbreviations).

- It will do number ranges on character fields with number pictures.

- It can make a "must fill" field (VALID LEN(TRIM(vchar)) > 0.

- It can interrupt processing during the READ to go off and do something completely different (like HELP) and more.

The list can go on and on. There is clearly more depth possible with the capabilities of the VALID function than there is with *dBase III Plus*. I hope that Ashton-Tate adds something like VALID to its program.

Post-Read Data Verification

Let us go back to Chapter 4 for a minute and review the program logic for editing within a loop as shown in Listing 5.4.

Between the READ and the exit prompts the developer has the opportunity to place any type of data verification routine needed. Each verification routine should be within its own loop that does not allow the user to proceed until the data is correct but allows termination of the edit without save. The data verification can take whatever form you wish, and can even include checking between fields within the READ.

The first type of data verification for discussion is the "must fill" field. The simplest way to make sure that at least *something* is in the fields is to test its length with a LEN(TRIM(variable)) <> 0 statement. This ensures that there is at least one character of some sort in the field. From this point on, further validation can be done.

It is a matter of strategy whether you test for the important fields during the data entry process with PICTURE and RANGE or after the initial READ is finished. I prefer the latter unless there is an overwhelming reason to do otherwise because it lets the operator finish the record before having his or her attention distracted by the errors that have been made. All errors can then be rectified by the operator looking at the screen while

Listing 5.4. Program Logic for Editing in a Loop

```
SAY <fixed text>

DO WHILE loop
  GETs
  READ SAVE
  Quit/Save/Re-edit

  DO CASE
    Q--quit & exit loop
    S--store data and exit loop
    R--loop
  ENDCASE

ENDDO

*** End Program Logic
```

---

making the corrections rather than going back and forth from an input form to the screen.

The obvious exception to my preference is the field that must be correct *before* other fields on the same sheet can be entered. An example of this is a quantity field that must be calculated before the proper discount code can be applied to it. If this is the case, the critical field(s) must be set up in their own READ loop and verified before going on to the main group of GETs.

Let's look at some of the data verification routines at our disposal.

A simple verification of a date entry to make sure that the date entered is a future date (greater than the system date) is shown in Listing 5.5. (To make this little routine more informative to the user, we will discuss it at the end of the chapter.)

You can also nest these error checking loops in your program. Suppose, for example, that we have three dates in a set of GETs, and that VDATE1 must be less than VDATE2, and VDATE2 must be less than VDATE3. A routine to check this is shown in Listing 5.6.

Listing 5.5. Date Verification Routine

```
IF vdate <= DATE()
  STORE .T. TO loop

  DO WHILE loop
    @ rr,cc GET vdate
    READ

    IF vdate > DATE()
      STORE .F. TO loop
    ENDIF

  ENDDO

ENDIF

***  End Date Verification Module
```

The module in Listing 5.6 throws processing into the main loop if either of the two opening conditions is met; VDATE1 greater than or equal to VDATE 2, or VDATE2 greater than or equal to VDATE3. The only

Listing 5.6. Multiple Date Comparison Routine

```
STORE .F. TO loop

IF vdate1 >= vdate2 .OR. vdate2 >= vdate3
  STORE .T. TO loop
ENDIF

DO WHILE loop
```

```
IF  vdate1 >= vdate2
  STORE .T. TO loop1

  DO WHILE loop1
    @ rr,cc GET vdate1
    @ xx,yy GET vdate2
    READ

    IF vdate1 < vdate2
      STORE .F. to loop1
    ENDIF

  ENDDO

ENDIF

IF  vdate2 >= vdate3
  STORE .T. TO loop1

  DO WHILE loop1
    @ xx,yy GET vdate2
    @ aa,bb GET vdate3
    READ

    IF vdate2 < vdate3
      STORE .F. TO loop1
    ENDIF

  ENDDO

ENDIF

IF vdate1 < vdate2 .AND. vdate2 < vdate3
  STORE .F. TO loop
ENDIF

ENDDO

*** End Date Comparison Routine
```

way out of the loop is the final IF statement, which tests that VDATE1 is less than VDATE2 and VDATE2 is less than VDATE3. While it might seem these two routines could be set up outside of the main DO LOOP, this is not the case. If this were allowed, you could have a valid comparison between VDATE1 and VDATE2, and then change VDATE2 to a date less than VDATE1 while correcting an invalid VDATE2/VDATE3 comparison. The outside loop prevents this from happening.

As a programmer, you should build in an escape from an impossible condition for your user. I recommend an ON ESCAPE exit without save, or allowing three tries at each loop (using an incrementing counter) before aborting the data entry and going back to the opening menu. If you program good error messages or have good help you should be able to guide the operator out of most trouble easily.

Let's turn now to the next form of data verification, lookup tables.

At their simplest, lookup tables are very easy to program. They consist of a separate data table with each valid entry represented in a record. Depending on whether the lookup table is short or long, the table can have an associated index to speed the search process.

A simple lookup procedure to validate the VSTATE (state) field is shown in Listing 5.7.

While it is possible to do this simple lookup using a substring comparison or an AT( ) string search of a 157 character string (50 states, DC, VI, and PR plus dashes between the state codes) there is a reason for doing it this way. You can also verify Zip codes using an expanded version of this table.

One nice thing that our Postal Service did when Zip codes were implemented is make sure that the codes within a state were contiguous. If you expand the lookup table from one field to three and include the minimum Zip code in field two (LOWZIP) and the maximum Zip code in field three (HIGHZIP) you can do the simple verification test as shown in Listing 5.8.

It should be obvious that the preceding two programs should be combined into one data verification routine. For those who are interested, the actual lookup table for this is shown in Listing 5.9.

We could write a book on the types and uses of lookup tables. They provide very powerful tools to the developer and are of inestimable value to the user. I prefer to have separate lookup tables for each functional area, while some people prefer to have a single table with a field acting as a code that "filters" in only those entries pertinent to the process. There are pros and cons to both approaches.

I use separate tables because I can limit the size of the fields to what

Listing 5.7.   State Lookup Module

```
(main program)
READ SAVE
STORE .T. TO loop

DO WHILE loop
  SELECT 2
  USE lookup INDEX state
  SEEK vstate

  IF .NOT. EOF()
    STORE .F. TO loop
  ELSE
    @ rr,cc GET vstate
    READ
  ENDIF

ENDDO
SELECT 1
USE <tablename>

*** End State Lookup Module
```

---

is necessary for a specific application, rather than have generic and overly large field lengths for most of the data entries. In addition, lookup is marginally faster on a smaller table, and editing and updating a table is easier. Last, if damage is done to a table, the table is easier to reconstruct.

An argument for a single large lookup table is that, from a programming standpoint, it is easier to manage and makes for fewer files in the total system. No argument on either of these points. To each his own, I suppose.

Until now we have been using lookup tables to validate data already entered. There is nothing that says that we cannot use the idea backward and use lookup tables to enter data. In some situations the improvements in both data entry efficiency and accuracy can be substantial. There is

Listing 5.8.   Zip Lookup and Check

```
(main program)
  READ SAVE
  SELECT 2
  USE lookup INDEX state
  SEEK vstate
  STORE .T. TO loop

  DO WHILE loop

    IF vzip > LOWZIP .OR. vzip < HIGHZIP
      STORE .F. TO loop
    ELSE
      @ rr,cc GET vzip
      READ
    ENDIF

  ENDDO

***  End ZIP lookup and Check Module
```

---

one problem, though; this type of data entry process will disrupt the single READ of all GETs in *dBase III Plus*. It is a fact of life that *dBase* just will not allow you to do anything else while you have a READ going on. Using this approach requires that the individual field be processed separately but, properly done, the savings can be worth the trouble.

If you have fewer than 20 items in your lookup table, it is easiest to set it up as a *dBase* data table with two fields: the first field will be the field trigger key, usually a single alpha character. The second field will be the actual field contents.

Assume that we wish to set up a city lookup table for our employee data file. We know that, with only one or two exceptions, all our employees live in only six different cities in the Phoenix area. This lookup table is shown in Listing 5.10. It should then be a simple matter to insert the following program that will allow us to select the proper city with a single keystroke. It should be simple but, unfortunately, *dBase*

Listing 5.9.   State Lookup Table with Zip Codes

Zip Codes By State

State	LOWZIP	HIGHZIP
PR	00600	00999
VI	00800	00899
MA	01000	02799
RI	02800	20999
NH	03000	03899
ME	03900	04999
VT	05000	05999
CT	06000	06999
NJ	07000	08999
NY	09000	14999
PA	15000	19699
DE	19700	19999
DC	20000	20599
MD	20600	21999
VA	22000	24699
WV	24700	26899
NC	27000	28999
SC	29000	29999
GA	30000	31999
FL	32000	34299
AL	35000	36999
TN	37000	38599
MI	38600	39799
KY	40000	42799
OH	43000	45899
IN	46000	47999
MI	48000	49999
IA	50000	52699
WI	53000	54999
MN	55000	56799
SD	57000	57799
ND	58000	58899
MT	59000	59999
IL	60000	62999
MO	63000	65899

```
KA      66000      67999
NB      68000      69399
LA      70000      71499
AR      71500      72899
OK      73000      74999
TX      75000      79999
CO      80000      81699
WY      82000      83199
ID      83200      83899
UT      84000      84799
AZ      85000      86599
NM      87000      88499
NV      88900      89899
CA      90000      96699
HI      96700      96899
GU      96900      96999
OR      97000      97900
WA      98000      99499
AK      99500      99999
```

Listing 5.10.   City Lookup Table

```
TRIGGER      CITY

    G        Glendale
    V        Paradise Valley
    P        Phoenix
    M        Mesa
    S        Scottsdale
    X        South Phoenix
    T        Tempe
    O        OTHER

*** End Lookup Table
```

complicates it by the lack of a good SAVE SCREEN utility and by the program's inability to interrupt a READ to do something else. As you can see, the excess code involved in rewriting the screen is burdensome, to say the least. Using a SAVE SCREEN function, we would not have to mess with the SAY/GETs as we do for this program Using *Clipper*'s VALID function, we could get around the READ problem also; later, we will discuss how to do it in *Clipper*.

Listing 5.11. Data Insert from Lookup Table

```
CLEAR
USE <tablename> INDEX name
STORE <fieldnames> TO <mvarnames>
STORE .T. TO loop

DO WHILE loop
  @ 02,26 SAY "EMPLOYEE DATA FILE"
  @ 03,05 SAY;
   "═══════════════════════════════════════════════════════"
  @ 05,05 SAY "Last Name:                    First Name:          "+;
           "      MI:"
  @ 07,05 SAY "Street Address:"
  @ 08,05 SAY "Street Address:"
  @ 10,05 SAY "City:                    State:      Zip Code:"
  @ 12,05 SAY "Home Telephone #:              Social Security #:"
  @ 14,05 SAY "Married Y/N:          Number of Dependents:"
  @ 16,05 SAY;
   "═══════════════════════════════════════════════════════"
  @ 18,05 SAY "Current Salary:        Date Last Raise:        Percent:"
  @ 20,05 SAY "Job Code:      Department:        Supervisor:"
  @ 22,05 SAY;
   "═══════════════════════════════════════════════════════"

  @ 05,16 GET vlname
  @ 05,50 GET vfname
  @ 05,71 GET vmi
  @ 07,21 GET vstadd1
  @ 08,21 GET vstadd2
  @ 10,11 SAY vcity
  @ 10,42 SAY vstate
  @ 10,58 SAY vzip
  @ 12,23 SAY vhtel
  @ 12,59 SAY vssn
  @ 14,18 SAY vmarried
  @ 14,51 SAY vdepends PICTURE "99"
  @ 18,21 SAY vcursal PICTURE "999999"
  @ 18,47 SAY vraisedat
  @ 18,67 SAY vraisepct PICTURE "99.9"
  @ 20,15 SAY vjcode
```

```
@ 20,33 SAY vdepart
@ 20,52 SAY vsuperv
READ SAVE

DO lookup

<repaint fixed text above>

@ 05,16 SAY vlname
@ 05,50 SAY vfname
@ 05,71 SAY vmi
@ 07,21 SAY vstadd1
@ 08,21 SAY vstadd2
@ 10,11 SAY vcity
@ 10,42 GET vstate
@ 10,58 GET vzip
@ 12,23 GET vhtel
@ 12,59 GET vssn
@ 14,18 GET vmarried
@ 14,51 GET vdepends PICTURE "99"
@ 18,21 GET vcursal PICTURE "999999"
@ 18,47 GET vraisedat
@ 18,67 GET vraisepct PICTURE "99.9"
@ 20,15 GET vjcode
@ 20,33 GET vdepart
@ 20,52 GET vsuperv
READ SAVE

ON ESCAPE
  STORE .T. TO loop1

  DO WHILE loop1
    @ 23,05 SAY "  A - Abort Edit    R - Re-Edit Record    S - Save Edits "
    WAIT "" TO vchoice

    DO CASE
      CASE UPPER(vchoice) = "A"
        @ 23,00 CLEAR
        STORE .F. TO loop
        RELEASE ALL LIKE V*
        EXIT
      CASE UPPER(vchoice) = "R"
        @ 24,00 CLEAR
        EXIT
      CASE UPPER(vchoice) = "S"
        @ 24,00 CLEAR
        USE UI INDEX LNAME
        SEEK MLNAME
       <replace fields with memvars>
        STORE .F. TO loop1
        STORE .F. TO loop

        IF mlname <> vlname
          REINDEX
        ENDIF
```

```
          RELEASE ALL LIKE V*
          RELEASE mlname
          @ 23,00 CLEAR
       OTHERWISE
       @ 24,00 CLEAR
       @ 24,10 SAY " Not A Valid Choice -- Try Again"
    ENDCASE

  ENDDO

ENDDO
RETURN

***  End Main Program

***  Lookup Program

CLEAR
SELECT 2
USE city INDEX trigger
LIST OFF
STORE "" TO vchoice
DO WHILE .NOT VCHOICE $ "GVPMSXTO"

  @ 23,00
  WAIT "             Enter Your City Choice: " TO vchoice
  vchoice = UPPER(vchoice)
  SEEK vchoice

  DO CASE
    CASE vchoice = "O"
      @ 22,00 CLEAR
      @ 23,10 say "Type in City: "  GET vcity
      READ
    CASE EOF()
      CLEAR
      @ 10,10 SAY "End Of File Encountered.  Please Notify Your System Manager"
      @ 14,10 Say "Please Enter City Name Manually"
      @ 16,10 SAY "CITY: " GET vcity
      READ
    OTHERWISE
      STORE city TO vcity
  ENDCASE

ENDDO
SELECT 1

***  End Lookup Program
```

To get around the *dBase* READ problem the main program actually does two separate READs, the first of only the first five fields with a SAY of all fields starting with the CITY field. The second READ starts after the VCITY field and includes a SAY of all the fields up to (and including) the now completed CITY field. This works, but it is is not a happy situation and it certainly takes more coding. If you wanted to "fool" your user, you would hve to take the SAYs and put them in inverse video, so they would have the appearance of READ fields. They would not, however, have the proper length, even if you did this.

The lookup table shown in Listing 5.10 includes a provision for typing in the name of a city that is not on the list, thereby making the possibility of an unexpected entry allowable. You could, if you wished, include a maintenance routine in the "O" option that would add the new city to the lookup table. All that would be necessary is to add an option asking "Add this City to the Lookup Table? (Y/N)", an APPEND BLANK, a STORE vcity TO CITY statement, a TRIGGER assignment (including a confirmation search to ensure that the trigger was not already in use), a STORE vtrigger TO trigger statement and, finally a trigger to the list of valid selections. To add a trigger, the list of valid choices must be set up as a memory variable, the new choice must be added to it, and the memvar must be SAVEd and RECALLed when the program is invoked.

What about *Clipper*? *Clipper* can do two things here that *dBase* cannot. First, it allows us to program our way around the problem of the two READs that *dBase* makes us go through, and second, we can do this with only one screen paint and a SAVE/RESTORE SCREEN. The key to the first is the VALID test that *Clipper* provides. We can use the function to "break" the user out of the READ and into the lookup program. To do this we test to see if the field has data in it and, if it does not, force the user into the lookup program. This is accomplished by creating a *Clipper* User Defined Function (UDF), which we will call NOLOOK, and using it as the VALID test for filling in the CITY field. One of the traits of the *Clipper* UDF is that the function returns a true/false value for the validation. In our example this function is named VTEST, and it must be made TRUE before the user will be allowed to move on. UDF can also pass other values to memory variables. The VCITY field is passed in this manner.

The UDF NOLOOK is shown in Listing 5.12.

There is one difference between *Clipper* and *dBase* when using this function. To start the lookup, there has to be an empty field. The user, if he or she wants to use the lookup table, has to hit the carriage return against the blank field. If he or she wants to type in the city, the NOLOOK function will not activate the lookup program. The "Type In City" option would no longer be necessary. The lookup does not even

Listing 5.12.   Clipper User Defined Function NOLOOK

```
FUNCTION nolook
PARAMETER vcity

IF LEN(TRIM(vcity)) > 0
  STORE .T. TO vtest
ELSE
  SAVE SCREEN
  DO lookup
  RESTORE SCREEN
  STORE .T. TO vtest
ENDIF

RETURN (vtest)

*** End UDF Nolook
```

---

have to go to a separate table, but can be written into the program as a "menu" routine, popping up on the screen wherever needed and disappearing when finished.

One of the truly powerful things about this simple user defined function is that it allows the programmer to interrupt a READ and do virtually any other programming job before going back to the READ. It is a shame that you cannot do this in *dBase*.

Error Message Communication

With *dBase*, you will almost always run into problems if you use the entire screen for data entry. This is an unfortunate fact, but one that is painfully true. Error messages are one of the main reasons for this problem. Several characteristics of the program make for this situation.

The first limitation that *dBase* imposes on the developer concerns using the RANGE clause in checking for a valid numeric or date entry. The only method that *dBase* provides to notify the user about an input value out of RANGE is the *dBase* RANGE prompt that is displayed on the right half of line 0. This RANGE message only shows up on the screen when SET SCOREBOARD is ON. If, by some unfortunate chance, you have elected to use line 0 in your screen all will be well until the error message is flashed. When it flashes, anything that you have to the right of column 38 will be overwritten. By itself this would not be too bad but, unfortunately, when you enter a valid number in the appropriate field the message is erased but nothing comes back in its place; you are left with a hole in the screen.

There are two different ways to solve this problem. The easiest solution is not to use line 0 when you design and code your screens. A second, less elegant solution is to eliminate all RANGE checking during the READ and check using a data validation loop of the memory variable before providing the user the opportunity to save the edited data.

The advantages of the second solution are many. First, as the contents of the message are now under your control, you can communicate more fully with the user. Second, you can place the message where you wish, freeing up line 0 for other uses. Third, you can limit the number of tries available to the user before either skipping the check and storing a null value in the field. As a developer, you could also decide that if the field is not filled in, the operation should be aborted or that a more detailed explanation of what is considered to be acceptable data for that field be given. Fourth, if you check after the fact, the "RANGE" does not have to be on a numeric field: you will have the ability to check ranges on either numbers in a character field or alpha data, things that are not legal using *dBase*'s RANGE clause.

The major disadvantage to this type of RANGE checking is that the code can get to be long. It is usually easier to set up the error check as a procedure and pass the necessary values as parameters. The programming for this procedure is shown in Listing 5.13. The procedure is passed the row and column coordinates of the invalid GET, the minimum and maximum of the acceptable range, and the error message. Three tries are allowed before the procedure is automatically ended and the value of VABORT is changed to .T.. With the abort flag on, the control is returned to the main program where the edit session is ended without a save, the operator is told what to do with the record, and the program goes to the top of the loop, ready for the next record.

As you can see, the procedure is generic and can be used to check any number of entries. The disadvantage is that the error checking does not take place during the READ. If this type of data validation is necessary, the only choice that you have is to go to *Clipper*, where a UDF can be defined similar to the procedure, and data can be validated using

Listing 5.13.   Data Validation Procedure

```
***  Main Program Segment

@ 19,21 GET vmvar
READ
PUBLIC vabort
STORE .F. TO vabort

IF vmvar <= 5 .OR. vmvar >= 10
  DO error with 19, 21, 5, 10
ENDIF

IF vabort
  @ 23,00 SAY "  PLEASE SEND INPUT SHEET BACK TO SALES FOR PROPER DATA"
  WAIT
  @ 23,00 CLEAR
  RELEASE ALL LIKE v*
  EXIT
ENDIF

*** End Main Program Segment

*** Procedure

PROCEDURE ERROR
PARAMETERS vrr, vcc, vmin, vmax

STORE "VALUE MUST BE BETWEEN " + LTRIM(STR(vmin)) + " AND " + LTRIM(STR(vmax));
TO vmessage
STORE 1 TO vcount

DO WHILE vcount < 4
  @ 23,00 CLEAR
  SET COLOR TO W+
  ?? CHR (7)
  @ 23,10 SAY vmessage
  SET COLOR TO W
  @ vrr,vcc GET vmvar
  READ

 IF vmvar >= vmin .AND. vmvar <= vmax
    @ 23,00 CLEAR
    EXIT
  ELSE
    vcount = vcount + 1
  ENDIF

ENDDO

IF vcount = 4
```

```
    STORE .T. TO vabort
    @ 23,00 CLEAR
ENDIF

RETURN

*** End Procedure
```

Clipper's VALID clause. If you do this, you will still have to pass parameters, but now only two: vmin and vmax. As the user is in the middle of the READ, the row and column coordinates of the GET are superfluous.

You will find it convenient to leave at least two lines open at the bottom of the screen for your prompts and error messages. Care must be taken when working with line 24, because a WAIT issued when the cursor is on this line will scroll the entire screen up one line. The results of this are somewhat confusing to the user, to say the least. If you find yourself in this situation, the only thing to do is to clear the screen and repaint it.

If you are going to be programming in a lot of error messages and prompts, I suggest that you write a procedure for the process and pass at least the message to the procedure when it is invoked. The process for showing messages on the screen then becomes much simpler.

Listing 5.14. Error Message Procedure

```
***  Main Program Segment

IF <error condition>
STORE .T. TO loop

  DO WHILE loop
    STORE "<message one>" TO vmess1
    STORE "<message two>" TO vmess2
    DO errmess WITH vmess1,vmess2
    @ rr,cc GET <mvar>
    READ
    @ 23,00 CLEAR
```

```
   IF .NOT. <error condition>
     STORE .F. TO loop
   ENDIF

 ENDDO

ENDIF

*** End Main Program Segment

*** Procedure

PROCEDURE errmess
PARAMETERS vmess1, vmess2

@ 23,00 CLEAR
?? CHR(7)
SET COLOR TO W+
@ 23,00 SAY vmess1
@ 24,00 SAY vmess2
STORE "" TO vmess1
STORE "" TO vmess2
RETURN

*** End Procedure
```

One final word on prompts and error messages. Always remember to CLEAR your messages from the screen when they are no longer valid, as you see in the example above. They will not clear themselves and can become dangerous if left on the screen when the condition that invoked them is no longer valid.

Handling Operator Errors

The best way to handle operator errors is to make sure that they do not happen in the first place. The second best way is to reduce the chance that they will happen by taking care when you program. The least desirable of all ways of handling operator errors is to try to recover from errors after they happen. All three ways will be discussed here.

Preventing User Errors

Making sure that operator errors do not happen is an art that comes with experience. The number of ways that people mess up a computer program is truly astounding. Simple things, like proper training in the care and handling of diskettes, can sometimes make the difference between successful implementations and those that do not work at all. Did you hear the one about the word-processing secretary who had a wonderful method of filing work in progress? She paper-clipped the diskette to the draft copy of the work so that she would not lose it. The paper clips came from the dispenser on her desk, the nice one that holds the paper clips up when you shake it . . . the magnetic one. Two guesses about the happened. The secretary got so upset when the computer refused to read the disk when she tried to revise her work that she finally went back to the typewriter and the system implementation was stopped dead in its tracks at the first stage.

Although training really has nothing to do with programming the user interface, I must stress that it is an integral part of program development. As the developer of custom software, you are familiar with all of the aspects of your program. The people who are going to use your program are not. It will save a lot of work if you spend the necessary time to bring your users up to minimum proficiency as you implement your system. If this is done properly, it will substantially improve the ease with which your system is brought up to speed.

Reducing the Chance of User Error

A second method of ensuring that mistakes do not happen is to design your programs to reduce the chances for operator error. You should always keep the operator informed about what is going on. In some instances, the computer can look as though it is "dead" while a long and complicated process is going on. In these cases, make it a point to program in informative prompts that tell the user that something is going on and, when possible, keep him posted as the process progresses. For example, you could use a series of "*"s that move across the screen as the task(s) are being completed. In this manner the user is kept informed enough so that he keeps his hands off the keyboard. The natural response when a computer does not seem to be doing anything is to hit some keys to try to "bring it back to life." All that happens is that the key presses sit in the keyboard buffer and come out after the current processing is finished. *dBase III Plus* has a command that allows the programmer to clear out the "typeahead" buffer. The command is CLEAR TYPE-AHEAD. I recommend its use in certain circumstances, such as a long indexing routine or a data backup.

Another type of error is the one that a developer should spend time dwelling on. When developing a system I try to think of every perverse way that an operator could mess up the program and then build in guards that stop the operator until the problem is resolved. Some basic error trapping routines were introduced in the previous chapters.

Some of the simplest and most important routines are those that ensure that the operator is giving valid responses to prompts. If the program is set up to respond to only a **Y** or an **N** key press, a routine must be built in to deal with a **T** or an **M** press as well. We can deal with the first of these situations by testing for a correct response within a DO LOOP and not allowing the user to exit until a correct key is pressed. We deal with the second situation by converting the user's response to uppercase by using the UPPER( ) function. We have also see how the AT( ) function can be used to test for a variety of responses and how the substring comparison operator ($) can be used in a similar fashion. In this chapter, we will discuss some of the more "interesting" situations that the user can get into, the problems that they cause, and some of the programming techniques that can be used to prevent disastrous results.

Unfortunately, *dBase III Plus* does not give you much help in dealing with operator errors. Fortunately, the program is flexible enough to allow you to program your own routines to handle these situations. Let us take a look at some of the more common operator errors and what you can do about the problems that arise.

Common Operator Problems and Solutions

Situation: Program calls for the operator to change diskettes and put a specific diskette in the disk drive before continuing with the program execution.

Problems: Operator can do one (or more) of at least three things. He or she can:

1. Not change the diskette before continuing.
2. Not put the right diskette in the drive and try to continue.
3. Take the diskette out but forget to put a new diskette in the drive before continuing with the program.

Solutions: 1. & 2. The easiest thing to do is to test for the existence of the destination program. If it is not present, a prompt can be given allowing the user to try a second diskette. The user cannot get out of the loop until the proper diskette is in the drive. You will note in the program shown in Listing 6.1 that the user is also given the option of quitting the process. This is to compensate for the inevitable situation where the user simply cannot find the right diskette.

Listing 6.1.   Error Trapping Routine for Wrong Disk

```
STORE .T. TO loop

DO WHILE loop

  IF FILE("<filename>")
    STORE .F. TO loop
  ELSE
    @ 23,00 CLEAR
    ??CHR(7)
    SET COLOR TO W+
    @ 23,10 SAY "WRONG DISK.  INSERT PROPER ONE AND PRESS A KEY TO CONTINUE"
    WAIT "            OR PRESS 'A' TO ABORT OPERATION" TO vchoice

    IF UPPER(vchoice) = "A"
      RETURN
    ENDIF

  ENDIF

ENDDO

***  End routine
```

---

3. If there is *no* disk in the drive, *dBase* will give you a prompt similar to the DOS "Not ready error reading Abort, Retry, Ignore?" prompt. The prompt will take care of the problem for you, but make sure that you repaint the screen before going on, because the *dBase* message stays on the screen. Unfortunately, the ON ERROR command does not do a good job on this problem: the error code returned is 12, which is the "Variable Not Found" code and is the same as the error code that would be returned in the first two instances as well. When the file is finally found, make sure that a complete CLEAR of the screen follows and that a "COPYING INFORMATION TO DISK" prompt is put up in the middle of the screen so that the operator knows what is going on. This will also get rid of the messages left on the screen.

Situation: Operator is supposed to backup daily transaction files to diskette. He places a diskette already full of information in the drive, and initiates the backup procedure.

Problem: The write will start and then the user will get a "disk full" error message. While the information has not been lost, it is better if the program checks first to make sure that there is enough space on the backup diskette to take the day's information.

Solution: Check first to find out the size of the daily file, then find out how much space is available on the destination diskette. If there is not enough space to copy the file, prompt for a new diskette. The programming for this is as shown in Listing 6.2.

The problem with this routine has to do with DISKSPACE( ). *dBase* will only give you the space available on the default drive. If you are copying information from a hard disk to a floppy located in Drive A, you will first have to SET DEFAULT TO A, measure the disk space available, and then reSET DEFAULT TO C. This presents no problem until you write an application that is designed to work on both floppy disk systems and hard disk systems. If you have this situation, I suggest that you put your drives into memory variables and specify them that way in the program to avoid trouble.

Clipper does not have the DISKSPACE( ) function built into it. It does have something like it in the extended library. The function is DISKSPACE(n) and works the same as does *dBase*'s function, except that you can specify the drive by putting a number in the parentheses.

Listing 6.2. Check for Enough Available Space

```
STORE .T. TO loop
STORE (32 * <# of fields in record) + 35 TO vheadsize
STORE RECSIZE() * RECCOUNT TO vtotrec
STORE vheadsize + vtotrec TO vtotsize

DO WHILE loop
  STORE DISKSPACE() TO vdisk

  IF vdisk < vtotsize
    ?? CHR(7)
    @ 23,00 CLEAR
    @ 23,10 SAY "NOT ENOUGH SPACE ON DISK.  INSERT NEW DISK AND PRESS ANY KEY"
    WAIT ""
    @ 23,00 CLEAR
  ELSE
    STORE .F. TO loop
  ENDIF

ENDDO

*** End check for space routine
```

Specifying 1 will give you the disk space of Drive A; using 2 will give you that space that is available on Drive B; 3 for Drive C, and so on.

Situation: Daily backup requires more than a single diskette.

Problem: Unlike the last situation, no matter what the operator does, he is going to run into a problem because his data simply will not fit on a single diskette. The data table has to be copied onto several diskettes.

Solution: Break the data table into chunks that will fit on diskettes. The following program routine will do this and inform the operator how many diskettes he or she will need.

Listing 6.3.   Multiple Diskette Backup Program

```
USE <tablename>
STORE RECSIZE() TO vrecsize
STORE RECCOUNT() TO vrecno
STORE INT(340000/vrecsize) TO vrecquan
STORE INT(vrecno/vrecquan) + 1 TO vdiskno
CLEAR
@ 10,10 SAY "You will need "+LTRIM(STR(vdiskno))+" diskettes to complete ";
              "this backup."
@ 12,10 SAY "Place diskette in drive A and press any key to start process."
GO 1

DO WHILE .NOT. EOF
   CLEAR
   @ 10,10 SAY "Copying data to diskette...   Please Wait"
   COPY NEXT vrecquan TO <backup>
   SKIP 1
   ? CHR(7)
   CLEAR
   @ 10,10 SAY "Copying completed.  Please remove this backup diskette"
   @ 12,10 SAY "and insert the next one. "
   @ 15,10 SAY "Press any key to re-start the backup process..."
   WAIT""
ENDDO

? CHR(7)
? CHR(7)
CLEAR
@ 10,10 SAY "Backup completed.  Please remove the last backup diskette"
@ 12,10 SAY "and place all backup diskettes in specified storage location."
@ 15,10 SAY "Press any key to go back to main program...."
WAIT ""
CLEAR
RETURN

*** End Multiple diskette backup program
```

Notice that the diskette size was specified at 340,000 bytes. A margin of error is always advisable. Notice also that the program SKIPs a record at the end of each diskette. This prevents the last record from being duplicated as the first record of the next backup diskette.

Situation: The operator is given the task of typing in the name of the daily backup file according to a preset code. He mistypes and the day's records are written on top of yesterday's, erasing the data completely.

Problem: With a day's transactions missing, it will be impossible to reconstruct the file from the last major system backup. If anything happens, data will be lost.

Solution: Have *dBase* assign the filename for you. *dBase* provides functions that allow you to get the month and day out of the system. Assuming that the system date is properly set (another check), you can assign the filename according to the date as shown in Listing 6.4.

The backup file for January 27th would be JAN27.BAK. This routine can easily be included in the backup programs listed below.

Situation: The operator inadvertently rests his thumb on the space bar and enters leading spaces in character fields.

Problem: Leading spaces to *dBase* are, unfortunately, just like any other character. They count. They mess up indexes. They mess up formatting. They should not get into a field. If you want further proof, just try to find "#Jones" when you are looking for "Jones".

Solution: Anytime you are dealing with a character field it is probably wise to use *dBase*'s LTRIM( ) function to get rid of any leading spaces that may have inadvertently crept in during data input. If this is done as a

Listing 6.4.   Date Assignment for Backup Files

```
STORE SUBST(CMONTH(DATE()),1,3) TO vmonth
STORE LTRIM(STR(DAY(DATE()))) TO vday
STORE vmonth + vday + ".BAK" TO vkey
COPY transact.dbf TO A:&vkey

*** End routine
```

---

matter of course, the leading blank problem will not exist. Do not do this with numeric data stored in a character field as you may completely mess up your intended formatting.

Situation: The operator is lazy and does not put in the system date when he turns on the computer.

Problem: If your application uses the system date for any reason, you probably do not want to have January 1, 1980 stamped on everything. If you are using a memory board with a time clock on it or if you are using a PC AT, which comes with a clock, the problem is less important, but still one that bears watching.

Solution: There are several things that can be done to "short circuit" the date problems. The first thing is to check for the system date. A simple routine at the beginning of your program will eliminate the January 1, 1980 problem (see Listing 6.5).

If you want to be a bit more careful with your date routine, you can take the date that the operator enters and do further checking to make sure the date is proper. If your system is installed in a business that works only Monday through Friday, the routine could look like Listing 6.6.

Listing 6.5.   Simple System Date Check

```
STORE CTOD("01/01/80") TO vdate

IF DATE() = vdate
   CLEAR
   @ 10,10 SAY "Before entering the system you must enter today's date."
   @ 12,10 SAY "As several system functions depend on this date, please "
   @ 14,10 SAY "take care to enter the date properly."

   DO WHILE DATE() = vdate
      ?
      ?
      RUN date
   ENDDO

   CLEAR

ENDIF

*** End System Date Check
```

Listing 6.6.   Extended Date Checking Routine

```
STORE CTOD("01/01/80") TO vdate
STORE .T. TO loop

DO WHILE loop

  IF DATE() = vdate
    CLEAR
    @ 10,10 SAY "Before entering the system you must enter today's date."
    @ 12,10 SAY "As several system functions depend on this date, please "
    @ 14,10 SAY "take care when you enter the date."

    DO WHILE DATE() = vdate
      ?
      ?
      RUN date
    ENDDO

    CLEAR

  ENDIF

  STORE DOW(DATE()) TO vday

  IF vday = 1 .OR. vday = 7
    CLEAR
    @ 10,10 SAY "The date that you have entered is a weekend date.  Enter the"
    @ 12,10 SAY "date again."
    ?
    ?
    RUN date
  ENDIF

  CLEAR
  @ 10,10 SAY "According to the system date, today is a " + CDOW(DATE())
  @ 12,10 SAY "Is this correct?  (Y/N)"
  STORE "" TO vcheck

  DO WHILE AT(vcheck,"YyNn") = 0
    WAIT "                          " TO vcheck
  ENDDO

  IF DATE() <> vdate .AND. vday <> 1 .AND. vday <> 7 .AND. UPPER(vcheck) = "Y"
    STORE .F. TO loop
  ENDIF

ENDDO

*** End Extended Date Checking Routine
```

Note that the routine gives the operator feedback on the day of the week and prompts for a confirmation of the day. Even if the operator cannot remember the date, he or she can almost always remember what day of the week it is.

Situation: Operator forgets to turn on the printer before invoking a print routine.

Problem: Depending on how the print routine is designed, the results of this action can be just annoying or can be disastrous. The *dBase III Plus* manual "suggests" that the only "safe" thing to do if this happens is to get the printer online and retry. What can happen (and sometimes does) is that the operator figures that the best thing to do is reboot and try again. This may present only minimal problems (such as unsaved memory variables) when you compare it to the possibility of leaving open data tables in memory and having the header information ruined.

Solution: There is a simple solution to this problem. I always save my memory variables to disk and send the printer an initialization string and a form feed before opening my data tables and starting my print routine. It may take a bit of extra time, but at least I have a bit more protection than I would have otherwise. If the system hangs up there are no open tables to be destroyed.

Clipper has a function called ISPRINT( ) that is supplied as part of its extended function library. The function returns a value of .T. if the printer is online and ready to receive. A simple routine like the following will save time and sorrow if you are using *Clipper*.

Listing 6.7.   *Clipper* Printer Ready Routine

```
@ 23,10 SAY "Make Sure Printer Is Ready and Press Any Key To Begin Printing."
@ 24,20 SAY "OR Press "A" T Abort Print Program"
STORE 0 TO key

DO WHILE key = 0 .OR. .NOT. ISPRINTER()
    STORE 0 TO KEY

    DO WHILE key = 0
       key = INKEY()
    ENDDO

    IF UPPER(CHR(key)) = "A"
       RETURN
```

```
'    ENDIF

ENDDO

@ 23,00 CLEAR
@ 23,30 SAY "Printing"
SET CONSOLE OFF
SET DEVICE TO PRINT

<continue program and print>

***  End Clipper Print Check Routine
```

As you can see, the program goes nowhere until the printer has been confirmed as being online and the operator has given a go-ahead to print.

Situation: The operator enters a code for a new customer, but the code already exists.

Problem: Every system should assign a unique code to each customer. Most systems assign this code based on their own programmed logic and do so in such a way that there is no possibility of duplicate numbers. Methods used include sequential numbering, use of telephone numbers, Zip code/name and many other possibilities. In some systems, however, the code is operator-assigned. Even when the code is given to the operator or when it is supplied from some external source and is *supposed* to be unique, it is still possible to have duplicate numbers. This possibility becomes even more likely when the operator assigns a "pet" number to the project himself. In cases like this, it is necessary to have a checking routine to ensure that the assigned code is not already in use.

Solution: A simple routine that should be included in a system that accepts record identification from the operator looks like Listing 6.8.

By inserting this routine, you will ensure that no two records in the system have the same record ID. The user will not see any of the error trapping unless something is wrong with an entry.

Situation: As always happens, the user gets into some situation where he or she feels that it is better to turn off the machine and start again rather than try to untangle the mess that he or she has made.

Listing 6.8.   Simple Record ID Number Check Routine

```
STORE .T. TO loop

DO WHILE loop
   @ 04,10 SAY "Assign the identification code that you wish to use"
   @ 05,10 SAY "for this new customer."
   @ 08,10 SAY "The code can contain alpna and numeric data and can"
   @ 09,10 SAY "be up to eight characters long."
   @ 11,10 SAY "Press <RETURN> to go back to main menu"
   @ 16,00
   ACCEPT "           ID CODE? " TO vchoice

   DO CASE
      CASE LEN(vchoice) = 0
         CLEAR
         loop = .F.
      CASE LEN(vchoice) > 8
         @ 20,5 SAY "ID CODE TOO LONG, RE-ENTER CODE"
         WAIT
         STORE "" TO vchoice
         @16,0 CLEAR
      OTHERWISE
         USE <table name> INDEX <index name>
         SEEK vchoice

         IF .NOT. EOF()
            @ 10,5 SAY "Selected id number is currently in use."
            @ 12,5 SAY "You will have to go back and start again."
            @ 15,5
            WAIT
         ELSE
            APPEND BLANK
            REPLACE <id> WITH vchoice
            DO <append routine>
            loop= .F.
         ENDIF

   ENDCASE

ENDDO

*** End Simple Record ID Check Routine
```

Problem: As has been stated throughout this book you cannot allow the user to summarily turn off the machine. If he or she does this, the risk of serious damage to your data files is great. If damage occurs, it may be difficult or impossible to repair. There are two main problems. The first has to do with the headers on open data files. The second has to do with open memory variables.

The data file problem is a real and serious one. When a table is opened the header and relevant data are written in to one of the *dBase* buffers. All changes that are made while the file is open are recorded in the header in memory. It is only when the file is closed that the header information is written back to the file so, if changes have been made while the file is open, the header on the disk will no longer match the header in memory. If the machine is turned off the header information no longer matches the data file and "unpredictable results may occur." This is one of the reasons that I recommend never leaving data tables open unless absolutely necessary.

The second problem can exist with memory variables. In many situations one or more memory variables may be used to govern some of the actions of a program. A memory variable may, for instance, be used as a counter when assigning invoice numbers, customer numbers, or other sequential identifiers. It may be used to carry the current balance of an account during processing. The values that these variables hold at the end of the day are written to a .MEM file when the system is shut down and read back into the program when the system loaded the next time it is used. If the computer is turned off before the values of these memory variables are saved, the system will be off.

Solution: There are different solutions for each of the problems mentioned. We will deal with them separately.

There are two possible scenarios for the first situation. The simplest is when the user gets stuck in a situation where he or she does not know what to do next. The most effective safeguard in this situation is providing the user with the help that he or she needs to rectify the situation without having to shut down the system. We will discuss the help options and programming in the next chapter so we will not deal with that here. In certain circumstances, however, the user will give up and just want to shut down. If this situation exists, you must provide him with a graceful (and safe) exit from your program.

One of the most typical cases is when a print routine is in progress. The user decides that he or she does not want to continue with the print routine. If no escape is provided, the only option that he or she has is to either turn off the machine or do a hot reboot (Control-Alt-Del). Either alternative may cause damage. In Chapter 2 we discussed a simple programming technique that allows the user to interrupt printing and abort the print run. (See the discussion of the ON KEY command.) If the user selects to abort the print run the ABORT module referred to in the ON KEY program would look like this:

Listing 6.9.　Abort Print Module

```
CLEAR
SET DEVICE TO SCREEN
SET COLOR TO R+6
@ 06,10 SAY "Program abort requested"
SET COLOR TO W
@ 10,10 SAY "Your options at this time are:"
@ 12,15 SAY "A  Abort printing and go back to the main menu"
@ 14,15 SAY "R  Restart printing"
@ 16,15 SAY "X  Exit back to the operating system"
STORE " " TO vchoice
@ 16,20 SAY "Your CHOICE: "

DO WHILE AT(vchoice,"ARX") = 0
   @ 16,34 GET vchoice PICTURE "!"
ENDDO

DO CASE
   CASE vchoice = "A"
      CLOSE DATABASES
      CLOSE PROCEDURE
      RETURN TO MASTER
   CASE vchoice = "R"
      RETURN
   CASE vchoice = "X"
      CLOSE DATABASES
      CLOSE PROCEDURE
      SAVE ALL LIKE <memvar prefix>
      CLEAR
      QUIT

ENDCASE

*** End Abort Print Module
```

Another danger zone exists while the user is in the middle of a READ. Sometimes the data on hand just will not fit into the data fields as defined and the user gives up in disgust. Another common problem occurs when the user is in the middle of a READ and decides that it is necessary to go back to the DOS prompt to run another program. In both of these cases there is the risk that the user will take the path of least resistance and Control-Alt-Delete rather than go through the proscribed shut-down procedures. The best cure for this situation was given in Chapter 4: Make sure that you do not work with field variables when doing your READ. Use only memory variables and make sure that all data tables are closed during a READ. If you make sure that you do this, your data tables will not be damaged when the user takes the hot-reboot option to exit your application.

The second problem that can exist is with memory variables. In many different types of systems, a memory variable(s) is used as a counter to keep track of number assignments, running totals, and other information that is used and incremented during the operation of the system. The normal procedure is to give these important memory variables a unique prefix and to save them to a .MEM file as a part of the system close down procedure. Obviously, this will not be of any help if the user hot reboots the system. The solution here is to save **all** of these memory variables back to disk each time that one of them changes.

Situation: User tires of waiting for an index to be rebuilt and hot reboots the system while indexing is in process.

Problem: Any time this happens, or any time that data is inserted into the data table while the index(es) are not active, the index(es) will be corrupted. They must be rebuilt if they are to work properly.

Solution: While there are many possible approaches to take to this situation, you will find that the best solution is to delete your index files and rebuild your indexes from scratch. This procedure can be invoked as part of an ON ERROR procedure where the return value for the ERROR( ) function is one of the indexing errors (values 112, 113, and 114 are the most probable). In this case the best thing to do is to delete all of the indexes from the application and start rebuilding them. The code in Listing 6.10 does this.

There are other cases where you have a bad index, but you will not get the indexing error. In this case, you will have to do something to get your indexes rebuilt outside of the programming in your application. I

Listing 6.10.   Index Rebuilding Procedure

```
PARAMETER verror

DO CASE
   CASE verror = 112 .OR. verror = 113 .OR. verror = 114
      CLEAR
      @ 10,10 SAY "Indexing error detected, please wait while indexes are
      @ 11,10 SAY "rebuilt.  The process will take a few minutes."
      SET CONSOLE OFF
      RUN DELETE *.NDX
      SET CONSOLE CN
      @ 14,10 SAY "Old index files deleted.  Building new index files."
      USE <tablename 1>
      INDEX ON <index expression> TO <indexanme 1>
      @ 16,10 SAY "*****"
      USE <tablename 2>
      INDEX ON <index expression> TO <indexname2>
      @ 16,15 SAY "*****"
      USE <tablename 3>
      INDEX ON <index expression> TO <indexname 3>
      @ 16,20 SAY "*****"
      USE <tablename 4>
      INDEX ON <index expression> TO <indexname 4>
      @ 16,25 SAY "*****"
      USE <tablename 5>
      INDEX ON <index expression> TO <indexname 5>
      @ 16,10 CLEAR
      @ 16,10 SAY "Indexing completed.  Press any key to go back to main program."
      WAIT ""

   CASE verror = 2
      <continue with other error cases>

ENDCASE
RETURN

*** End Indexing Error Procedure
```

---

recommend a "self-healing" approach to this problem. Include the module shown in Listing 6.11 at the beginning of your programs.

If a problem exists, the user simply deletes the named index file from the disk and starts the application. The program, sensing the absence of the file, deletes all index files and rebuilds all the indexes.

Situation: Unauthorized changes are being made to your data tables.

Listing 6.11.   Index "Self-Healing" Module

```
IF .NOT. FILE("<indexname.ndx>")
  SET CONSOLE OFF
  RUN DELETE *.NDX
  SET CONSOLE ON
  @ 14,10 SAY "Building new index files."
  USE <tablename 1>
  INDEX ON <index expression> TO <indexname 1>
  @ 16,10 SAY "*****"
  USE <tablename 2>
  INDEX ON <index expression> TO <indexname2>
  @ 16,15 SAY "*****"
  USE <tablename 3>
  INDEX ON <index expression> TO <indexname 3>
  @ 16,20 SAY "*****"
  USE <tablename 4>
  INDEX ON <index expression> TO <indexname 4>
  @ 16,25 SAY "*****"
  USE <tablename 5>
  INDEX ON <index expression> TO <indexname 5>
  @ 16,10 CLEAR
  @ 16,10 SAY "Indexing completed.  Press any key to start program."
  WAIT ""

ENDIF

*** End Self-Healing Index Module
```

Problem: The data included in your application is extremely valuable and you cannot afford to have someone mess it up. You need to have controls built into the system to prevent this from happening.

Solution: Password protection is the root of the solution to this problem. A simple and effective password routine is included in Listing 6.12.

If you are designing an application that has need of password protection, you will find that this will work for most situations. I prefer to use passwords embedded in a program file and use the AT() verification for the simple reason that, when compiled, the passwords are included in the .EXE file as opposed to being in a separate lookup data table and are therefore more secure. You must make sure that you provide enough passwords to cover each of the operators so that each will have a unique code.

Listing 6.12.   Simple Password Routine

```
CLEAR
@ 10,10 SAY "ACCESS TO VARIOUS LEVELS OF THIS PROGRAM ARE PROTECTED."
@ 12,15 SAY "Type in your password to gain entry to system."
@ 14,30
STORE "    " TO vpass
STORE 1 TO vcount
DO WHILE vcount <= 3
   SET CONSOLE OFF
   ACCEPT TO vpass
   SET CONSOLE ON

   IF AT(UPPER(vpass), "AAA@BBB@CCC@DDD") = 0
     ? chr(7)
     @ 20,20 SAY "INCORRECT PASSWORD, TRY AGAIN."
     vcount = vcount + 1
   ELSE
     @ 20,20 SAY "ACCESS GRANTED"
     @ 22,20 SAY "Press any key to continue..."
     WAIT ""
     CLEAR
     DO <main program>
   ENDIF

? CHR(7)
? CHR(7)
? CHR(7)
CLEAR
@ 10,10 SAY "UNAUTHORIZED ACCESS ATTEMPTED."
@ 12,10 SAY "RETURNING TO DOS."

*** End Password Module
```

This unique operator code can be of further use to you as you program your system. You can easily set up levels of access within the program by dividing the codes into the proper groups and verifying the password in a DO CASE structure instead of the IF structure shown in Listing 6.12. If you do this, you can set up another memory variable and store a value to it so that program module access and editing rights are restricted. In its simplest form a logical access variable (VEDIT in the example shown in Listing 6.13) will do.

Listing 6.13.   Edit Access Restriction

```
IF vedit
  @ 10,10 SAY "Amount of last payment: " GET vpayment
  @ 12,10 SAY "Amount of current payment: " GET vcpay
  READ
ELSE
  @ 10,10 SAY "Amount of last payment: " + vpayment
  @ 12,10 SAY "Amount of current payment: " + vcpay

ENDIF

*** End Edit Access Restriction
```

If VEDIT is TRUE then the operator is allowed to enter or change information in the two fields shown. If VEDIT is FALSE, the operator can view the information, but cannot change it.

Conclusion

This chapter deals with only a few of the problems that you may encounter when developing and working with systems in the field. I continue to learn new ways of avoiding problems, and build up my own library of tools to include in applications. As I said at the beginning of the chapter, I am always amazed at the ways that people have of messing up programs. I look at it as a challenge to design trapping routines that eliminate the possibility of this happening.

Operator Help

Help screens for the operator are difficult to design and a real project to program. I try to stay away from supplying context-sensitive help within my programs for several reasons, the biggest two of which are stated in the sentence above. Help can be a bottomless pit, taking much unproductive programming time.

This is not to say that you should avoid designing help systems for your applications. Quite the contrary, this should always be at the top of the developer's mind. When you are programming, you should be constantly thinking about what the operator sees and what he or she is going to do next. Anytime there could be the slightest doubt about what step to take next, the developer should think about improving the flow of the program to eliminate these moments of indecision. In other words, the best help function that the developer can build into a program is a logical program flow that the operator can follow either intuitively or explicitly without having to resort to help screens. A simple example will serve to make this point. When you stop the program and WAIT for a keyboard response to continue, it is normal practice to put in the valid responses

Y/N for the operator to choose from. Not including them in the prompt "Do You Want To Continue?" makes the operator more nervous than he or she should be.

The second type of help that the developer should consider is assistance for an operator who has made an input mistake and isn't sure of which corrective action to take. As was mentioned in Chapter 5, *dBase* does not allow you to interrupt a READ so, if you program your validation as PICTURE and RANGE statements, you will not be able to give the user much help if he or she is confused. If you program your validation routines after the READ, you will be able to provide substantial help (see Chapter 5). More advanced help is available if the user gets "stuck" in one of these routines. It is a simple matter to program in a **HELP** key that invokes help from one of the help files discussed in this chapter.

Throughout this book I have given examples of program feedback to the operator. When the operator requests a record but it is not found, the name that was typed for the request is flashed back up on the screen for the operator to look at. When the program is indexing, a note is flashed on the screen. Most of the time if a mistake is made, the operator can check the error and go back and try again. All of this type of feedback comes under the broad heading of operator help.

The "logical flow" of screens that we keep discussing includes an appropriate menu structure to clearly lead the operator to the proper choice without having to search through every sub-sub-menu in the system. It makes more sense, for example, to have the "Print Checks" option on the "Process Checks" menu screen than it does to have it located with "Reports" in a completely different section of the application. To the developer the latter case may make more sense, as printing checks involves the printer and the printer online check routine is located in the "Reports" module but, to the operator, this makes no sense at all. The operator can also be told where he or she is in the system and what the highlighted option does by using prompt lines. This is demonstrated in the horizontal bounce bar menu structure and the special *Clipper* menu that appears in Chapter 3 (Listings 3.7 and 3.8).

One last point must be made about programming help into your applications; any online help facility is no substitute for properly written documentation and instructions on the use of your application. Online help should be secondary to written documentation and should provide only the information necessary for the completion of the immediate task at hand. One of the best forms of online help that I have seen consisted primarily of page references to the manual for the appropriate information. Crude, but totally effective.

Unfortunately, no matter how hard you try, there are times when some type of operator help is needed. *dBase III Plus* directly and indirectly provides extensive help programming capabilities. *Clipper* and *Quicksilver* provide even more for the developer to choose from.

Basic Operator Help Systems

The simplest type of on-screen operator help system is associated with choice menus. A HELP option can be programmed as a valid menu choice that calls a simple help file to give information about the menu choices. When the user is finished looking at the help program, control is RETURNed to the menu for further action. The help given in this type of file is nothing but a series of TEXT...ENDTEXT blocks with a WAIT command to control paging (if necessary).

A simple help program looks like Listing 7.1.

This works quite well if there is only one menu, but quickly becomes a burden if there are more than two menus that require help. If this is the case, the developer has two choices open if he decides that he likes this simple approach to help. The first and easiest option is to provide several different help programs (uniquely named) and simply call

Listing 7.1.   Simple Help Program

```
CLEAR
TEXT

    There are four options that are available to you from this menu.

    The first option is .............
    The second option is ...........
        etc.

    Press any key to go back to the Menu......

ENDTEXT
WAIT""
RETURN

*** End Simple Help Program
```

the proper one for the menu that is on the screen at that time. The second, more elegant solution is to have a single file, with blocks of text associated with the proper menus filed under separate CASE statements of a DO CASE structure. The calling program issues a "DO help WITH "xx "command where "xx" corresponds to the appropriate CASE statement in the help program and the desired text is flashed on the screen. As before, more than one screen help can be shown using the WAIT statement as a paging device.

The help file now looks like Listing 7.2.

If you need to have more than 99 help screens in your application, simply change the passed parameter to three digits.

Listing 7.2.   Expanded Help Program

```
CLEAR
PARAMETER vhelp

DO CASE
   CASE vhelp = 1
      TEXT
         <information associated with first help screen>
      ENDTEXT
      WAIT
      RETURN
   CASE vhelp = 2
      TEXT
         <information associated with second help screen>
      ENDTEXT
      WAIT
      RETURN
   CASE vhelp = 3
      TEXT
         <information associated with third help screen (part one)>
      ENDTEXT
      WAIT
      TEXT
         <information associated with third help screen (part two)>
      ENDTEXT
      WAIT
      RETURN
ENDCASE

*** End Expanded Help Program
```

Advanced Help Systems

The programs shown in Listing 7.1 and Listing 7.2 will give you generalized menu help that is context-specific only to the menu currently on the monitor. If you are using a bounce bar menu you can do two different things to provide help. First, you can provide one or more prompt lines with each of the options, as was done with the horizontal menu program shown in Listing 3.8. If only a small quantity of information needs to be presented, this is probably the best method. There is also a second option that offers a much more powerful help function to your users. It is possible to make help specific to the highlighted option by including the CASE number of the currently highlighted option in the parameters that you pass. This requires that two paremeters be passed — the screen number and the CASE number — and that help be triggered by a separate, nonmenu key press. The help screen file would be exactly the same except that a single variable would be constructed from the two passed parameters (screen number and option number) before searching for the appropriate CASE.

The menu program with option-sensitive help looks like Listing 7.3.

Listing 7.3. Main Menu with Option-Sensitive Help

```
vchoice = 6
key = 24
vmenu = "1"
valchoice = "AEDPBX"
DO WHILE .T.

   DO WHILE key <> 13

      SET COLOR TO W
      CLEAR
      @ 00,23 SAY " ┌──────────────────────────────┐ "
      @ 01,23 SAY " │                              │ "
      @ 02,23 SAY " │   USER INTERFACE IN dBASE III │ "
      @ 03,23 SAY " │                              │ "
      @ 04,23 SAY " │     BOUNCE BAR DEMO MENU     │ "
      @ 05,23 SAY " │   WITH CONTEXT-SENSITIVE HELP │ "
      @ 06,23 SAY " └──────────────────────────────┘ "
      @ 08,24 SAY " A    ADD A NEW RECORD "
      @ 10,24 SAY " E    EDIT AN EXISTING RECORD "
      @ 12,24 SAY " D    DELETE AN OLD RECORD "
      @ 14,24 SAY " P    PRINT REPORTS "
      @ 16,24 SAY " B    BACKUP DATABASE "
      @ 19,32 SAY " X    EXIT FROM SYSTEM "
```

```
@ 23,10 SAY " Press F-1 to Get Further Information on Highlited Option"
SET COLOR TO W/

DO CASE
   CASE vchoice = 1
     @ 08,24 SAY " A     ADD A NEW RECORD "
   CASE vchoice = 2
     @ 10,24 SAY " E     EDIT AN EXISTING RECORD "
   CASE vchoice = 3
     @ 12,24 SAY " D     DELETE AN OLD RECORD "
   CASE vchoice = 4
     @ 14,24 SAY " P     PRINT REPORTS "
   CASE vchoice = 5
     @ 16,24 SAY " B     BACKUP DATABASE "
   CASE vchoice = 6
     @ 19,32 SAY " X     EXIT FROM SYSTEM "
ENDCASE

DO CASE
   CASE key = 28
     DO help WITH vmenu, vchoice
     key = 0
     LOOP
   CASE AT(UPPER(CHR(key)),valchoice) > 0
     vchoice = AT(UPPER(CHR(key)),valchoice)
     EXIT

     CASE key = 24 .OR. key = 4 .OR. CHR(key) = ' '

       IF vchoice = 6
         vchoice = 1
       ELSE
         vchoice = vchoice + 1
       ENDIF

     CASE key = 5 .OR. key = 19

       IF vchoice = 1
         vchoice = 6
       ELSE
         vchoice = vchoice - 1
       ENDIF

   ENDCASE

   SET COLOR TO +W/B

   DO CASE
      CASE vchoice = 1
        @ 08,24 SAY " A     ADD A NEW RECORD "
      CASE vchoice = 2
        @ 10,24 SAY " E     EDIT AN EXISTING RECORD "
      CASE vchoice = 3
        @ 12,24 SAY " D     DELETE AN OLD RECORD "
      CASE vchoice = 4
        @ 14,24 SAY " P     PRINT REPORTS "
```

```
      CASE vchoice = 5
         @ 16,24 SAY " B    BACKUP DATABASE "
      CASE vchoice = 6
         @ 19,32 SAY " X    EXIT FROM SYSTEM "
   ENDCASE

   STORE INKEY() TO key

   DO WHILE key = 0
      key = INKEY()
   ENDDO

   IF key < 0
      key = 0
   ENDIF

ENDDO

SET COLOR TO W

DO CASE
   CASE vchoice = 1
      DO add
   CASE vchoice = 2
      DO edit
   CASE vchoice = 3
      DO delete
   CASE vchoice = 4
      DO print
   CASE vchoice = 5
      DO backup
   CASE vchoice = 6
      DO exit
   ENDCASE

ENDDO

***  End Bounce Bar Program With Option Sensitive Help
```

There are four major differences between this program and the standard bounce bar menu program that appears in Listing 3.5.

The first difference is that the entire screen has to be repainted every time the operator presses a navigation key. This is made necessary by the added help function that CLEARs the screen before it paints the help messages. The DO loops now encompass the whole screen painting portion of the program.

The second difference is that the menu is named in the memory variable VMENU and the menu name is passed to the help program when help is invoked.

The third difference has to do with the INKEY( ) loop. When you press **F1**, INKEY( ) passes the value 28 to the key. This is not a problem and the CASE statement will be evaluated with no difficulty. Unfortunately, **F1** is located right next to **F2** and that key (along with the other eight function keys) returns a negative number. The CHR( ) function, designed to work on ASCII values from zero to 255, chokes on negative numbers. The IF key < 0 (then) key = 0 statement handles this problem.

The fourth difference is the heart of the change: the "CASE key = 28" statement in the navigation loop. As you can see, if the **F1** key (28) is pressed, the help program is invoked with the screen number (01) and the currently selected option (vchoice) being passed.

The help program skeleton looks like Listing 7.4.

Note that the passed parameters VMENU (character) and VCHOICE (numeric) must be combined to make a single character string (VHELP-SCR) before the program can start searching for the appropriate CASE.

Any number of different help screens relating to different menus can be included in this type of help program.

So far we have been dealing with a linear approach to help. When the user asks for some help, the help program is invoked and a specific piece of information is given. The help program is, however, inflexible in how the information is presented.

There are several improvements that can be made to the help program that make it more productive for users. You might want to construct the help file so that the user can page back to a previous screen. Using the current help structure, the user must first exit help and then re-invoke it to see a previous screen again. You might want to have an automatic cross referencing system that allows the user to select more than one screen (or subject) of help after the original screen(s) of help have been viewed. Finally, you might want to construct a help index and allow the user to "browse" through the help file to find out about your application.

Paging back and forth within a single help subject can be accomplished two ways. The first method involves a completely different structure for the help file and uses the *dBase III Plus* editor to page back and forth through the file.

Up until this point we have been looking at the help program as a .PRG file that consists of a collection of CASE statements. The help program in this example is different: it is a program that accepts the passed

Listing 7.4. Option-Sensitive Help Program

```
PARAMETERS vmenu, vchoice
CLEAR
STORE vmenu+LTRIM(STR(vchoice)) TO vhelpscr

DO CASE
  CASE vhelpscr = "11"
    TEXT
      <help screen one>
    ENDTEXT
    WAIT
    RETURN
  CASE vhelpscr = "12"
    TEXT
      <help screen two>
    ENDTEXT
    WAIT
    RETURN
  CASE vhelpscr = "13"
    TEXT
      <help screen one>
    ENDTEXT
    WAIT
    RETURN
  OTHERWISE
    @ 12,10 SAY "NO HELP AVAILABLE"
    ?
    WAIT
    RETURN
ENDCASE

*** End Help Program
```

---

parameters, assembles the search string and then searches a data table for the correct data record. The data table of two fields. The first field is the help identifier and is indexed. The second field contains the help messages and is stored as a MEMO field.

Once the proper record is found, the contents of the second field (the MEMO field) can be viewed using all the scrolling features of the editor. There are several advantages to this type of approach. The most important one is that you can program in flexibility so that the viewer can page back and forth between records (screens) and view all information that is needed any number of times. This is not possible using the CASE structure. Second, the developer can program as many different routines as are necessary to assist the user in navigating through the help program. The help program can contain its own navigation aids to help the user move through all the information that is stored there.

There are two disadvantages to this type of help structure. The first is that when the user is in the help screens he or she is using the editor and can change data that is stored in the help file. You must try to make certain that changes made to the help file are discarded and that the contents of the MEMO field remain unchanged. To do this, you should prompt the user to use **Escape** to get out of both the MEMO field and to get back to the program. Listing 7.5 shows this. The second disadvantage is that, in order to get into the MEMO field, the user is first presented with the required format screen (see Listing 7.6 for the format screen programming and Figure 7.2 for the screen shot of the format screen) and then must press **Control-PgDn** to enter the MEMO field. Figure 7.1 shows an actual help screen including the *dBase III Plus* navigation keys on the

Listing 7.5. Help Program

```
PARAMETERS vmenu, vchoice
SET ESCAPE OFF
SET FORMAT TO <help format filename>
USE help INDEX <help index name>
STORE vmenu+LTRIM(STR(vchoice)) TO vhelpscr
SEEK vhelpscr
READ

RETURN

*** End Help Program
```

Listing 7.6.   Help Program Format File

```
CLEAR
@ 05,10 SAY "To enter the help program, press Control + PgDn"
@ 08,10 GET <helpfield>
@ 12,10 SAY "PRESS ESCAPE TO EXIT FROM THE HELP SCREEN"
@ 14,10 SAY "PRESS ESCAPE TO RETURN TO THE PROGRAM"


*** End Help Program Format File
```

To enter the help program, press Control + PgDn

memo

PRESS ESCAPE TO EXIT FROM THE HELP SCREEN

PRESS ESCAPE TO RETURN TO THE PROGRAM

Figure 7.1.   Help Program Screen

the top of the screen. To turn the navigation key help box off, make sure that you have SET MENU OFF.

The flexibility that is gained by doing this is offset by the incremental time necessary to program it. If there is a lot of information, I suggest that the developer seriously evaluate what information is necessary to have online and what should appear in written documentation.

If you wish to stay with the text block help file structure you can still program the paging function into your help program where necessary using an INKEY( ) bounce program.

The basic help program is still a collection of DO CASE statements but, within a single DO CASE statement, you are free to add whatever programming that you need.

Let us re-do the help screen that is used in Figure 7.2 using the approach shown in Listing 7.7.

Edit: HELP

```
┌─────────────────────┬───────────────────┬─────────────────┬─────────────────────────┐
│ CURSOR:  <-- -->    │       UP  DOWN    │    DELETE       │ Insert Mode:     Ins    │
│ Char:        ← →    │ Line:    ↑    ↓   │ Char:     Del   │ Insert line:      ^N    │
│ Word:   Home End    │ Page: PgUp  PgDn  │ Word:     ^T    │ Save: ^W  Abort:Esc     │
│ Line:     ^←  ^→    │ Find:     ^KF     │ Line:     ^Y    │ Read file:        ^KR   │
│ Reformat: ^KB       │ Refind:   ^KL     │                 │ Write file:       ^KW   │
└─────────────────────┴───────────────────┴─────────────────┴─────────────────────────┘
```

PRINT ALL HELP

When you direct the program to PRINT ALL please make sure that you have enough continuous sheet paper in the printer to print the file.

Make sure that the printer is turned on and that you have aligned your paper at Top Of Form properly before starting to print.

You will then be asked to confirm that the printer is on before you start printing. At that time you will be given the following prompt:

    <<<< Press the PgDn Key to see the next help screen >>>>

Figure 7.2.   Help Screen

Listing 7.7.   Help Screen Paging Program

```
PARAMETERS vmenu, vchoice
STORE vmenu+LTRIM(STR(vchoice)) TO vhelpscr

DO CASE
  CASE vhelpscr = 13
    CLEAR
    TEXT
       <help text>
    ENDTEXT
    WAIT

  CASE vhelpscr = 14
    CLEAR

    STORE 1 TO vscreen
    DO WHILE .T.
      DO CASE
        CASE vscreen = 1
          CLEAR
          TEXT




                  PRINT ALL  HELP

          When you direct the program to PRINT ALL please make sure that
```

you have enough continuous sheet paper in the printer to print
the file.

Make sure that the printer is turned on and that you have aligned
your paper at Top Of Form properly before starting to print.

You will then be asked to confirm that the printer is on before
you start printing. At that time you will be given the following
prompt:

          Press any key to begin printing

     <<<< Press the PgDn Key to see the next help screen >>>>

     <<<< Press Escape to go back to the program >>>>
```
     ENDTEXT

  CASE vscreen = 2
     CLEAR
     TEXT
```

                   PRINT ALL   HELP (ctd.)

After you have struck a key, the printer will start printing your
report.

If, for any reason, you run out of paper or if something else
happens to stop your print run, the program will wait for you
to insert more paper before going on with the print run.

If you need to stop the print run, you can do so by pressing the
Escape key. You must then answer the prompt that follows with
a "C" to cancel the printing program.

     <<<< Press the PgUp Key to see the previous help screen >>>>

     <<<< Press Escape to go back to the program >>>>

```
     ENDTEXT
  ENDCASE

  STORE 0 TO key
DO WHILE KEY = 0
     STORE INKEY() TO key
  ENDDO

  DO CASE
     CASE key = 3
       IF vscreen = 2
         vscreen = 1
       ELSE
```

```
            vscreen = vscreen + 1
         ENDIF
      CASE key = 18
         IF vscreen = 1
            vscreen = 2
         ELSE
            vscreen = vscreen - 1
         ENDIF
      CASE key = 27
         RETURN
      ENDCASE

   ENDDO

 CASE vhelpscr = 21
    <text>

ENDCASE

RETURN

*** End Help Screen Paging Program
```

The navigation DO CASE structure includes both the **PgUp** and **PgDn** key presses even though the user only needs to move back and forth between two screens in this case. This structure will take care of situations requiring three or more help screens to completely discuss a subject.

The two screens that this program generates are shown in Figures 7.3 and 7.4

```
                PRINT ALL  HELP
When you direct the program to PRINT ALL please make sure that
you have enough continuous sheet paper in the printer to print
the file.

Make sure that the printer is turned on and that you have aligned
your paper at Top Of Form properly before starting to print.

You will then be asked to confirm that the printer is on before
you start printing.  At that time you will be given the following
prompt:

          Press any key to begin printing


    <<<< Press the PgDn Key to see the next help screen >>>>

    <<<< Press Escape to go back to the program >>>>
```

Figure 7.3.   Screen Shot of First Help Screen

```
        PRINT ALL   HELP (ctd.)

After you have struck a key, the printer will start printing your
report.

If, for any reason, you run out of paper or if something else
happens to stop your print run, the program will wait for you
to insert more paper before going on with the print run.

If you need to stop the print run, you can do so by pressing the
Escape key. You must then answer the prompt that follows with
a "C" to cancel the printing program.


  <<<< Press the PgUp Key to see the previous help screen >>>>

  <<<< Press Escape to go back to the program >>>>
```

Figure 7.4.   Screen Shot of Second Help Screen

In some applications you may find that it would be beneficial to have a cross-referencing on some or all of your help screens. You can program this feature in by adding a cross-referencing module in the help screens that should be cross-referenced. The program to do this is included as Listing 7.8.

Notice that the whole of the help program is now contained in a loop. Each of the CASEs will now have to have its own RETURN command. The loop is necessary to continue processing if a cross-reference is requested. Pressing the **F1** key activates the CASE key = 28 case and resets the variable VHELPSCR to the appropriate value and passes control back to the outside loop. In the next iteration of the loop, the requested screen(s) are shown. Any number of different cross-references can be included in this type of structure by assigning separate trigger keys to them and including them in the DO CASE structure after the INKEY( ) loop.

Finally, you may want to allow your user access to all the help screens that you have in your system from some type of help index. This can be programmed as a bounce bar menu that is entered from within help. There are two main differences in this program. The first is that the whole program is now contained inside a loop and processing continues until the user presses the **Escape** key. The second difference is that instead of having WAIT statements in each CASE and waiting there for a key press to RETURN you to the program, the initial program pause is in an INKEY( ) loop. This INKEY( ) loop either places the user in the help selection menu (if the **F1** key is pressed) or returns the user to the program (if the **Escape** key is pressed).

Listing 7.8.   Help Cross-Referencing Program

```
DO WHILE .T.
<starts just as in figure 7.9 above>
..........
          If you need to stop the print run, you can do so by pressing the
          Escape key.  You must then answer the prompt that follows with
          a "C" to cancel the printing program.


              <<<< Press F-1 to view Help on printing one record >>>>

              <<<< Press the PgUp Key to see the previous help screen >>>>

              <<<< Press Escape to go back to the program >>>>

          ENDTEXT
       ENDCASE

       STORE 0 TO key
    DO WHILE KEY = 0
          STORE INKEY() TO key
       ENDDO

       DO CASE
          CASE key = 28
             vhelpscr = <screen for help on printing one record>
             EXIT
          CASE key = 3
             IF vscreen = 2
               vscreen = 1
             ELSE
               vscreen = vscreen + 1
             ENDIF
          CASE key = 18
             IF vscreen = 1
               vscreen = 2
             ELSE
               vscreen = vscreen - 1
             ENDIF
          CASE key = 27
             RETURN
       ENDCASE

     ENDDO

   CASE vhelpscr = 21
      <text>

  ENDCASE

ENDDO

*** End Cross-Referencing Help Program
```

Listing 7.9.   Help Index Program

```
PARAMETERS vmenu, vchoice
STORE vmenu+LTRIM(STR(vchoice)) TO vhelpscr

DO WHILE .T.
  DO CASE
    CASE vhelpscr = 13
      CLEAR
      TEXT
        <help text>
      ENDTEXT

    CASE vhelpscr = 14
      CLEAR
      TEXT
        <help text>
      ENDTEXT

    CASE <all other cases>
  ENDCASE

  @ 24,10 SAY "Press F-1 for Help Menu, Escape to return to program."

  STORE 0 TO key
  DO WHILE key = 0
    STORE INKEY() TO key
  ENDDO

  DO CASE
    CASE key = 27
      CLEAR
      RETURN
    CASE KEY = 28
      vchoice = 1
      key = 0
      SET COLOR TO W/N
      CLEAR
      @ 01,24 SAY " ┌──────────────────────────────┐ "
      @ 02,24 SAY " │                              │ "
      @ 03,24 SAY " │    DEMONSTRATION PROGRAM      │ "
      @ 04,24 SAY " │                              │ "
      @ 05,24 SAY " │        HELP INDEX            │ "
      @ 06,24 SAY " │                              │ "
      @ 07,24 SAY " └──────────────────────────────┘ "
      @ 08,10 SAY " ┌─────────────────────────────────────────────────┐ "
      @ 09,10 SAY " │ Help is available on the following list of subjects. │ "
      @ 10,10 SAY " │                                                 │ "
      @ 11,10 SAY " │ Highlight your choice and press the Carriage Return to │ "
      @ 12,10 SAY " │     view the information available on your choice.  │ "
      @ 13,10 SAY " └─────────────────────────────────────────────────┘ "
      @ 15,01 SAY;
```

```
                "Adding new customers                    Printing all invoices"
   @ 17,01 SAY "Editing existing customer records        "+;
                "Valid data entries for input fields"
   @ 19,01 SAY "Deleting customers from the file         "+;
                "Finding a specific record in the file"
   @ 21,01 SAY "Printing a single invoice                "+;
                "System backup"
   @ 23,23 SAY "Return to the program"

DO WHILE key <> 13
   SET COLOR TO W/N

   DO CASE
      CASE vchoice = 1
         @ 15,00 SAY " Adding new customers "
      CASE vchoice = 2
         @ 17,00 SAY " Editing existing customer records "
      CASE vchoice = 3
         @ 19,00 SAY " Deleting customers from the file  "
      CASE vchoice = 4
         @ 21,00 SAY " Printing a single invoice "
      CASE vchoice = 5
         @ 15,41 SAY " Printing all invoices "
      CASE vchoice = 6
         @ 17,41 SAY " Valid data entries for input fields "
      CASE vchoice = 7
         @ 19,41 SAY " Finding a specific record in the file "
      CASE vchoice = 8
         @ 21,41 SAY " System backup "
      CASE vchoice = 9
         @ 23,22 SAY " Return to the program "
   ENDCASE

   DO CASE
      CASE key = 24 .OR. CHR(key) = ' '
         IF vchoice = 9
           vchoice = 1
         ELSE
           vchoice = vchoice + 1
         ENDIF
      CASE key = 4
         IF vchoice <= 4
           vchoice = vchoice + 4
         ELSE
           vchoice = vchoice - 4
         ENDIF
      CASE key = 5
         IF vchoice = 1
           vchoice = 9
         ELSE
           vchoice = vchoice - 1

         ENDIF
      CASE key = 19
         IF vchoice > 4
           vchoice = vchoice - 4
         ELSE
           vchoice = vchoice + 4
   ENDCASE
```

```
      SET COLOR TO N/W

      DO CASE
        CASE vchoice = 1
          @ 15,00 SAY " Adding new customers "
        CASE vchoice = 2
          @ 17,00 SAY " Editing existing customer records "
        CASE vchoice = 3
          @ 19,00 SAY " Deleting customers from the file  "
        CASE vchoice = 4
          @ 21,00 SAY " Printing a single invoice "
        CASE vchoice = 5
          @ 15,41 SAY " Printing all invoices "
        CASE vchoice = 6
          @ 17,41 SAY " Valid data entries for input fields "
        CASE vchoice = 7
          @ 19,41 SAY " Finding a specific record in the file "
        CASE vchoice = 8
          @ 21,41 SAY " System backup "
        CASE vchoice = 9
          @ 23,22 SAY " Return to the program "
      ENDCASE

      STORE INKEY() TO key
      DO WHILE key = 0
        key = INKEY()
      ENDDO

  ENDDO

  DO CASE
     CASE vchoice = 1
       vhelpscr = 11
     CASE vchoice = 2
       vhelpscr = 12
     CASE vchoice = 3
       vhelpscr = 13
     CASE vchoice = 4
       vhelpscr = 14
     CASE vchoice = 5
       vhelpscr = 23
     CASE vchoice = 6
       vhelpscr = 24
     CASE vchoice = 7
       vhelpscr = 25
     CASE vchoice = 8
       vhelpscr = 31
     CASE vchoice = 9
       RETURN
  ENDCASE

  ENDCASE

ENDDO

*** End Help Index Program
```

If you compare the navigation DO CASE structure in this help index program to the one in the bounce bar menu program featured in Listing 3.5, you will find that there are two differences. The first difference is the absence of keyboard triggers for help. The only way that the user can call a help screen is by moving the light bar with the cursor keys. The second difference is that the four cursor keys (left, right, up, and down) all have different effects. In the bounce bar menu program pushing either the **up arrow** or the **right arrow** key has the same effect. In this menu selection program, pushing the **right arrow** key will move the light bar to the other option on the same row. Pushing the **left arrow** key has exactly the opposite effect. As there are only two columns in this example the opposite effect is actually the same effect. If there were three columns of choices, the results would be different. This logic makes it easier to move around a complicated menu structure as a major help index might be.

One thing to remember is that *dBase III Plus* does a lousy job of trapping the left arrow key press. I included the programming for the **left arrow** key because I would probably compile this type of application and therefore would not have this problem. If the application were to be run under *dBase III Plus*, I would most probably leave out the CASE key = 19 statements.

The help index screen generated by this program looks like Figure 7.5.

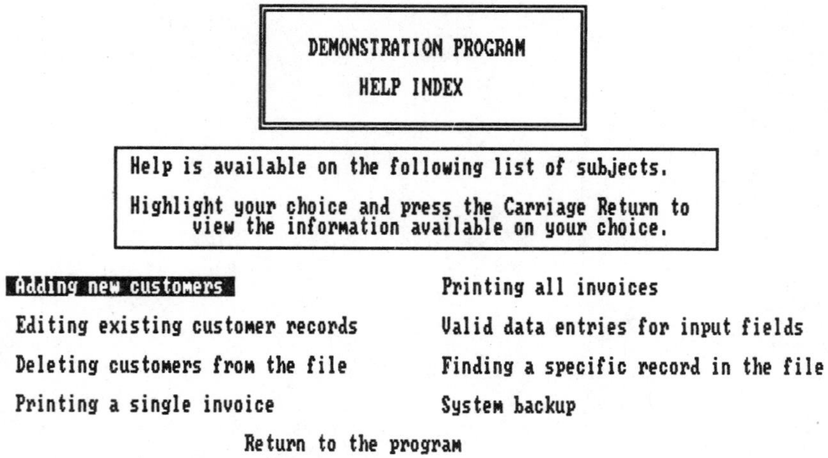

```
          +-------------------------------------+
          |      DEMONSTRATION PROGRAM          |
          |           HELP INDEX                |
          +-------------------------------------+
```

```
   +-------------------------------------------------------+
   | Help is available on the following list of subjects.  |
   | Highlight your choice and press the Carriage Return to|
   |      view the information available on your choice.    |
   +-------------------------------------------------------+
```

Adding new customers   Printing all invoices

Editing existing customer records   Valid data entries for input fields

Deleting customers from the file   Finding a specific record in the file

Printing a single invoice   System backup

                   Return to the program

Figure 7.5.   Help Screen Index

An area where help is needed is when a user gets stuck in a data entry field and cannot figure out what to do. *dBase III Plus* will not let the user get out of a READ temporarily so that you can program in specific help at the moment that it is needed in the middle of filling in a data screen. There are two different solutions to this problem. You can either provide a HELP option as one of the choices at the end of the READ (which the user can **Escape** to when needed and then return to the same screen using the re-edit option) or you can set up all data checking after the READ and provide the option of going directly to HELP from within the error checking routine. Either way will work, but neither provides immediate help on the spot. To do this, you need to use *Clipper*.

Using Compiled Programs

Quicksilver acts just like *dBase III* except that instead of CLEARing the screen and repainting it as you must do with *dBase*, you can use the WINDOW commands and have pop-up help show up all over the screen. When used automatically with the post-READ error checking routines, it works exceptionally well. As *Quicksilver* does not erase the main screen (Window 0), it is not necessary to go through the same screen repainting routines that are discussed above.

Clipper is a completely different story. The developer can SAVE SCREEN before invoking the help program and RESTORE SCREEN after the program is done so the cumbersome screen repaints that are necessary with *dBase III Plus* are not necessary with *Clipper*. Also, *Clipper*'s VALID function, which will allow the developer to interrupt a READ and do some other task before coming back to the same spot in the READ, can also be used to provide context-sensitive help *at the point where it is needed*.

Clipper also provides you with another possibility for providing help to the user: the **F1** key. *Clipper* uses the **F1** key in a different fashion than *dBase III Plus* does. When the user presses **F1** while the program is waiting for the input of a variable, *Clipper* invokes the help program and automatically passes three variables. The three variables are the name of the calling program (character), the source code line number of the calling program (numeric), and the name of the memory variable that is waiting for user input (character variable.) All three parameters must be passed, but you must use discretion in what you include in your help program. The associated help file must receive the three passed parameters and should execute a SAVE SCREEN command before going on to the DO CASE help section of the program. The help screens can be complete screens, multiple screens, or small boxes of help over-layed on top of the existing screen. As the entry screen is SAVEd, it can be RESTOREd at the end of the help session.

Clipper's **F1** function works only when the user is at a point where input to a memory variable is expected, but you can develop a single help program that contains help for the **F1** source as well as for other sources. All you have to do is make sure that three variables are passed and that they conform to the types listed above.

Data Viewing

Once the user has filled a database with massive amounts of information and all that information has been checked to make sure it is valid, it would be nice if the application provided some way for the user to view his data in the ways that are most useful. It does the user no good to be presented with masses of unsorted information. In order to be useful to the user, information must be sorted and selected according to specific criteria.

There are several database management programs on the market that advertise that you can give a search phrase in English — like "Show me the last name of all salesmen in the Northeast Region who are single and have exceeded their quota for the year by at least 20%" — and the program will execute the search without any problem. This is true to a certain extent (depending on what our grammar is like and which program you use) but, in the end, you still have to comply to a specific set of grammar rules or find that you have data that does not meet what you thought your search criteria were. For example, the "at least" before the 20% means "greater than or equal to." If you forgot to put it in you might

might only get those salesmen whose sales exactly equaled 120% of quota.

We will not deal with this type of program in this book. Instead, we will concentrate on developing programs for sorting and selecting data using what Ashton-Tate provides in the *dBase III Plus* language. We will first discuss a method for finding a specific record when the correct spelling of the name is not known. Next we will discuss simple ways of developing search criteria and, finally, we will develop a generalized search program that allows users to enter their own customized search criteria.

SOUNDEX Search

One of the frustrating moments of any computer database search happens when you know that the record has to be there, but you do not find it when you are searching for a specific name. What has probably happened is that the name that the operator entered does not exactly match the name in the database. If, for example, the operator is searching for the name "Simmons" but the name is actually "Symmons" no match will be found. A routine to handle this problem was developed over 20 years ago and has been improved on over the years by several people. It is called the SOUNDEX algorithm, which takes words and reduces them to codes depending on their sounds.

The SOUNDEX procedure is as follows:

```
    1. Eliminate all non-alpha characters
    2. Desensitize case (convert all characters to upper-
case)
    3. Move first letter of the word to result
    4. Change the remaining letters according to the fol-
lowing:

        a. B,F,P & V          = 1
        b. C,G,J,K,Q,S,X & Z  = 2
        c. D & T              = 3
        d. L                  = 4
        e. M & N              = 5
        f. R                  = 6
        g. A,E,I,O,U,Y,H & W  = 0
```

```
5,  All zeros are eliminated
6,  Identical digits are combined
7,  The result is added to the first letter (step 3)
8,  The result is then trimmed to the requisite length
```

(Wiederhold, Gio DATABASE DESIGN McGraw-Hill 1983 p, 655)

*** End SOUNDEX Procedure

It has been found that the complete SOUNDEX code is not necessary to achieve a satisfactory search "hit" rate. The trim length (referred to in Step 8 above) is usually either four characters or five in length. Depending on your application you might want to use the longer length but most people that have studied the subject extensively recommend a length of four characters, so we will use this length in our example.

The result of applying the SOUNDEX algorithm to both "Simmons" and "Symmons" is the same: a SOUNDEX code of "S52". Going through the procedure step by step we get the following code after Step 4:

```
S + 055052
```

After Step 5 the code would look like this:

```
S + 5552
```

After Step 6 the code looks like this:

```
S + 52
```

After Step 7 the code is now:

```
S52
```

Step 8 is not needed in this case because the length of the code is less than the four digits specified.

If we were searching from "Symmons" we would "hit" if we searched for the SOUNDEX code as both Symmons and Simmons have the same SOUNDEX code.

The *dBase III Plus* routine to generate the SOUNDEX code is as shown in Listing 8.1.

Listing 8.1. *dBase* SOUNDEX Routine

```
STORE UPPER(vlname) TO vlname
STORE LEN(vlname) TO vlen
STORE SUBSTR(vlname,1,1) TO vsound
STORE 2 TO vcount
STORE 0 TO vlast

DO WHILE vcount <= vlen
   STORE SUBSTR(vlname,vcount,1) to vlet

  DO CASE
    CASE vlet $ "BFPV"
      STORE 1 TO vval
    CASE vlet $  "CGJKQSXZ"
      STORE 2 TO vval
    CASE vlet $ "DT"
      STORE 3 TO vval
    CASE vlet $ "L"
      STORE 4 TO vval
    CASE vlet $ "MN"
      STORE 5 TO vval
    CASE vlet $ "R"
      STORE 6 TO vval
    OTHERWISE
      vcount = vcount + 1
      LOOP
  ENDCASE

  IF vval = vlast
    vcount = vcount + 1
    LOOP
  ELSE
    vsound = vsound + STR(vval,1)
```

```
    IF LEN(vsound) = 4
       EXIT
    ENDIF

    vlast = vval

   ENDIF

   vcount = vcount + 1

ENDDO

***   End SOUNDEX Routine
```

If this were to be set up as a separate program or as a procedure, the passed parameter would be VLNAME. VSOUND would also have to be made PUBLIC so that the results would be available to the calling program.

How should the SOUNDEX code be used? First, the SOUNDEX code must be included in the appropriate data table and the table must be indexed on the code. When new names are added to the table, the last name must be converted to its SOUNDEX code and stored. Second, when searching for a record by a person's last name, the SOUNDEX code does not come into play at all unless the search using the last name fails. If this happens the routine in Listing 8.2 would be invoked.

You would be surprised at how many times this type of search is invoked and how much time it can save.

Simple Data Query Routines

The least complicated data query routines simply set a filter on the data table(s) and present only the data that satisfies the filter criteria. Only a single filter can be set in a data table at any time, but the filter criteria can include conditions on more than one field using the logical operators .AND., .OR., and .NOT.. Comparisons are made using the relational operators <, <=, =>, >=, and <> and, in the case of the logical data type, the logical operators "True" (implied) and .NOT. ("SET FILTER

Listing 8.2.   SOUNDEX Search Routine

```
<do normal search routine>
IF EOF()
  ? CHR(7)
  @ 22,00 CLEAR
  @ 23,10 SAY "SOUNDEX Search Commencing"
  DO soundex WITH vlname, vsound
  SET INDEX TO vsound
  SEEK vsound

  IF EOF()
    @ 23,00 CLEAR
    WAIT "         SOUNDEX Search Failed.  Press any key to continue..."
    <return to program to try a new name or quit>
  ELSE
    @ 23,00 CLEAR
    @ 23,10 SAY "First SOUNDEX Match --  (N)ext  (P)revious  (E)dit  (Quit)"
    <do record positioning and edit/quit>
  ENDIF

ENDIF

*** End SOUNDEX Search Routine
```

TO married" would show only those employees who are married; "SET FILTER TO .NOT. married" would show only those employees who are single.) A single field can also have more than one criterion: salary > 25000 AND salary < 50000 will show all employees with salaries between $25,000 and $50,000.

A simple routine that allows the user to set a single filter on a specified field is usually all that is necessary to satisfy most needs. A program to do just this with the simple STATE data table that we discussed in Chapter 5 would look like Listing 8.3.

Only one filter can be set on a data table at one time. The filter criteria, however, is limited only to the maximum length of a *dBase III Plus* command (254 characters) so the actual filter can be set on two or more fields at the same time. You can also set filters between fields so that, for instance, only those records where Current Bonus is less than

Listing 8.3.   Simple Data Filter Routine

```
CLEAR
USE state
@ 04,10 SAY "Please Enter Your Search Criteria"
@ 06,10 SAY "You can search on the following fields:"
@ 08,10 SAY "   STATE,  LOWZIP,  HIGHZIP"
STORE .T. TO loop

DO WHILE loop
   STORE "          " TO vsearch
   STORE "      " TO vmin
   STORE "      " TO vmax
   @ 10,10 SAY "Search on: " GET vsearch
   READ
   STORE TRIM(UPPER(vsearch)) TO vsearch

   IF vsearch $ "STATE LOWZIP HIGHZIP"
      STORE .F. TO loop
   ELSE
      ? CHR(7)
      @ 12,10 SAY "Not a valid field.  Retype your entry"
   ENDIF

ENDDO

@ 12,00 CLEAR
@ 12,10 SAY "Greater than or equal to: " GET vmin PICTURE "!!!!!"
@ 14,10 SAY "Less than or equal to: " GET vmax PICTURE "!!!!!"
READ
SET FILTER TO &vsearch >= "&vmin" .AND. &vsearch <= "&vmax"

< continue with processing>

***  End Filter Routine
```

Previous Bonus are shown. A filter can also be set on each of the linked files.

Complex Filter Assembly Program

So far we have dealt with only a single, simple filter condition. It is possible to set up complex filter conditions. A problem in doing this is an application is that the operator is the one that must assemble the filter conditions. What usually happens is that something goes wrong, the filter is set improperly, and the data that is extracted is not what was needed in the first place. What *is* needed is a way to reduce the chances for operator error. The following program is designed to do just that. The program develops a complete statement for use by the SET FILTER TO command (Listing 8.4).

This program is designed to call up the first 20 fields in a data table (if there are that many) and establish a filter criterion for different values on several different fields. The only limitation is on the length of a single *dBase* command and that has been taken into account near the end of the program with the "IF LEN(vcrit) > 220" structure that limits the length of VCRIT to less than the maximum length of a *dBase* command line, including the "SET FILTER TO" part of the statement. The limit of 20 fields is arbitrary and can be changed easily by modifying the first part of the program.

The program uses the FIELD( ) function to get into the data table and extract the necesssary information about the field type and length in order to execute the proper CASE statement.

If you are going to use this program, make sure that the fields that you might want to set up conditions on are among the first 20 fields and that the field names are clearly understandable to the user, as the program simply pulls the names directly from the data table. In operation, the screen looks like Figure 8-1. As you can see, the table used in this example is the Employee Data Table with several of the field names changed to improve readability. The filter set will allow only those single employees whose last names start with the letter J or later, who live in Los Angeles, and make $25,000 or more. To take off or reset the filter, simply invoke the program again.

An alternative to using this type of program is to "hard wire" a query program to a specific data table. If you do this you can use

Listing 8.4. Complex Filter Program

```
USE <table name>
CLEAR
STORE 1 TO vfieldno
STORE " " TO vtest
DO WHILE .T.
  SET CONSOLE OFF
  STORE FIELD(vfieldno) TO vtest

  IF LEN(vtest) = 0
    EXIT
  ENDIF

  vfieldno = vfieldno + 1

ENDDO

SET CONSOLE ON
vfieldno = vfieldno - 1

IF vfieldno <= 20
  STORE vfieldno TO vcount
ELSE
  STORE 20 TO vcount
ENDIF

STORE 1 TO vno
DO WHILE vno <= vcount

  DO WHILE vno <= 10 .AND. vno <= vcount
    @ vno+1,05 SAY vno PICTURE "99"
    @ vno+1,10 SAY FIELD(vno)
    vno = vno + 1
  ENDDO

  DO WHILE vno > 10 .AND. vno <= vcount
    @ vno-9,40 SAY vno PICTURE "99"
    @ vno-9,45 SAY FIELD(vno)
    vno = vno + 1
  ENDDO

ENDDO

STORE 1 TO vno
STORE "" TO vcrit

STORE .T. TO loop
DO WHILE loop

  STORE 0 TO vchoice
  @ 13,10 SAY "Press Carriage Return to Return/Eliminate Filter Criteria"
```

```
@ 23,00 CLEAR
@ 23,10 SAY "Chose Field for Filter Criteria: " get vchoice;
            PICTURE "99" RANGE 1, vfieldno
READ
STORE FIELD(vchoice) TO vname
@ 13,00 SAY SPACE(70)
@ 13,30 SAY "FILTER CRITERIA"
@ 14+vno,10 SAY FIELD(vchoice)

DO CASE
  CASE vchoice = 0
    CLEAR
    STORE "" to vcrit
    EXIT
  CASE TYPE(FIELD(vchoice)) = "L"
    @ 23,00 Clear
    STORE .T. TO vlogic
    @ 23,10 SAY "Logical Data Type: Search for True? (Y/N): " get vlogic;
                PICTURE "Y"
    READ

    IF vlogic
      @ 14+vno,20 say "TRUE"
      STORE vcrit + "&vname" TO vcrit
    ELSE
      @ 14+vno,20 SAY "FALSE"
      store vcrit + ".NOT. " + "&vname" TO vcrit
    ENDIF
  CASE TYPE(FIELD(vchoice)) = "C"
    STORE vcrit +  "&vname" TO vcrit
    STORE LEN(&vname) TO vlen
    @ 23,00 CLEAR

    STORE .T. TO loop1
    DO WHILE loop1
      STORE " " TO vchoice
      @ 23,00 SAY "Choices  (B) Beginning With   (F) Finishing With";
                  "(E) Equal to: " GET vchoice PICTURE "a"
      READ

      IF upper(vchoice) $ "BFE"
        EXIT
      ELSE
        ? CHR(7)
      ENDIF

    ENDDO

    DO CASE
      CASE UPPER(vchoice) = "B"
        @ 14+vno,20 SAY ">="
        STORE vcrit + " >= " TO vcrit
      CASE UPPER(vchoice) = "F"
        @ 14+vno,20 SAY "<="
        STORE vcrit + " <= " TO vcrit
      CASE UPPER(vchoice) = "E"
```

```
      @ 14+vno,20 SAY "="
        STORE vcrit + " = " TO vcrit
   ENDCASE

   STORE SPACE(vlen) TO vchoice
   @ 23,00 CLEAR
   @ 23,10 SAY "Enter Boundry Value: " GET vchoice
   READ
   @ 14+vno,25 SAY vchoice
   STORE TRIM(vchoice) TO vchoice
   STORE vcrit + CHR(34) + VCHOICE + CHR(34) + " " TO vcrit
CASE TYPE(FIELD(vchoice)) = "N"
   STORE vcrit + "&vname" TO vcrit
   @ 23,00 clear

   STORE .T. TO loop1
   DO WHILE loop1
     STORE " " TO vchoice
     @ 23,00 SAY "Choices: (L) Less Than    (G) Greater Than";
                 "(E) Equal to   (N) Not Equal to"
     @ 24,00 SAY "        (D)  Less or Equal to     (U) Greater or Equal";
                 " to: " GET vchoice
     READ

     IF UPPER(vchoice) $ "LGENEDU"
       EXIT
     ELSE
       ? CHR(7)
     ENDIF

   ENDDO

   DO CASE
     CASE UPPER(vchoice) = "L"
       @ 14+vno,20 SAY "<"
       STORE vcrit + " < " TO vcrit
     CASE UPPER(vchoice) = "D"
       @ 14+vno,20 SAY "<="
       STORE vcrit + " <= " TO vcrit
     CASE UPPER(vchoice) = "E"
       @ 14+vno,20 SAY "="
       STORE vcrit + " = " TO vcrit
     CASE UPPER(vchoice) = "G"
       @ 14+vno,20 SAY ">"
       STORE vcrit + " > " TO vcrit
     CASE UPPER(vchoice) = "U"
       @ 14+vno,20 SAY ">="
       STORE vcrit + " >= " TO vcrit
     CASE UPPER(vchoice) = "N"
       @ 14+vno,20 SAY "<>"
       STORE vcrit + " <> " TO vcrit
   ENDCASE

   STORE 000000 TO vchoice
   @ 23,00 CLEAR
   @ 23,10 SAY "Enter Boundry Value: " GET vchoice
```

```
  READ
  @ 14+vno,25 SAY LTRIM(STR(VCHOICE))
  STORE vcrit + LTRIM(STR(VCHOICE)) + " "  TO vcrit
CASE TYPE(FIELD(vchoice)) = "D"
  STORE vcrit + "&vname" TO vcrit
  @ 23,00 clear

  STORE .T. TO loop1
  DO WHILE loop1
    STORE " " TO vchoice
    @ 23,00 SAY "Choices:  (B) On or Before Date  (A) After Date : ";
            GET vchoice
    READ

    IF UPPER(vchoice) $ "BA"
      EXIT
    ELSE
      ? CHR(7)
    ENDIF

  ENDDO

  DO CASE
    CASE UPPER(vchoice) = "B"
      @ 14+vno,20 SAY "<="
      STORE vcrit + " <= " TO vcrit
    CASE UPPER(vchoice) = "A"
      @ 14+vno,20 SAY "<"
      STORE vcrit + " > " TO vcrit
  ENDCASE

  STORE "01/01/01"TO vdate
  STORE CTOD("01/01/01") TO vchoice
  @ 23,00 CLEAR
  @ 23,10 SAY "Enter DATE: " GET vchoice
  READ
  STORE DTOC(vchoice) TO vdate
  STORE 'CTOD("&vdate")' TO vchoice
  @ 14+vno,25 SAY vchoice
  STORE vcrit + vchoice  TO VCRIT

ENDCASE

@ 23,00 CLEAR
IF LEN(vcrit) > 220
  EXIT
ENDIF

STORE .T. TO loop1
DO WHILE loop1
  STORE "Y" TO vchoice
  @ 23,10 SAY "Add Another Filter Criteria? (Y/N) "  GET vchoice PICTURE "a"
  READ

  IF UPPER(vchoice) $ "YN"
    EXIT
  ELSE
```

```
      ? CHR(7)
   ENDIF

ENDDO

IF UPPER(vchoice) = "N"
   EXIT
ENDIF

@ 23,00 CLEAR
STORE .T. TO loop1
DO WHILE loop1
   STORE "A" TO vchoice
@ 23,10 SAY "Enter Your Choice for Logical Connector:  (A) And  (0) or  : "
GET vchoice
   READ

   IF UPPER(vchoice) $ "AO"
      EXIT
   ELSE
      ? CHR(7)
   ENDIF

ENDDO

DO CASE
   CASE UPPER(vchoice) = "A"
      @ 14+vno,38 SAY "AND"
      STORE vcrit + " .AND. " TO vcrit
   CASE UPPER(vchoice) = "0"
      @ 14+vno,38 SAY "OR"
      STORE vcrit + " .OR. " TO vcrit
ENDCASE

STORE vno + 1 TO vno

ENDDO

SET FILTER TO &vcrit

***  End Complex Query Program
```

a version of a set of simple menu programs to build up your filter criteria.

Graphics

Every once in a while you will be faced with a situation in which it is necessary to work with graphics. *dBase III Plus* does not do graphics. Or

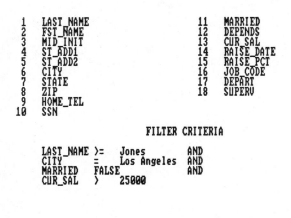

```
 1  LAST_NAME            11  MARRIED
 2  FST_NAME             12  DEPENDS
 3  MID_INIT             13  CUR_SAL
 4  ST_ADD1              14  RAISE_DATE
 5  ST_ADD2              15  RAISE_PCT
 6  CITY                 16  JOB_CODE
 7  STATE                17  DEPART
 8  ZIP                  18  SUPERV
 9  HOME_TEL
10  SSN
```

FILTER CRITERIA

```
LAST_NAME  >=   Jones          AND
CITY       =       Los Angeles AND
MARRIED    FALSE              AND
CUR_SAL    >    25000
```

Add Another Filter Criteria? (Y/N) y

Figure 8.1.   Set Filter Screen

at least it was not intended to do them. Fortunately the program is so flexible that you can do some very simple graphics within the program.

The most commonly used graph type is the bar graph, and *dBase III Plus* can imitate this type of graph by simply painting the fill-in character (usually ASCII character 219) in the graphics mode or an * if you are going to print the output on a nongraphics printer.

The program to draw a bar chart is relatively simple. The parameters needed are the number of columns and the specific values for each of the columns. With this data, *dBase* will be able to paint the appropriate size bars. The first thing that you must do is STORE the actual data points from the data table into the appropriate memory variables and start work with these data points. From that starting point the program to develop a bar graph for six data points looks like Listing 8.5.

The program can control the minimum and maximum values for the Y axis, so the graph can be scaled. Titles can be edited with each iteration of the program and the bar character and the graph outline can be changed from a block black character (ASCII 219) and line draw characters to an * for the bar and the | and − characters for the graph so it can be printed using the IBM system's PrintScreen function on a printer that is not capable of printing the IBM extended graphics characters.

The six input values for this graph come from the data table and are STOREd in the six starting memory variables. As a starting point for the graph, the program determines the maximum value of the data points and uses this value for VMAX. The user then has the option to change this value and the minumum value for the graph before viewing.

Listing 8.5.   Simple Bar Graph Program

```
CLEAR
STORE <val1> TO vcol1
STORE <val2> TO vcol2
STORE <val3> TO vcol3
STORE <val4> TO vcol4
STORE <val5> TO vcol5
STORE <val6> TO vcol6

STORE SPACE(40) TO vtitle
STORE SPACE(10) TO vstitle1
STORE SPACE(10) TO vstitle2
STORE SPACE(10) TO vstitle3
STORE SPACE(10) TO vstitle4
STORE SPACE(10) TO vstitle5
STORE SPACE(10) TO vstitle6
STORE CHR(219) TO vchar
STORE .F. TO vprint
STORE 0 TO vmax
STORE 0 TO vmin

STORE 1 TO vcount
DO WHILE vcount <= 6

   STORE "vcol" + LTRIM(STR(vcount)) TO vrec
   IF &vrec > vmax
     STORE &vrec TO vmax
   ENDIF

   vcount = vcount + 1

ENDDO

STORE .T. TO loop
DO WHILE loop

   @ 02,10 SAY "Please enter/change any of the values listed below:"
   @ 05,10 SAY "Graph Title: " GET vtitle
   @ 07,10 SAY "Column 1 Title: " GET vstitle1
   @ 08,10 SAY "Column 2 Title: " GET vstitle2
   @ 09,10 SAY "Column 3 Title: " GET vstitle3
   @ 10,10 SAY "Column 4 Title: " GET vstitle4
   @ 11,10 SAY "Column 5 Title: " GET vstitle5
   @ 12,10 SAY "Column 6 Title: " GET vstitle6
   @ 14,10 SAY "Maximum Value for graph: " GET vmax PICTURE "999999"
   @ 15,10 SAY "Minimum Value for graph: " GET vmin PICTURE "999999"
   READ
   @ 17,10 SAY "Prepare Graph for PrintScreen? " GET vprint PICTURE "Y"
   READ
   CLEAR

IF vprint
  STORE "*" TO vchar
```

```
     STORE "¦" TO vvert
     STORE " " TO vcor
     STORE "-" TO vhor
ELSE
     STORE CHR(219) TO vchar
     STORE CHR(179) TO vvert
     STORE CHR(192) TO vcor
     STORE CHR(196) TO vhor
ENDIF

STORE TRIM(vtitle) TO vhead
STORE INT((80 - LEN(vhead))/2) TO vpos
@ 00,vpos SAY vhead

@ 02,06 SAY vvert
@ 03,06 SAY vvert
@ 04,06 SAY vvert
@ 05,06 SAY vvert
@ 06,06 SAY vvert
@ 07,06 SAY vvert
@ 08,06 SAY vvert
@ 09,06 SAY vvert
@ 10,06 SAY vvert
@ 11,06 SAY vvert
@ 12,06 SAY vvert
@ 13,06 SAY vvert
@ 14,06 SAY vvert
@ 15,06 SAY vvert
@ 16,06 SAY vvert
@ 17,06 SAY vvert
@ 18,06 SAY vvert
@ 19,06 SAY vvert
@ 20,06 SAY vvert
@ 21,06 SAY vvert
@ 22,06 SAY vcor+REPLICATE(vhor,70)

STORE vmax - vmin TO vrange
@ 02,00 SAY vmax PICTURE "999999"
@ 07,00 SAY .75 * (vrange) PICTURE "999999"
@ 12,00 SAY .50 * (vrange) PICTURE "999999"
@ 17,00 SAY .25 * (vrange) PICTURE "999999"
@ 22,00 SAY vmin PICTURE "999999"

STORE 1 TO vcount
STORE vmax - vmin TO vrange
DO WHILE vcount <= 6

   STORE "col" + LTRIM(STR(vcount)) TO vrec
   STORE "vstitle" + LTRIM(STR(VCOUNT)) TO vsub
   STORE &vrec - vmin TO vquant
   STORE ROUND((vquant/vrange) * 20,0) TO vsize
   SET DECIMAL TO 0

   DO WHILE vsize > 0
     @ (22-vsize),(12*(vcount-1)+08) SAY REPLICATE(vchar,8)
     vsize = vsize - 1
```

```
    @ 23,(12*(vcount-1)+08) SAY &vsub
  ENDDO

  vcount = vcount + 1

ENDDO

STORE "" TO vresp
WAIT ""
@ 23,00
WAIT "          RUN ANOTHER ITERATION OF THIS GRAPH? (Y/N) " TO vresp
IF UPPER(vresp) = "N"
  EXIT
ENDIF
CLEAR

ENDDO

*** End Simple Graph Program
```

The height of each bar is determined by the number of lines that the bar should occupy, with 20 lines being 100 percent of the range. Building the bars is then nothing more than a brute printing routine.

The data entry screen (filled) looks like Figure 8.2.

The Graphics output of the program looks like Figure 8.3 on the screen.

When the user wants to print the graph on a printer that cannot print the PC's extended graphic set, the output character can be changed to the

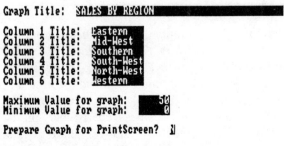

Figure 8.2. Bar Graph Data Entry Screen

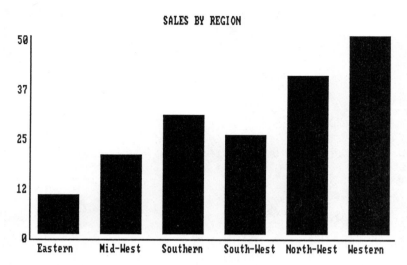

Figure 8.3.   Screen Shot of Bar Graph

* character for printing. Note that the program has an additional WAIT "" at the end of the graph writing portion of the program *before* the prompt appears asking the user if he or she is interested in another iteration of the program. This is done so that the prompt does not appear on a PrintScreen dump to the printer.

Such a dump looks like Figure 8.4.

You will notice tha the program ROUNDs the Y-axis values before they are presented. This is fine for graphs with a large range — greater than 10. If the graph were to be used in a program where the range of values is small, the ROUND function would have to be modified to include the appropriate number of decimal places.

Extended Graphics

If your needs are greater than those supplied by the above program, Ashton-Tate has just put out the *Tools for "C" Graphics Library* that allows you to do both low-level and high-level graphics. The extension requires a PC system with 512K of memory minimum and recommends a graphics adapter (EGA or Hercules preferably). With this in mind the library provides the most used type of business charts: bar charts, stacked bar charts, line and marked point charts and X/Y charts (which are close to being the same thing), high/low/close charts, and pie charts.

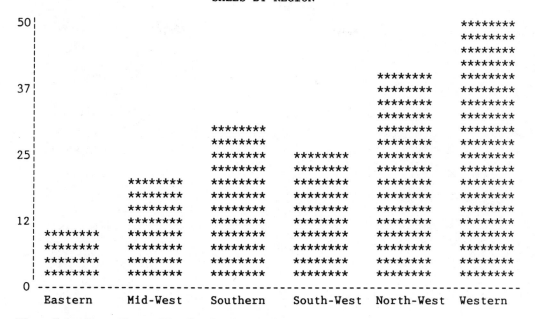

Figure 8.4. Screen Dump of Bar Graph Using PrintScreen

Ashton-Tate has, wherever possible, included some close approximations to these chart types for those of you that do not have a graphics adapter. The monochrome charts are obviously not in color and can only use the normal screen coordinates so they are, at best, an approximation. If detail and accuracy is not essential and if the number of different data points is limited, these approximations should work satisfactorily. The sample monochrome stacked bar chart (Figure 8.13) shows one of the limitations of the monochrome equivalent: the three numbers that are "stacked" are too small for the program to handle, so only one comes out. The sample monochrome marked point chart (Figure 8.9) shows another problem with the monochrome equivalents of the graphics charts. It appears that the program cannot handle negative numbers: Product 4's sales (represented as "#") show constant at zero when they should be trending negative.

Figures 8.5 through 8.15 show the graphics presentation of some of the different chart types that are included in the product and (where available) the monochrome equivalent of the same graph. Note that the "Cake" (a rectangular one) Chart is the only way that you can get a representation of shares of a total in monochrome.

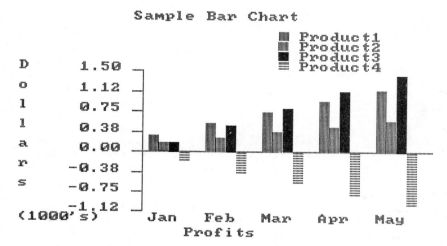

Figure 8.5. Simple Bar Chart in Graphics Mode

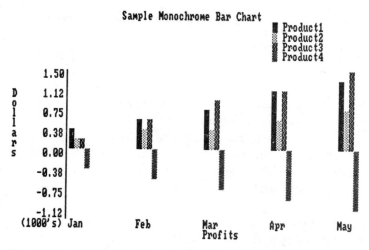

Figure 8.6. Simple Bar Chart in Text Mode

If you want to print out the graph, Ashton-Tate provides support for the Epson FX and MX printers and the IBM Graphics Printer only. It would be nice if they were to extend the list of printers supported to include a few other popular models. The graphics and monochrome images shown above are actually screen shots that were printed on a

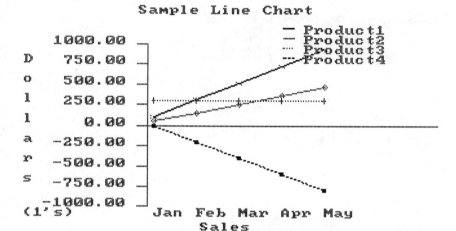

Figure 8.7. Line Chart in Graphics Mode

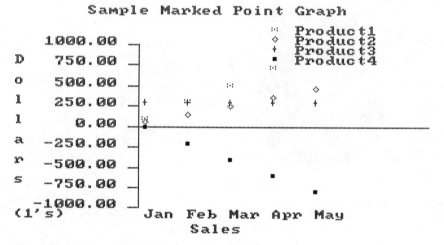

Figure 8.8. Marked Point Chart in Graphics Mode

Hewlett-Packard LaserJet using a screen print utility: they are not print outputs from the program.

For those who wish to venture deeper, the low-level graphics functions can be used with the high-level graphics functions that were used to create the charts in Figures 8.5 through 8.15. If you use them, you can improve the look of your graphs with better labeling and custom graphics.

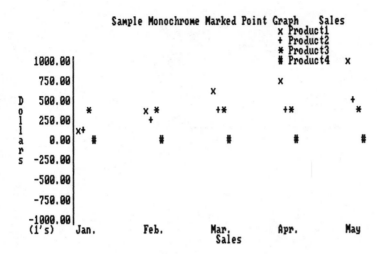

Figure 8.9. Marked Point Chart in Text Mode

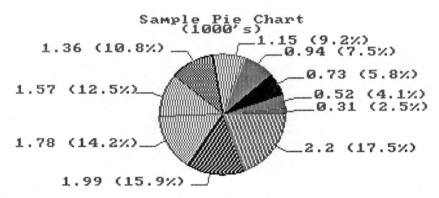

Figure 8.10. Pie Chart in Graphics Mode

If you are interested in doing this, be prepared to spend some time and effort to master the subject.

The price for all this is $89.95, a bargain if you need the features provided. Be prepared to spend more than an hour or two going through the manual, for it is not written in terms that are easily understood. The *Tools for "C" Graphics Library* is a companion volume to the original *dBase Tools for "C"* and works in a similar manner. If you are familiar with how *dBase* handles the creation of arrays and how data is passed back and forth, the learning process will be considerably shortened.

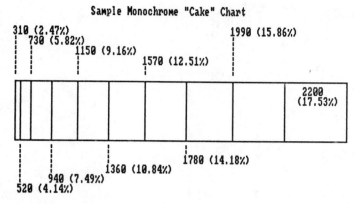

Figure 8.11.   "Cake" Chart in Text Mode

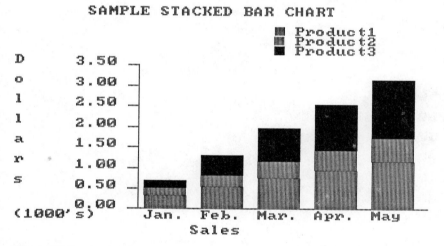

Figure 8.12.   Stacked Bar Chart in Graphics Mode

A third alternative for presenting graphics in *dBase III Plus* is Fox & Geller's dGRAPH for *dBase*. The product is a stand-alone package that can be invoked from within *dBase* if so desired. It works independently of *dBase* to evaluate data contained in *dBase* files before it presents them on the screen (or to the printer) as either line, bar, or pie charts. Fox & Geller include a fourth type of graph called the "Pie Bar" graph. It can best be described as a single stacked bar laid out on its side. It looks something like the "Cake" Chart shown in Figure 8.11.

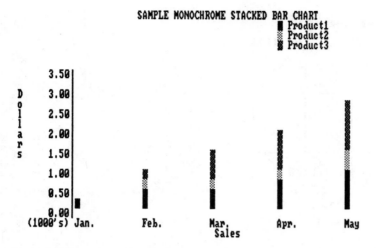

Figure 8.13.   Stacked Bar Chart in Text Mode

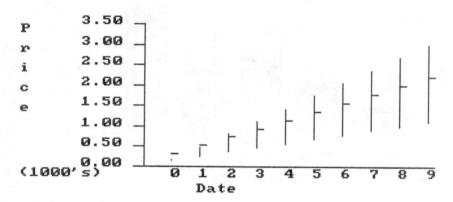

Figure 8.14.   High/Low/Close Chart in Graphics Mode

dGRAPH is interesting in that it can actually take input data and make modifications and calculations on it before showing the results on the screen. Custom legends can also be added to improve the quality of the work for presentations. The quality of printed output is dependent on the quality of the output device that you have. The suggested retail price of the program is $295.00.

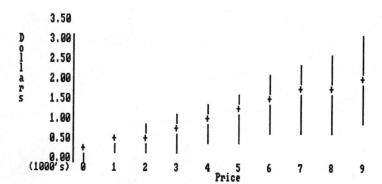

Figure 8.15.   High/Low/Close Chart in Text Mode

Data Reporting

Even if you develop the best application in the world it is worth very little if you cannot "get it on paper" in the form of a report. This chapter deals with developing the reports needed to get information out of your program.

There are three different ways to develop your reports. You can use the report generator included with *dBase III Plus*, you can purchase an "add-on" package from a third party vendor, or you can program the reports yourself. All three of these methods have advantages and each of them has disadvantages.

dBase III Plus Report Generator

There are two big advantages to the *dBase III Plus* report generator. First, it is free; it is included in the package with the database program. Second, it is easy to learn and easy to use.

There is one great disadvantage to the *dBase III Plus* report generator: it is, to put it kindly, limited in scope. Ashton-Tate's *dBase* manual dedicates 15 pages (about nine after you take out the pictures) to their report generator which should be an indication of its power.

Reports created by using the CREATE REPORT command are stored as a special file type (.FRM extension) and are invoked using the REPORT FORM <filename> command. Reports can be sent to the printer or to a named file for later printing.

The *dBase III Plus* report generator allows you to vary the page width and length, the number of characters on a line, the number of printed lines per page, the right and left margins, and whether the body of the report will be printed single or double spaced. You also have the option in the report setup section of the program to specify form feeds before the first page prints and after the last page is printed. You can also specify something called "Plain Page." If you elect this option the header information is only printed on the first page, and page numbers and the system date are not printed. The report title and the individual column headings can be a maximum of four lines of text each.

Figure 9.1 shows the *dBase III Plus* Report Generator's Options menu set up for a report on our Employee Data File.

The report generator centers the title between the left and right margins. If you find that you need the title information on the left or right side of the report you cannot do it with the program. As mentioned

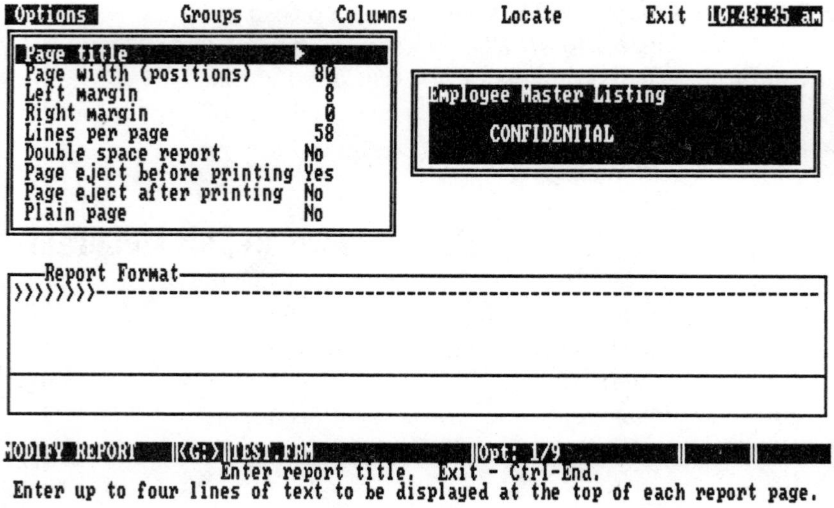

Figure 9.1.   Options Screen with *dBase III Plus* Report Generator

earlier, the Plain Page option takes out the title information on all but the first page, eliminates page numbers, and takes out the system date but if you wanted to remove *only* the system date from the report you would be out of luck. If, for some reason, you needed to print a report using cut sheet paper, you would not be able to use the report generator, as there is no option for making the printer pause between pages.

Reports developed using the report generator are limited to two levels of subtotalling, a single line of data per record, only simple mathematics (no conditional tax calculations for example) in calculated fields, and do not allow for any text enhancements such as bold printing of titles. Reports are also limited to the columnar report format; such things as custom invoicing are difficult or impossible to do using the program.

Figure 9.2 shows that our report is to be grouped by job code and subgrouped by supervisor.

Now that the outline of the report has been specified, we get to the meat of the report generator: the information from the data table. As you can see from Figure 9.3, there is only the most limited flexibility available with the *dBase III Plus* report generator. Only one line per record is allowed and limited flexibility is given on where and how it is presented.

There are ways to get around some of the limitations to the report generator, but they must all be considered workarounds. If, for instance, you must have conditional record selection based on multiple criteria,

```
Options      Groups        Columns        Locate       Exit  10:46:38 am
            ┌──────────────────────────────────────────────────┐
            │ Group on expression      JCODE                    │
            │ Group heading            Job Code                 │
            │ Summary report only      No                       │
            │ Page eJect after group   No                       │
            │ Sub-group on expression  SUPERV                   │
            │ Sub-group heading        Supervisor Name          │
            └──────────────────────────────────────────────────┘


┌─Report Format──────────────────────────────────────────────────────┐
│>>>>>>>>────────────────────────────────────────────────────────────  │
│                                                                      │
│                                                                      │
└──────────────────────────────────────────────────────────────────────┘

MODIFY REPORT    KG>TEST.FRM                    Opt: 6/6
    Position selection bar - ↑↓.  Select - ◄┘.  Leave menu - ↔.
    Enter text to be displayed at the beginning of each sub-group.
```

Figure 9.2.   Grouping Screen with *dBase III Plus* Report Generator

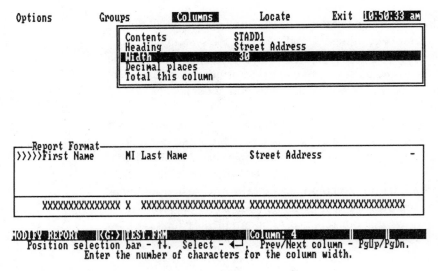

Figure 9.3.   Report Body for *dBase III Plus* Report Generator

or need to have different pieces of information included in a single column depending on some outside criteria, the easiest way to get this done and to compensate for the limitations of the report generator is to create a temporary data table (call it PRINT) and do all your sophisticated calculations and conditional merging while you are writing data to the file. You would then use the report generator to develop your output from this temporary file. This still does not answer the problems of formatting your reports the way that you would like.

Third Party "Add-On" Packages

One of the nice things about the whole *dBase* series has been that there are enough customers in the marketplace to make it worth peoples' while to develop products that do the things that Ashton-Tate forgot to do or did not do well. Report generation is one area in which this is true.

Two add-on packages are worth commenting on here. Fox & Geller's *QUICKREPORT for dBase* is the first that will be discussed and Concentric Data System's *R&R Relational Report Writer* is the second. These packages are both stand-alone report writers that work with *dBase* files. Both products have their own executable load module (.EXE file) that can be invoked either from within *dBase III Plus* or from the DOS prompt. Both programs develop their own special report files that use the information supplied in *dBase* files to write their reports.

To develop the reports, the programs are invoked from the DOS prompt, the reports specified and, finally, saved to disk. These report formats are then run either directly from DOS or invoked from with *dBase*. If the report files are called from *dBase*, the .EXE file is then loaded and the report is then written. *It is important to note that* dBase III Plus *remains inactive while the report is being developed and while it is being printed*. Both products require memory beyond that taken by *dBase III Plus* and neither write any code that can be directly interpreted by *dBase*. The programs are report *writers*, not report code generators.

Quickreport

Fox & Geller, Inc. is one of the original add-on firms for *dBase*. Their product line now includes everything that you could possibly want for *dBase*. *Quickreport* (suggested retail price — $295) is their report writer and it works with up to six different data tables at one time. It allows the developer to create reports that can break on up to 16 different fields if that is ever necessary. Calculated fields and conditional processing are built into the product, as are special printer features such as bold, italics, underlining, condensed print, and any supported combination of the above.

Quickreport is a menu driven program and is therefore relatively easy to learn. It suffers the same problem that I have found with other programs that are similarly constructed: you have to continually go back and forth between your work and the menus in order to get anything done and, unless you are paying attention, you can get lost in what options are on or off at any one time.

Figure 9.4 shows *Quickreport* database setup menu. In this particular example, only one data table is used, (our employee database) but by simply specifying which tables to use, several files can be linked. When multiple files are specified, all the fields available for a report will be shown in the lower box.

Figure 9.5 shows one of the biggest advantages that an add-on report writer has over the *dBase III Plus* report generator: it has the ability to print multiple line reports. Here we have constructed a report where each record occupies four lines. Any number of different formats, including full page formats are allowed.

As can be seen in Figure 9.6 the sort order for our report is on Job

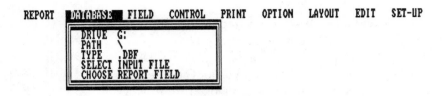

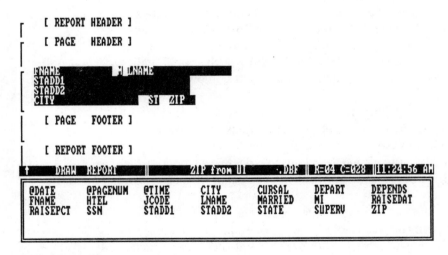

Figure 9.4. *Quickreport* Setup

Figure 9.5. *Quickreport* Sample Report

Code with a secondary sort by Supervisor. Unlike the *dBase III Plus* report generator, where only two levels of sorting are allowed. *Quickreport* will allow for a maximum of 16 different sorting and page breaking criteria.

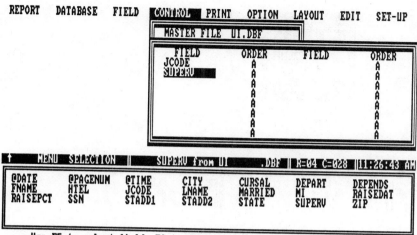

Figure 9.6. *Quickreport* Sorting Screen

Printers supported include the Epsons, Okidatas, NEC Pinwriter, 7710, and 3550, Anadex, C.Itohs, Brother, TI-855, Qume, Diablo, and HP ThinkJet. You are also allowed to define your own printer specifications as well. Figure 9.7 shows the text enhancements that are available using *Quickreport*. This must be constrasted against the *dBase III Plus* report generator, which does not allow for any text enhancements at all.

One of the reasons to use a report writer is for the improvement in report formatting that they can give your reports. With *Quickreport*, formatting options include custom formatting of headers and footers, separate headers and footers for each group, sub-group, sub-sub-group, sub-sub-sub-group (and so on). Any size paper can be accommodated and, unlike the *dBase III Plus* report generator, you can use cut sheet paper because the program contains a pause option. *Quickreport* allows you to suppress repeated values so that in a report that includes the state of residence of your employees, you can suppress the "CA" for those employees who live in California and still have the "AZ" show up when the state changes (this assumes that you have the STATE field included in your index so that the data is sorted). Data can either be left or right justified or centered within the column width specified. Figures 9.8 and 9.9 show some of the formatting options that are available to you with *QuickReport*.

The *Quickreport* manual (125 pages long with a sample program

Figure 9.7.   *Quickreport* Text Enhancements

REPORT   DATABASE   FIELD   CONTROL   PRINT   **OPTION**   LAYOUT   EDIT   SET-UP

```
┌──────────────────────────────────────────┐
│ SUPPRESS REPEATED VALUES              N   │
│ JUSTIFY                               L   │
│ DECIMAL PLACES FOR ROUNDING           0   │
├──────────────────────────────────────────┤
│ DATE FORMAT        YYYYMMDD               │
│ NEGATIVE #'s       -999.99                │
│ SINGLE ZERO        0                      │
│ THOUSANDS          NO FORMAT              │
│ FLOATING           NO FORMAT              │
│ DECIMAL CHAR       .                      │
│ FILL CHAR          space                  │
└──────────────────────────────────────────┘
```

↑   MENU SELECTION   ‖   ZIP from U1   .DBF ‖ R=04 C=028 ‖11:28:35 AM

```
┌────────────────────────────────────────────────────────────────────────┐
│ @DATE        @PAGENUM    @TIME     CITY      CURSAL     DEPART    DEPENDS │
│ FNAME        HTEL        JCODE     LNAME     MARRIED    MI        RAISEDAT│
│ RAISEPCT     SSN         STADD1    STADD2    STATE      SUPERV    ZIP     │
│                                                                          │
└────────────────────────────────────────────────────────────────────────┘
```

Specify whether spaces should be printed if a field's value doesn't change

Figure 9.8.   *Quickreport* Formatting Options

section) is not the easiest to understand. All the information is there, but not necessarily in a format that lends itself to quick comprehension. I often found myself unable to quickly find out what I needed to know.

The product of a *Quickreport* session is a single file with a .QR

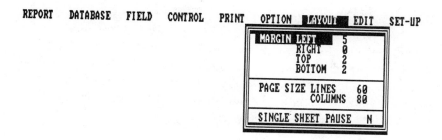

Set the number of blank spaces on the left border of the report

Figure 9.9. *Quickreport* Formatting Options

extension. This file can be invoked with *Quickreport* allowing the product to be run from within *dBase III Plus*.

As mentioned above, *Quickreport* is a stand-alone product and, if run from inside *dBase III Plus* requires an *additional* 256K of memory on top of the 256 required by *dBase*. Fox & Geller includes a sample of their runtime version of *Quickreport* which will run reports but will not crate them. If you use QRRUN.EXE the memory requirement shrinks to 128K above that used by the system, *dBase* and whatever else you have loaded (RAM disks, spelling checkers, spoolers, etc.). If you intend to use *Quickreport* to develop and run the reports for your applications, you should know that you can purchase additional copies of the *Quick-report* runtime module from Fox & Geller for $59 each. Quantity discounts are available. Interested parties should contact Fox & Geller directly at their offices in New Jersey (201) 794-8883.

R&R Relational Report Writer

The R&R Relational Report Writer was introduced by Concentric Data Systems in 1986 and provides an interesting alternative to *Quickreport*. The product is available for $99. For an extra $50 you can get a *Clipper* runtime module that will execute reports developed using the R&R

Relational Report Writer. The Report Writer requires a minimum of 205K of available memory to operate in the stand-alone mode (with a recommendation for at least 225K if possible) and the same plus *dBase*'s 256K to operate from within *dBase*. Concentric supplies a runtime module that allows the user to execute (but not configure) reports. The runtime module requires a minimum of 160K of available memory from within *dBase* in order to run, but the vendor recommends 187K for best performance.

The separate *Clipper* runtime module requires more memory than does the *dBase* runtime module. A minimum of 210K above that taken by the application is needed to run the program. Larger reports require as much as an additional 20K of memory to execute. As the base memory requirements of *Clipper* vary according to the application size and how it was complied (with or without overlays) the total memory needed to run Relational Report Writer varies.

The produce installation program that comes with R&R Relational Report Writer is well thought out and provides for user defined default directory and path, user specified memo editor, monitor type, printer count (one or two) and type (55 of the most popular plus a custom installation option for those with unusual printers). The installation program even allows for users to go in and change the printer escape codes used in the selected printer files if they are not to their liking.

Concentric has done a good job on their manual. It is well written and well documented. I found that I had little trouble finding what was needed in its 230 pages when it was necessary to go there to look up something. As can be seen for the listing of online help available, (Figure 9.10) one does not have to go to the manual too often.

If you have used Lotus Development Corporations 1-2-3 spreadsheet program you will feel right at home with the R&R Relational Report Writer. It has the look, feel and, wherever possible, the logic of this product. I found that I was able to decipher much of what was available by simply going through the menus at the top of the page. Figure 9.11 shows you what a report outline looks like.

I found that I needed more time to figure out what you could do with R&R Relational Report Writer than it did when I was looking at *Quick-report*. This is partly true because there is a lot more that you *can* do. R&R Relational Report Writer will use up to the maximum of 10 different data tables, will do up to eight levels of sub-totalling, will do calculated fields, and will include data on an if/then decision basis. Figure 9.12 shows the R&R Relational Report Writer sort fields selection screen. Choices are made simply by moving the cursor to the appropriate field.

Type / for command menu. Press F1 for help, F10 to insert field   Line: 1 Col: 1   HELP

Help Index

From each screen, you can select help for highlighted topics.

Calculated Fields	Margins
Character Functions	Math Functions
Control Panel	Modes
Database Command	Move Command
Date Functions	Multifile Reports
Edit Keys	Page Size
Entering Text	Pointing in a Pull-Down Menu
Exiting from R&R	Print Command
Field Command	Query Command
Global Command	Report Command
Help Screens	Selecting Commands
Identification Functions	Selecting Databases
Line Command	Sort-Group Command
LOWMEM indicator	Special Test Functions
Main Command Menu	Total Fields

Figure 9.10.   R&R Relational Report Writer Help Index

Field Move Line Sort-Group Query Print Database Report Global Exit   MENU
Insert, Calculate, Total, Width, Format, Attribute, Erase

```
Header ||···Master·listing·for·Employee·Data·File
Header ||
1▼LNAM ||···Last·name····.'XXXXXXXXXXXXXXXXXX
Body   ||
Body   ||   'XXXXXXXXXXXX  'XXXXXXXXXXXXXXXXXX  'XXXXXXXXXXXXXXXXXX  'X
```

Figure 9.11.   R&R Relational Report Writer Sample Report

The page size for reports can be specified, margins, lines per inch, pause between pages, indentation, and whether to use compressed print are some of the options that the user has. Figure 9.13 shows the page setup screen for R&R Relational Report Writer.

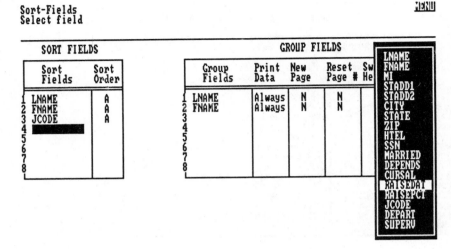

Figure 9.12.   R&R Relational Report Writer Sort Field Screen

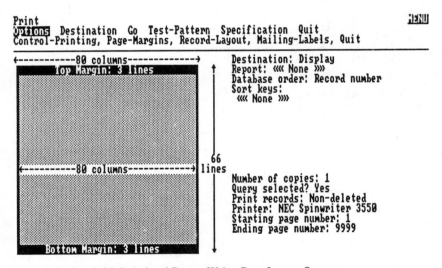

Figure 9.13.   R&R Relational Report Writer Page Layout Screen

R&R Relational Report Writer has an excellent filter capability. It is intuitive, and provides an excellent additional feature when creating reports. Figure 9.14 shows a filter criteria session where the user is about to select a greater than or equal to the salary figure of 25,000. Note that

```
Query
Enter value: 25000                                        EDIT
```

```
Select·all·records·where (LNAME is·equal·to "Jones") and·where (FNAME
is·less·than "Bob") or·where
```

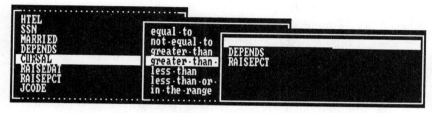

Figure 9.14.   R&R Relational Report Writer Set Filter Screen

R&R Relational Report Writer gives you the capability of making filter comparisons across fields as well.

One interesting characteristic to R&R Relational Report Writer is that the program stores reports in "Libraries" with any number of reports stored together and accessible through the program.

Concentric Data Systems supplies a runtime module with their program and expressly grants you the right "to permit others to use copies of Runtime for the purpose of printing reports from report format files created by the product."

The Do-It-Yourself Method

As I have said before, one of the nice things about *dBase III Plus* is that there always seems to be at least one way of getting done what you need to do. It may not be the easiest, but it can be done. This is as true with report output as it is with other areas of the program.

Most of the time, I design and implement my own report formats as DBASE.PRG files. One of the benefits to this approach is that I can compile the formats and maintain them inside the .EXE load module, thereby reducing the number of programs that need to be distributed and reducing the total code size. The cost that is associated with this is the extra time that I spend programming my reports. What I gain is complete control over the look and feel of the output of my program.

I wish to discuss two different types of reports here: the first is the simple data table output report, and the second is the more complicated full-page formatted output.

Simple Data Table Output

When I say "Simple Data Table Output," the word "Simple" can be deceiving. Complicated calculations and decision rules can be included in the processing that leads up to this simple output. "Simple" refers only to the fact that the report is columnar in nature and that (usually) each record in the data table(s) occupies only one line.

The first thing that must be done is to determine the order of the report and what records are going to be printed. This is done by setting up the proper index for the report and applying the proper filter criteria to the data table(s) that are included in the report. We have already discussed filter criteria and developed a program to set them in place on a data table in Chapter 10 so we will not go into further detail here. We have not yet discussed indexing and a brief discussion of this subject is necessary here.

The index that is used to properly order a report is probably not an index that is used in normal program operation. I usually construct a special index for each report so that information can be ordered the way that I need it for output. I create the indexes at the time that the report is requested and then get rid of it after the report is processed. In this manner I can be absolutely certain that the index is current. I use the module in Listing 9.1 to create and get rid of the indexes.

Indexes should be constructed in the same order as the report is to be sorted. The primary sort is the first field in the index, the secondary sort is the second field in the index expression and so on. Make sure that you have constructed a valid expression for your index by converting all fields to the same data type (usually character).

The next thing that must be done is test to make sure that the printer is on. We discussed in Chapter 6 that you should make sure that the printer is on while all data tables are closed so that you are not faced with the loss of data table headers. I do this by sending a form feed to the printer after prompting the user to make sure that the printer is on. If there is a problem, the program will hang up with no data at risk. A hot re-boot from this situation may be annoying, but it will not normally

Listing 9.1.   Report Index Handling Module

```
CLEAR
@ 10,10 SAY "Please wait while databases are sorted for this report"

USE <datatable>
INDEX ON <filed1> + <field2> + <field3> (etc.)  TO <indexname1>

@ 12,10  SAY "Data sorting is 50% completed"
USE <datatable2>
INDEX ON <filed6> + <field7> + <field8> (etc.)  TO <indexname2>

CLOSE DATABASES

<do printer test routine>
<do report processing

ERASE <indexname1>
ERASE <indexname2>

*** End Report Index Handling Module
```

---

cause too many problems. The routine that I use for this is as shown in Listing 9.2.

Once the index is created and the printer has been found to be on, the report can be constructed. Constructing a report is not that difficult. You simply have to imagine that what you are doing is going to go to the screen with a few minor differences. We will discuss these before going into detail about the actual report.

The first thing that must be done if we are going to get printed output is make sure that output goes to the printer. The command to accomplish this is SET DEVICE TO PRINT. This command is different from SET PRINT ON in that the SET DEVICE TO PRINT redirects the results of all SAYs to the printer. SET PRINT ON routes all unformatted output (such as the results of a LIST command) to the printer, but does nothing with SAYs. As reports are always formatted with SAYs, we use the SET DEVICE command.

The second thing that must be done is change the way that the program looks at rows and columns. The screen is mapped for 80 columns and 25 rows but a piece of paper may be much larger (or smaller) than that. If it is smaller, the absolute positioning method will work without

Listing 9.2.   Printer Testing Routine

```
STORE .T. TO loop
DO WHILE loop
  CLEAR
  @ 10,10 SAY "Make sure that your printer is on and has paper loaded."
  SET COLOR TO R+
  @ 14,10 SAY "IT IS VERY IMPORTANT THAT YOU CHECK"
  SET COLOR TO W
  @ 20,10 SAY "        Printer on and ready? (Y/N)  :  "
  ?
  SET CONSOLE OFF
  STORE "" TO CHECK
  WAIT "" TO CHECK
  SET CONSOLE ON
  CLEAR

  IF UPPER(CHECK) = "Y"
    loop = .F.
  ELSE
    RETURN <to calling program>
  ENDIF

ENDDO

CLEAR
@ 10,10 SAY "MAKE SURE THAT CONTINUOUS FEED PAPER IS POSITIONED AT "
@ 12,10 SAY "THE TOP OF THE FORM"
@ 15,15 SAY "PRESS ANY KEY TO START PRINTING"
WAIT ""
CLEAR
@ 10,30 SAY "PRINTING"
SET CONSOLE OFF
SET DEVICE TO PRINT
@ 00,00 SAY "PRINTER TEST"
@ 01,00 SAY ""
EJECT

<start report routine>

*** End Printer Testing Routine
```

---

any problems. If the paper is larger (as is 8 1/2 inch by 11 inch typing paper) this method will not work. A different method is needed.

All output starts at the top of the page (or the point on the page that has been aligned as "top of form"). On a standard sheet of paper (11 inches long) using six lines per inch, there are 66 lines on a page. Each line (row) of a page is printed in sequence (line 1, line 2, line 3, etc.). *dBase* allows you to either name these rows directly (up to 25) using the absolute reference system or name them *relatively* using the PROW( ) function. The PROW( ) function allows the program (and therefore the printer) to look at output using the current row as a base. PROW( ) is the current line (PresentROW.) PROW + 1 is the next line down from the current line. PROW( ) + 6 is six lines further down. As long as you do not advance a line, you will be able to print out fixed text and data from fields using the column coordinates associated with the present row. **@ PROW( ),20 SAY "Hello"** will print out the word "Hello" at column 20 of the line that the printer is currently on. **@ PROW( ) + 1,20 SAY "Hello"** moves the carriage down one line before printing the word. It therefore becomes a simple matter to SAY your fixed text on one line and then SAY all the information from the data record that you want on that same line using individual SAY statements that position the information where it is supposed to be.

The following set of SAYs:

```
@ PROW(),00 SAY "First Name:          Last Name: "
@ PROW(),12 SAY fname
@ PROW(),39 SAY lname

*** End Sample Format using PROW() Function
```

will give you the following output using the name of Sam Jones.

```
First Name: SAM          Last Name: Jones

*** End Sample Output Using PROW() Function
```

If more than one name is to be printed, the PROW( ) function for the first line would be changed to PROW( ) + 1 in order to move the printhead down to the next line before typing the next name on the list.

When you have SET DEVICE TO PRINT activated, you are also not limited to 80 columns. If you are doing a report on standard paper, using 10 characters to an inch you will find that 80 will do fine. If you are going to be using compressed print, or if you will be formatting reports on 14 inch wide paper, you will need more than 80 spaces. Fortunately, you have 256 columns (zero to 255) to play with, more than enough to use compressed print on wide paper. As with the ROW( )/PROW( ) pair, there is a PCOL( ) function to complement COL( ). Location on a line can be addressed in relation to the current location of the printhead. **@PROW( ),PCOL( ) + 5 SAY "There"** will print the word "There" five spaces to the right of the last position of the printhead (column position).

A few words of caution are needed. First, make sure that you print everything that you want printed on one line before going on to the next. Issuing a row coordinate that is less than the current row (or issuing a PROW( ) − 1 command) will cause the current page to eject before the program seeks the proper line number. Avoid issuing negative PCOL( ) commands in your programs. They will work only on those printers that allow for the carriage to travel right to left. Results on certain printers are unpredictable. Finally, you cannot just go on and on with relative positioning. You still have to count lines and make a page break using the EJECT command. This is where the print loops come in.

Every time that you move the printhead down a line using the @ PROW( ) + 1,cc command, you have to account for that move with a counter. Setting and using this counter gets into the heart of developing simple line reports with *dBase III Plus*.

In reality, developing reports in *dBase III Plus* is simply a matter of setting up and keeping track of where you are in a series of loops. This simplest report has no breaks in it for data sections and contains no totals on any of the columns. It provides us with a look at the simplest output structure (Listing 9.3).

Even at the simplest level we have a report that does several things for us. It gives us a title on each page, lists the page number of the report, gives us column headings and places the associated data under the proper column.

Notice that the report is processed inside two loops, the outer, that keeps processing going as long as we are not at the end of the file, and an inner loop that controls page breaks in the report. The inner loop also

Listing 9.3. Simplest Line Report Structure

```
STORE 1 TO vpage
DO WHILE .NOT. EOF()

  @ 03,05 SAY "Sample Report
  @ 03,70 SAY "Page " + LTRIM(STR(vpage))
  @ 05,05 SAY "First Name     Last Name              Supervisor"
  @ 06,00

  STORE 1 TO vcount
  DO WHILE vcount < 50 .AND. .NOT. EOF()
    @ PROW()+1,05 SAY fname
    @ PROW,25 SAY lname
    @ PROW,45 SAY superv
    SKIP 1
    STORE vcount + 1 to vcount
  ENDDO

  STORE vpage + 1 to vpage
  EJECT

ENDDO

*** End Simplest Line Report Program
```

---

tests for the End Of File condition so that processing stops at the moment
that EOF( ) is encountered. As we develop more complex reports each
nested loop will also test for the break conditions of the outer loops in
order to ensure that the report is paged properly. There are two counters
in this report, a page counter (VPAGE) used to place the page number on
the top right of each page, and the line counter (VCOUNT) used to control the number of records that are printed on each page.

Notice also that each page of the report starts with fixed title text and
is located with absolute reference to the starting line of the page (Top Of
Form). Printing starts on the fourth line from the top and is indented five
spaces using an absolute column reference of "05." The left margin can
be set using the SET MARGIN TO nn where "nn" is a number indicating

the offset from absolute zero. This works fine with *dBase* but does not work at all with *Clipper* when using the SET DEVICE TO PRINT command. If you need to have the option of setting the left margin with *Clipper* you need to add the routine shown in Listing 9.4 to your print program.

All that this program segment does is accept a numeric value from the user and use it as a constant value (vlm) that is then added to each of the column coordinates. It is a workaround at best, but at least it gives you the possibility of changing your left margin setting.

Notice also that the listing of information from the data records starts with the SAYing of field FNAME at column position five. The row is determined by the PROW( )+1 statement that instructs the printer to advance a line before printing the field. Notice that each successive SAY is given a row reference of PROW( ), meaning that no line feed is issued. If you wanted to have a space between each record printed (a double spaced report) you would simply change PROW( )+1 for the SAY of field FNAME to PROW( )+2. If this is done, it is also necessary to change the maximum count for the inner loop to 25 from 50 to take this fact into account.

If you need to have the ability to print this report on cut sheet paper instead of continuous feed paper you can add this feature by simply adding the routine shown in Listing 9.5 to your program.

From this point it is not difficult to start extending our formatting capabilities to places that the *dBase* report generator will not let you go. Headers and footers can be of any size and can be placed where you want them on the report. Each record can take up two (or more) lines on the

Listing 9.4. *Clipper* Set Left Margin Routine

```
CLEAR
STORE 0 TO vlm
@ 10,10 SAY "What left margin do you want? (0 to 10 spaces)" GET vlm RANGE 0,10
READ

<set up the rest of the print program>

@ rr,(cc+vlm) SAY.......

*** End Clipper Set Left Margin Routine
```

Listing 9.5. Printer Pause Routine

```
CLEAR
STORE .T. TO vpause
@ 10,10 SAY "Pause printer between pages?  (Y/N) " GET vpause PICTURE "l"
READ

<printer program up to....>

   STORE vcount + 1 to vcount
 ENDDO

 STORE vpage + 1 to vpage
 EJECT
 IF vpause
   SET DEVICE TO SCREEN
   SET CONSOLE ON
   @ 10,10 SAY "Place new sheet of paper in printer, align it properly,"
   @ 12,10 SAY "and press any key to re-start printing."
   WAIT ""
   @ 10,00 CLEAR
   @ 10,10 SAY "Printing..."
   SET CONSOLE OFF
   SET DEVICE TO PRINT
 ENDIF

ENDDO

*** End Printer Pause Routine
```

---

page and can be formatted as you want. Totals, sub-totals, sub-sub-totals and more can be included in the report. You are now limited only by the time that it takes to set up your program.

Let us look at some of the more complex report programming that is available using the .PRG file method of report generation.

1. Report Breaks

Even simple reports sometimes require that separate groupings of information be "broken" into discrete units. The easiest example of this using our employee database is a listing of employees by job code. In order to list each job code separately the file must first be indexed by job code (and most probably by last name if you want the report to be in alphabetical order). To break the report by job code you would use the following program structure shown in Listing 9.6.

Listing 9.6.   Single Report Break Coding

```
STORE 1 TO vpage
DO WHILE .NOT. EOF()
  STORE jcode TO vjcode

  DO WHILE jcode = vjcode .AND. .NOT. EOF()
    STORE O TO vcount

    DO WHILE jcode = vjcode .AND. vcount < 50 .AND. .NOT. EOF()
      @ rr,cc SAY (heading text)
      @ PROW()+1,cc SAY (report fields)
      vcount = vcount + 1
      SKIP 1
    ENDDO

  EJECT
  vpage = vpage + 1

  ENDDO

ENDDO

*** End single report break coding
```

The key to this coding is the contents of the JCODE field. The first instruction inside the outside loop is to store the value of JCODE to a memory variable VJCODE. Processing of the inside loops is then controlled by whether the value of JCODE for the record to be processed is the same as the value stored in VJCODE. If it is, processing continues. If it is not, a page break occurs. The new value for JCODE is stored in VJCODE and processing starts over again.

If you wanted to have the report broken out by job code and by supervisor a fourth loop would be necessary and you would have to make sure that the index for the report was constructed to include the SUPERV filed as the second part of the index expression. The coding for this would look like Listing 9.7.

The inside loop breaks pages, the second loop breaks by supervisor,

Listing 9.7.   Double Report Break Coding

```
STORE 1 TO vpage

DO WHILE .NOT. EOF()
  STORE jcode TO vjcode

  DO WHILE jcode = vjcode .AND. .NOT. EOF()
    STORE superv TO vsuperv

    DO WHILE jcode = vjcode .AND. superv = vsuperv .AND. .NOT. EOF()
      STORE 0 TO vcount

      DO WHILE jcode = vjcode .AND. superv = vsuperv .AND. vcount < 50 .AND;
.NOT. EOF()

        @ rr,cc SAY (heading text)
        @ PROW()+1,cc SAY (report fields)
        vcount = vcount + 1
        SKIP 1
      ENDDO

      EJECT
      vpage = vpage + 1

    ENDDO

  ENDDO

ENDDO

*** End double report break coding
```

---

the third loop by job code and the outside loop terminates the report program when EOF( ) is reached. Note that for each successive loop the outside conditions are included as part of the loop termination condition. This is to ensure that (in this case) the report does not continue on the same page with employees of a different job code who happen to have the same supervisor (as might happen if processing continued within the inside loops).

It is a simple matter to break on four or even five or six different criteria, the only thing to watch out for is where you are in your loops and make sure that the values for each of your break criteria are updated when necessary.

2. Report headings, sub-headings, and sub-sub-headings

Once you have set up your report to break at the proper places, you probably want to remove from the body of the report those fields that serve as breaks. These repetitive values are best put into headings and sub-headings at the top of each page. A report format that includes Job Code and Supervisor's Name in the heading information looks like Listing 9.8.

Footings could be easily included just before the EJECT in the inside loop.

3. Suppressing Repetitive Values

In certain circumstances you will want to suppress repetitive values of a field in a report. If, for example, you have a report that is sorted by customer by state and by city, you may want to suppress the repetitive state values in your report. To do this you must set up a memory variable and suppress printing if the current value of the variable is equal to the current value of the field. The program segment would look like Listing 9.9.

All that this program segment does is test to see if the value of STATE in the current record is the different from the one stored in the memory variable VSTATE. If the values are different, the STATE field from the current record is printed and the value of the memory variable is updated for the new situation.

4. Sub-totals and Totals

We can also include a sub-sub-total, sub-total and grand total of salaries for the listed employees with little problem. The code now looks like Listing 9.10.

Counters have been set up at the appropriate points in the program to keep track of the sub-sub-totals, sub-totals, and grand total salaries. These counters are also reset at the appropriate spots to keep track of the next set of numbers.

The only thing that is slightly tricky is where the sub-totals are printed. As you can see from the report, there is a two level IF/ENDIF construct that is used to print both the sub-sub-totals and sub-totals on the bottom of the appropriate page. The grand total still falls on a separate page. If you wanted to include the grand total on the bottom of the last page, you could do it by simply including a third IF/ENDIF inside the other two instructing the program to toal and print the grand total.

Listing 9.8.   Double Report Break Coding with Headings

```
STORE 1 TO vpage

DO WHILE .NOT. EOF()
  STORE jcode TO vjcode

  DO WHILE jcode = vjcode .AND. .NOT. EOF()
    STORE superv TO vsuperv

    DO WHILE jcode = vjcode .AND. superv = vsuperv .AND. .NOT. EOF()
      STORE 0 TO vcount

      DO WHILE jcode = vjcode .AND. superv = vsuperv .AND. vcount < 50;
               .AND. .NOT. EOF()

        @ 02,40 SAY "EMPLOYEE MASTER LISTING
        @ 04,45 SAY "CONFIDENTIAL"
        @ 06,10 SAY "JOB CODE:"
        @ 06,22 SAY jcode
        @ 07,10 SAY "Supervisor's Name:"
        @ 07,31 SAY superv
        @ 08,10 SAY "-------------------------------------"
        @ PROW()+1,cc SAY (report fields)
        vcount = vcount + 1
        SKIP 1
      ENDDO

      EJECT
      vpage = vpage + 1

    ENDDO

  ENDDO

ENDDO

*** End double report break coding with headings
```

---

5. Print Enhancements

So far everything that we have printed is in normal type. It is quite possible that you will want to improve the look of your report by including some of the printer enhancements that are available on your output device. The *dBase III Plus* report generator does not allow for you to do this, but it can be done with ease inside a .PRG report file.

When you have SET DEVICE TO PRINT, you can just as easily

Listing 9.9.   Suppress Repetitive Values

```
DO WHILE (break point criteria) .AND. .NOT. EOF()
   (processing)
   IF state <> vstate
     @ rr,cc SAY state
     STORE state TO vstate
   ENDIF
   (continue processing)
SKIP 1
ENDDO

*** End Suppress Repetitive Values
```

Listing 9.10.   Double Report Break Coding with Headings and Totals

---

```
STORE 1 TO vpage
STORE 0 TO vtsal

DO WHILE .NOT. EOF()
  STORE jcode TO vjcode
  STORE 0 TO vstsal

  DO WHILE jcode = vjcode .AND. .NOT. EOF()
    STORE superv TO vsuperv
    STORE 0 TO vsstsal

    DO WHILE jcode = vjcode .AND. superv = vsuperv .AND. .NOT. EOF()
      STORE 0 TO vcount

    DO WHILE jcode = vjcode .AND. superv = vsuperv .AND. vcount < 50 .AND;
.NOT. EOF()
        @ 02,40 SAY "EMPLOYEE MASTER LISTING"
        @ 04,45 SAY "CONFIDENTIAL"
        @ 06,10 SAY "JOB CODE:"
        @ 06,22 SAY jcode
        @ 07,10 SAY "Supervisor's Name:"
        @ 07,31 SAY superv
        @ 08,10 SAY "----------------------------------------"
        @ PROW()+1,cc SAY (fields included in report)
        vcount = vcount + 1
        vsstsal = vsstsal + cursal
        SKIP 1
      ENDDO
```

```
   IF vcount = 50 .AND. superv = vsuperv
     EJECT
   ELSE
     @ PROW()+1,20 SAY "Sub-Sub-Total Salary: "
     @ PROW(),50 SAY vsstsal
     vstsal = vstsal + vsstsal
     IF jcode <> vjcode
       @ PROW()+1,20 SAY "Sub-Total for Job Code:"
       @ PROW(),50 SAY vstsal
     ENDIF
     EJECT
   ENDIF
   vpage = vpage + 1

 ENDDO

ENDDO

vtsal = vtsal + vstsal

ENDDO

@ 06,20 SAY "Grand Total Company Salaries:"
@ 06,60 SAY vtsal

***  End double report break coding with headings and totals
```

send printer codes in the middle of your SAYs as you can text. If, for example, you are using a NEC 3550 printer and wanted to have the fixed text come out in shadow (bold) print, you could very easily send the printer code (Esc G (CHR(27) + CHR(71) for dBASE)) at the start of your fixed text SAYs and send the cancel shadow mode code (Esc H) at the end of text that you wanted highlighted. This would work but it would become tiresome rather quickly. A better way to invoke this code is to set up the codes that you want to use as memory variables and then include the macro expansions of the memory variables in your text (see Listing 9.11).

The "of bold" will come out in shadow print. You must remember to place these printer macros in a SAY when you are using SET DEVICE TO PRINT because only the SAY statements are sent to the printer.

These printer codes can be set up as public variables and declared at the beginning of the program. If this is done they will be available for all output requirements. If your application is going to be used with several different machines you may want to develop an installation program

Listing 9.11.   Text Enhancements in Reports

```
STORE "CHR(27)+CHR(71)" TO mdbo
STORE "CHR(27)+CHR(72)" TO mdob

SET DEVICE TO PRINT
SET CONSOLE OFF
@ 4,10 say "This is a test " + &mdbo + "of bold " + &mdob + "printing."
SET DEVICE TO SCREEN
SET CONSOLE ON

*** End Text Enhancements in Reports
```

---

that allows the user (or you) to set up these codes in a memory variable file (.MEM) that is recalled when the program is booted. In this fashion, the same program can be used in several different environments.

Complex Report Formatting

We have already introduced several sophisticated formatting options that have allowed us to develop complex reports using .PRG command files. The programming techniques discussed above will most probably be all that you will ever need for reporting but they do not deal directly with another very important area of reporting; the full page report. An invoicing program is an example of this.

There are two different situations that need to be discussed here. The first involves reports where there are already pre-printed forms and it is simply a question of making sure that the information that is going to be printed fits in the appropriate places. The second instance is where there is no report, and you need to create the report and fill it in at the same time.

In the first instance, your most important tool will be the type ruler. With it you will be able to locate the proper row and column positions for all information that will be filled in from the data record. It is then a simple task to construct the proper @ rr,cc SAYs for the data fields. The only piece of advice to make your life easier is to start your measurements not from the top of the page, but from a reference point further down the page at a point where the typehead will be when the top of the page is flush with the top of the typehead mechanism. This makes it easier for the operator to properly line up the page in the printer.

The second instance, where you will have to design the form as well as where to print in the data is both easier and harder than the first case. It is easier in that all referencing is within the program, so you do not have to worry about where a form is positioned. It is more difficult because you have to design the form yourself.

After much trial and error I have found that the easiest way to design a full page form is to use a screen generator and split the page into three parts (top, middle and bottom) to accommodate the 25 line maximum on the screen generator. I can then merge the three screens into one single file for the full page, convert the absolute references to relative ones (using the @ PROW( ) + n function) and then merge in the SAY statements for the data fields behind each fixed text statement. It takes some work to assemble the total entity, but the project can be shortened if you use a word processor that has a good search and replace function (to change the absolute references to relative ones) and split screen editing (to merge in the data field SAYs behind the fixed text SAYs). I have also found that it is always a good idea to make backup copies at frequent intervals to ensure that not too much effort is lost when you make a fatal error.

As an example, Listing 9.12 is a program for printing an invoice form and filling it in with data from an invoice file.

The program shown in Listing 9.12 will print invoices from a daily transaction file that is linked to the customer file through a customer ID number. The program shows both the full page report logic in the first half of the program, and the invoicing logic in the second half.

As you can see, each of the lines of fixed text is incremented using the PROW( ) + 1 command. Behind each line of fixed text comes the associated information from the data tables. You can create a full page this fashion.

This particular report is not exactly a "full page" report. There is a variable nature to it as well. As we are preparing an invoice from a transaction file and as each item ordered is considered to be a transaction, the program "collects" all items that have the same invoice number and prints them all on one or more pages. In this example, if more than 40 items are ordered, the program loops and creates a second page for the same invoice number. When the next item contains a different invoice number, processing of that particular order terminates, and the total is printed on the next several lines of that page.

Listing 9.12.   Full Page Invoicing Report Program

```
DO WHILE .NOT. EOF()
  STORE 1 TO vpage
  STORE invno TO vinvno
  STORE 0 TO vtot

  @ 04,40 SAY "INVOICE NUMBER:"
  @ PROW(),57 SAY invno
  @ PROW()+1,00 SAY;
  "┌─────────────────────────────────────╥─────────────────────────────────────┐"
  @ PROW()+1,00 SAY;
  "│ INTERNATIONAL WIDGETS COMPANY        ║                                     │"
  @ PROW()+1,00 SAY;
  "│ 300 West 45th. Street                ║       Order Line:   (800) 234-5600  │"
  @ PROW()+1,00 SAY;
  "│ Anywhere, NE  45678                  ║  Customer Service:  (800) 234-5678  │"
  @ PROW()+1,00 SAY;
  "└─────────────────────────────────────╨─────────────────────────────────────┘"

  @ PROW()+1,00 SAY;
  "┌─────────────────────────────────────┬─────────────────────────────────────┐"

  @ PROW()+1,00 SAY;
  "│ BILL TO:                            │ SHIP TO:                            │"

  @ PROW()+1,00 SAY;
  "├─────────────────────────────────────┼─────────────────────────────────────┤"

  @ PROW()+1,00 SAY;
  "│                                     │                                     │"
  @ PROW(),02 SAY custfile->custbt
  @ PROW(),41 SAY custfile->custst

  @ PROW()+1,00 SAY;
  "│                                     │                                     │"
  @ PROW(),02 SAY custfile->btadd1
  @ PROW(),41 SAY custfile->stadd1

  @ PROW()+1,00 SAY;
  "│                                     │                                     │"
  @ PROW(),02 SAY custfile->btadd2
  @ PROW(),41 SAY custfile->stadd2

  @ PROW()+1,00 SAY;
  "│                                     │                                     │"
  @ PROW(),02 SAY custfile->btcity
  @ PROW(),19 SAY custfile->btstate
  @ PROW(),22 SAY custfile->btzip
  @ PROW(),41 SAY custfile->stcity
  @ PROW(),53 SAY custfile->ststate
  @ PROW(),56 SAY custfile->stzip

  @ PROW()+1,00 SAY;
  "└─────────────────────────────────────┴─────────────────────────────────────┘"
  @ PROW()+1,00 SAY;
  "┌─────────────┬───────────────────────┬─────────────┬─────────────┐"
  @ PROW()+1,00 SAY;
```

```
"|Quant| Description                                      |Unit Pr.|Total    |"
@ PROW()+1,00 SAY;
"|     |                                                  |        |         |"

  DO WHILE invno = vinvno .AND. .NOT. EOF()
    STORE 1 TO vcount

    DO WHILE invno = vinvno .AND. vcount < 40 .AND. .NOT. EOF()
      @ PROW()+1,00 SAY "|        |"+SPACE(55)+"   |        |         |"
      @ PROW(),01 SAY quan
      @ PROW(),07 SAY desc
      @ PROW(),56 SAY unitpr
      @ PROW(),65 SAY quan * unitpr

      vtot = vtot + quan * unitpr
      vcount = vcount + 1
      SKIP 1

      IF invno <> vinvno
        @ PROW()+1,00 SAY;
"|                                                         |        |         |"

        @ PROW()+1,00 SAY;
"|                          TOTAL FOR THIS ORDER           |        |         |"
        @ PROW(),65 SAY vtot

        @ PROW()+1,00 SAY;
"|                                                         |        |         |"
        EJECT
        EXIT
      ENDIF

      IF vcount = 40
        @ PROW()+1,00 SAY;
"|                                                         |        |         |"

        @ PROW()+1,00 SAY;
"|                          PAGE NUMBER:                   |        |         |"
        @ PROW(),49 SAY vpage

        @ PROW()+1,00 SAY;
"|                                                         |        |         |"
        EJECT
      ENDIF

    ENDDO

    vpage = vpage + 1

  ENDDO

ENDDO

***  End Full Page Invoicing Report Program
```

For those of you who are interested, a completed invoice using this report program would look like Figure 9.15.

There can be no doubt that there is some extra work involved when you program your reports this way. You will, however, find that it is worth the effort. The strongest argument for doing your reports this way is that once you have finished, you have a simple .PRG file that can be modified just like any other program file and can be compiled as an integral part of an .EXE load module, saving space and the memory that would be required to run reports through an add-on report writer.

```
                            INVOICE NUMBER:  123456

INTERNATIONAL WIDGETS COMPANY
300 West 45th. Street                  Order Line:   (800) 234-5600
Anywhere, NE  45678              Customer Service:   (800) 234-5678


BILL TO:                      SHIP TO:

Bobson Marine Products          Bobson Marine Products
123 Marina Way                  123 Marina Way
Bali Hai Marina                 Bali Hai Marina
Long Beach       CA 98765       Long Beach       CA 98765


Quant  Description                           Unit Pr. Total

    5  Wonder Bilge Pumps 50 GPM                21.20   106.00
   23  Everlasting Life Preservers              10.50   241.50
   50  Now You See It Emergency Flares           2.50   125.00

                        TOTAL FOR THIS ORDER             472.50


***  End Full Page Invoice
```

Figure 9.15.   Completed Invoice

Development Tools

Probably one of the first things that a person does after buying *dBase III Plus* is look for good development tools to make the process of coding easier. The three biggest categories of development tools are screen generators, application generators, and report writers. While there are other programs available to do many other things with *dBase*, the bulk of the market is in the areas of screen, application and report generation.

We have already discussed three different report programs in Chapter 9: the *dBase III Plus* report format generator, Fox & Geller's *Quickreport* and Concentric Data Systems R&R Relational Report Writer. We will not discuss these further here.

The two remaining areas, screen generators and application generators are separate and distinct functions, but some products tend to fit into both categories. All applications have data entry programs and therefore much of the programming produced by these products has to do with putting information on the screen and getting it back to the data tables. Except for the *dBase III Plus* Screen Painter, the programs that we will look at are, at a greater or lesser extent, application generators.

As this book is about programming the user interface, not building applications, we will spend our time reviewing how these programs work in building this interface and mention only in passing some of the other capabilities of the products.

In order to have some level of comparability between products, we will use as our example the simple data entry screen that is shown in Figure 4.2 and supported with the code of Figure 4.3. We will go through the development process step by step, and point out some of the strengths and weaknesses of each of the products evaluated.

dBase III Plus Screen Painter

The *dBase III Plus* Screen Painter is a surprisingly versatile little program that makes screen painting quite easy. It is menu driven, easy to learn, easy to use, and is a vast improvement over the utility that was provided with *dBase III*. Best of all, it is free. The entire "documentation" for the screen painter is contained in the six pages covering it in the directory of commands. As the product is very easy to use, you will not have too much trouble figuring it out. One thing that still stumps me: how do you erase a line that you decide is in the wrong place? I finally had to dump the file that I was working on and start over again. I would have simply removed the spurious data from the format file, but the .SCR file would not have been updated.

The product is invoked within *dBase III Plus* using the CREATE SCREEN command (or MODIFY SCREEN to recall a screen format that has already been developed). The output from the product is a .FMT file that is linked to the CREATE SCREEN .SCR file. Output is automatic when you save the screen and, whenever a change is made in the .SCR file, the format file is updated to take this change into consideration. Unfortunately, the reverse is not true: if you make changes in the format file, the .SCR file is not updated and, if any further modification are made to the screen using MODIFY SCREEN, the changes made in the .FMT file will be overwritten and lost.

When you enter the program you are presented with the first logical choice: what data table to use. You can either select from an existing .DBF file (as seen in Figure 10.1) or you can create a data table inside the screen painter. Any number of data tables can be included in a screen format, it is simply a question of going back to the Set Up menu and changing the active data table (see Figure 10.1).

Once you have selected the active data table, you then select the

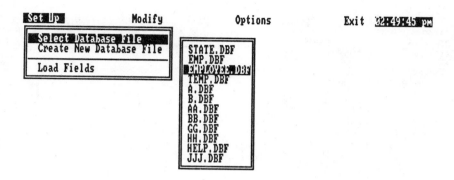

Figure 10.1.   Create Screen Data Table Selection

fields from that table that you want to include in your screen and place them on the "blackboard", or working area of the product. I found that it was better to go to the blackboard first, move the cursor to an empty area of the screen and then go back and select a group of fields that I wanted to work on. Figure 10.2 shows that all fields in the data table up to JCODE have been selected. When you toggle back to the blackboard these descriptions and a field space the size of the data field will be transferred.

Operating the *dBase III Plus* Screen Painter is easy. You simply type in fixed text, move the cursor to the first position of the field that you wish to have associated with that text and press the carriage return to lock on to it, move the cursor (the field does not move with the cursor, it stays where it is) to the spot on the screen where you want the field to appear, and then press the carriage return to move the field to that location. Figure 10.3 shows the screen halfway completed.

The *dBase III Plus* Screen Painter uses a blackboard area of 20 lines, line 1 to line 20 on the screen. The top line and the bottom four lines are used by the program and are not available to the developer. What this does is limit the view available to less than the full screen. Figure 10.3 shows this. If you need more than 20 lines, the blackboard area scrolls up and down, giving you access to more than the 20 lines

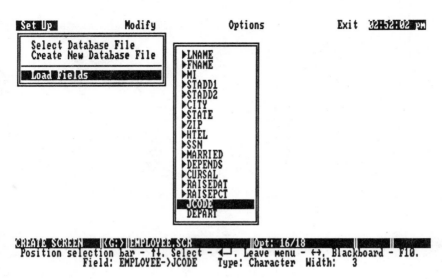

Figure 10.2.   Selecting Data Fields for Transfer to the Blackboard

Figure 10.3.   Half Completed Screen

shown. Figure 10.4 shows this scrolling; the top of the screen has moved off the screen. This is not too much of a problem, for if you must see the entire screen you can easily save your work (which automatically generates the proper .FMT file and drops you back to the *dBase* dot prompt),

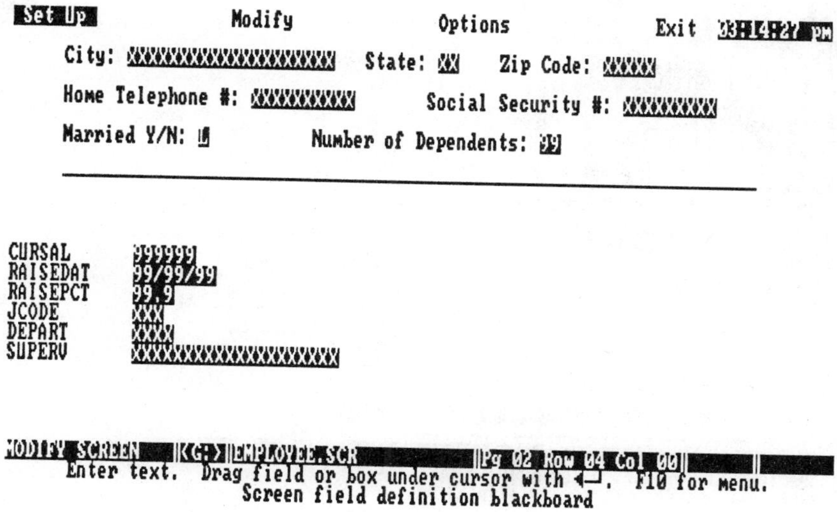

Figure 10.4. Blackboard Scrolling

and type APPEND. As your data table is already open (the screen painter does this) and as *dBase* automatically SETs FORMAT TO your screen file, you will immediately see the current state of your work.

The *dBase III Plus* Screen Painter will develop data entry screen format files of more than one page. As you scroll down through the screen the program automatically puts in a READ statement after each 25 lines. Multi-page format files are generated automatically.

Once you have placed your field where you want it on the screen, the *dBase III Plus* Screen Generator gives you the flexibility to make the field a SAY instead of a GET, allows you to change the display width, and allows you to attach PICTURE functions, symbols, and RANGEs (for numeric fields) to control the display of the field and the data that will be accepted into it. Figures 10.5, 10.6, and 10.7 give you some idea of the program's capabilities. Notice that the level of help given makes referring to the manual almost unnecessary.

Once you have completed your screen, you simply leave the *dBase III Plus* Screen Generator and your format file is automatically generated. Listing 10.1 shows the format file that is generated.

The generated code is not the most efficient. Each piece of fixed text and each field occupies a separate line and both are mixed. It is difficult to visualize anything from this file because the format (fixed text statements) is broken up too much, and it is difficult to do anything about the

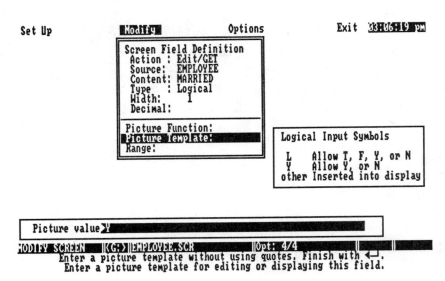

Figure 10.5. Adding Picture Symbols to a Logical Data Field

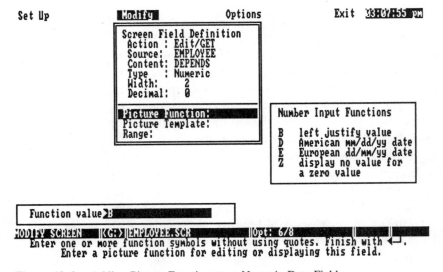

Figure 10.6. Adding Picture Functions to a Numeric Data Field

order in which data fields are processed unless you strip them all out and place them together in the proper order at the end of the file.

An extra added feature that the *dBase III Plus* Screen Generator gives you is an ASCII text file describing the screen and the location and

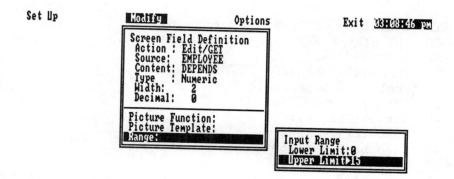

Figure 10.7.   Adding Range Values to a Numeric Data Field

Listing 10.1.   Finished Format File

```
@  2, 26   SAY "EMPLOYEE DATA FILE"
@  5,  5   SAY "Last Name:"
@  5, 16   GET   EMPLOYEE->LNAME
@  5, 37   SAY "First Name:"
@  5, 49   GET   EMPLOYEE->FNAME
@  5, 66   SAY "MI:"
@  5, 70   GET   EMPLOYEE->MI
@  7,  5   SAY "Street Address:"
@  7, 21   GET   EMPLOYEE->STADD1
@  8,  5   SAY "Street Address:"
@  8, 21   GET   EMPLOYEE->STADD2
@ 10,  5   SAY "City:"
@ 10, 11   GET   EMPLOYEE->CITY
@ 10, 34   SAY "State:"
@ 10, 41   GET   EMPLOYEE->STATE
@ 10, 47   SAY "Zip Code:"
@ 10, 57   GET   EMPLOYEE->ZIP
@ 12,  5   SAY "Home Telephone #:"
@ 12, 23   GET   EMPLOYEE->HTEL
```

```
@ 12, 40  SAY "Social Security #:"
@ 12, 59  GET   EMPLOYEE->SSN
@ 14,  5  SAY "Married Y/N:"
@ 14, 18  GET   EMPLOYEE->MARRIED  PICTURE "Y"
@ 14, 29  SAY "Number of Dependents:"
@ 14, 51  GET   EMPLOYEE->DEPENDS
@ 18,  5  SAY "Current Salary:"
@ 18, 21  GET   EMPLOYEE->CURSAL
@ 18, 30  SAY "Date Last Raise:"
@ 18, 47  GET   EMPLOYEE->RAISEDAT
@ 18, 58  SAY "Percent:"
@ 18, 67  GET   EMPLOYEE->RAISEPCT
@ 20,  5  SAY "Job Code:"
@ 20, 15  GET   EMPLOYEE->JCODE
@ 20, 21  SAY "Department:"
@ 20, 33  GET   EMPLOYEE->DEPART
@ 20, 40  SAY "Supervisor:"
@ 20, 52  GET   EMPLOYEE->SUPERV
@  3,  5  TO  3, 70      DOUBLE
@ 16,  5  TO 16, 70
@ 22,  5  TO 22, 70

***  End Format File
```

content of all information that shows up on it. Listing 10.2 shows you this file.

There are several things that the *dBase III Plus* Screen Generator does not do. It does not work with colors. Any use of color has to be typed in. It only generates .FMT files. If you want to use the screens in a .PRG file, you will have to go in and manually insert the .FMT file where it belongs. This would not be too much of a problem if you could go back and modify the altered .FMT file, but you cannot. The program works from the .SCR file, which you cannot modify. Lastly, the program only works with fields from a data table. If you want to work with memory variables, you will have to go in and change the data table alias (in our example EMPLOYEE->) into the identifier that you use to identify memory variables. Initializing the memory variables, storing data from the data table(s) to them and then saving them back is work that you must do yourself.

Listing 10.2.   ASCII Text File Describing Screen Format.

```
Field definitions for Screen: employee.scr
```

Page	Row	Col	Data Base	Field	Type	Width	Dec
1	5	16	EMPLOYEE	LNAME	Character	20	
1	5	49	EMPLOYEE	FNAME	Character	15	
1	5	70	EMPLOYEE	MI	Character	1	
1	7	21	EMPLOYEE	STADD1	Character	30	
1	8	21	EMPLOYEE	STADD2	Character	30	
1	10	11	EMPLOYEE	CITY	Character	20	
1	10	41	EMPLOYEE	STATE	Character	2	
1	10	57	EMPLOYEE	ZIP	Character	5	
1	12	23	EMPLOYEE	HTEL	Character	10	
1	12	59	EMPLOYEE	SSN	Character	9	
1	14	18	EMPLOYEE	MARRIED	Logical	1	

```
PICTURE  Y
```

Page	Row	Col	Data Base	Field	Type	Width	Dec
1	14	51	EMPLOYEE	DEPENDS	Numeric	2	0
1	18	21	EMPLOYEE	CURSAL	Numeric	6	0
1	18	47	EMPLOYEE	RAISEDAT	Date	8	
1	18	67	EMPLOYEE	RAISEPCT	Numeric	4	1
1	20	15	EMPLOYEE	JCODE	Character	3	
1	20	33	EMPLOYEE	DEPART	Character	4	
1	20	52	EMPLOYEE	SUPERV	Character	20	

```
Content of page :  1
```

```
                         EMPLOYEE DATA FILE


    Last Name: XXXXXXXXXXXXXXXXXXXX First Name: XXXXXXXXXXXXXXX  MI: X

    Street Address: XXXXXXXXXXXXXXXXXXXXXXXXXXXXXX
    Street Address: XXXXXXXXXXXXXXXXXXXXXXXXXXXXXX

    City: XXXXXXXXXXXXXXXXXXXX   State: XX    Zip Code: XXXXX

    Home Telephone #: XXXXXXXXXX      Social Security #: XXXXXXXXX

    Married Y/N: X         Number of Dependents: XX


    Current Salary: XXXXXX   Date Last Raise: XXXXXXXX   Percent: XXXX

    Job Code: XXX  Department: XXXX   Supervisor: XXXXXXXXXXXXXXXXXXXX
*** End of ASCII file
```

In summary, the *dBase III Plus* Screen Generator is a good program if you are not going to be spending too much time working with *dBase III Plus* program generation. It has some limitations, but none that are serious. If you are planning to do a lot of work developing applications in *dBase III Plus*, I would recommend a more complete product.

dGENERATE

dGENERATE is a product from the mind of Tom Rettig, the creator of the original *dBase* program and one of the heavyweights in the industry. If the name *dGENERATE* shows something about his sense of humor, his newest product, Free Base, should set you chuckling also. *dGENERATE* is in the public domain and is therefore available to anyone who has a friend with a copy, anyone who has access to the November and December, 1985 issues of *The Data Based Advisor* and is an excellent typist, or anyone who has $15 to send to *The Data Based Advisor* for volume 311 of their program library (1975 Fifth Ave., San Diego, CA 92101 — order phone 800-336-6060). If you spend your $15, you will receive not only the *dBase* source code, but also a compiled copy of the product.

The documentation states: "You are encouraged to freely distribute copies of *dGENERATE* to anyone you choose, as long as you do not charge for it and the original copyright notice and registration information remain intact . . . You are invited to become a registered *dGENERATE* by sending $15 to us at the above address, for which we will send you a disk containing the latest version of all the files listed below. Registration also entitles you to full technical support by telephone, mail, Compu-Serve, and the Source . . . . We feel that *dGENERATE* belongs to the entire *dBase* community and your feedback is highly valued. . . ."

But what about the product? *dGENERATE* is a very good screen code generator and a bit more. It is easy to learn and easier to use than it is to explain. Its function is a bit spartan, but it gets the job of basic screen generation done with no trouble.

dGENERATE is structured so that you create screens using your own word processing program. By doing this you avoid the difficulty that normally accompanies the use of different cursor control commands. Creating and editing the screen is a snap for this reason. Provision has been made for memory resident editors, such as *SideKick* as well.

As you can see from Figure 10.8, *dGENERATE* does more than simply create screens. It writes four different types of programs from the

```
dGENERATE - - MAIN MENU - - 4:14:33 PM - - 01/22/87
=================================================================


    1 - (C)reate a new screen-form      5 - (D)OS access

    2 - (E)dit existing screen-form      6 - (S)etup new parameters

    3 - (G)enerate screen-form code      7 - (R)egistration information

    4 - (M)ake memvars from fields       0 - (Q)uit to DOS



=================================================================
              Select an action by number or letter...
```

Figure 10.8.   *dGENERATE* Main Menu

information provided on your screen. The first takes your screen information and develops a simple data entry/edit program. The second type opens and closes a database file. The third program created is a menu program and the fourth is a report program that allows you to include relative (PROW( )) addressing in the file.

You can customize *dGENERATE* to meet your individual needs. The setup menu is shown in Figure 10.9.

When it comes to laying out a screen, *dGENERATE* is a bit different from other screen generators. A completed screen is included as Figure 10.10.

The information included on the screen is sparse. The top two lines of the display belong to the editor used to create the screen, XyWrite III. The third line is XyWrite's ruler line. If your word processor does not have a convenient ruler line, *dGENERATE* has an option in the setup menu to include one in the file for you (see Figure 10.9). All fixed text is simply typed in as you would type anything else on your word processor. The open curly bracket "{" sign that you see signifies a GET. If you wanted to SAY a field, you would use a "}". (Both of these symbols can be changed to suit the individual user's needs.) The lowercase a, b, c and so on that you see after the bracket are the fields. This is the heart of *dGENERATE*.

When you create a new screen, *dGENERATE* searches the fields in the named data table (only one per screen) and inserts a list of all fields

```
d G E N E R A T E  - -  Setting Up dGENERATE - -   4:12:08 PM  - -  01/22/87
==============================================================================
⟨A⟩ --⟩ Characters used to denote GETs:▓ and SAYs:▓
⟨B⟩ --⟩ Character used for the initialization code:▓
⟨C⟩ --⟩ Size of screen-form in ROWs:▓24▓ and COLumns:▓80▓

⟨D⟩ --⟩ Relative Addressing?:▓
⟨E⟩ --⟩ Ruler line in screen-form?:▓
⟨F⟩ --⟩ Delimiters on?:▓
⟨G⟩ --⟩ Fill screen-form with blanks?:▓
⟨H⟩ --⟩ Help screens on?:▓

⟨I⟩ --⟩ Default file extensions for drawing screens:▓DGS▓, code generated:▓DGP▓
                                           memvar names generated:▓DGM▓

⟨J⟩ --⟩ Characters used to make up ruler in COLumn zero:▓, every ten:▓123456789▓

⟨K⟩ --⟩ Characters used for left and right delimiters:▓▓
⟨L⟩ --⟩ Character used for marquee lines in this program (ASCII value):▓61▓
⟨M⟩ --⟩ Filename of word processor used for editing screen-forms:▓▓▓▓
==============================================================================
      Choose item to change by letter, ⟨T⟩ to use these ⟨T⟩emporarily,
      ⟨S⟩ to ⟨S⟩ave as system defaults, or ENTER to abort any changes.
```

Figure 10.9.   *dGENERATE* Setup Menu

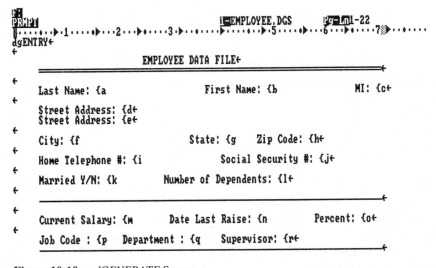

Figure 10.10.   *dGENERATE* Screen

as part of the footer of the screen file. The user then designates an identifier for each of the fields and GETs (or SAYs) using this identifier. The footer for the EMPLOYEE screen is included as Listing 10.3.

The first part of the footer lists each of the fields that is included in

Listing 10.3.   Employee Data Screen Footer

```
dgDEFINE -- Begin definitions in the first column.  Example syntax follows:
<definition symbol> [<memvar> ] <expression> [PICTURE/FUNCTION <template>]
a m_lname  Lname
b m_fname  Fname
c m_mi  Mi
d m_stadd1  Stadd1
e m_stadd2  Stadd2
f m_city  City
g m_state  State
h m_zip  Zip
i m_htel  Htel
j m_ssn  Ssn
k m_married  Married PICTURE "Y"
l m_depends  Depends
m m_cursal  Cursal
n m_raisedat  Raisedat
o m_raisepct  Raisepct
p m_jcode  Jcode
q m_depart  Depart
r m_superv  Superv

dgFILE employee.dbf


Begin options in the first column, one per line.
Code generating options are: dgENTRY, dgMENU, and dgREPORT, one per screen.
File opening option is: dgFILE <database filename>, one per screen.

parameters: { }   80   24   F F
             ! ! ! !    !    ! !
GET Symbol-' ! ! ! !    !    ! '-Ruler line (T/F)
SAY Symbol---' ! !      !    '---Relative Addressing (T/F)
Initialization ! !      '-------Form Length (rows: 1..999)
        Symbol-' '----------Form Width (columns: 1..254)

*** End Employee Data Screen Footer
```

---

the specified data table. As I requested the use of memory variables, the memory variables have also been created. The next thing to do is to specify the identifier for that field. I elected to use alpha characters, but any keyboard key can be used. Next any PICTURE functions or symbols and RANGEs can be entered. I did this with the MARRIED field.

The last part of the footer is the generation parameters. Here, they have been left at the default settings to generate a dgENTRY program.

The program generated is included as Listing 10.4.

As with the *dBase III Plus* Screen Painter, the code that *dGENERATE* generates is fractured. The first text is broken up by each GET, and GETs read from the same line first. The comments that I made about the code in the last section apply here also.

The program includes a simple data entry algorithm to edit, save edits, and quit the program. Note under the SAVE case that the program says "Add replace statements here." *dGENERATE* helps you here also.

dGENERATE will create a memory variable package from a data table for you. As you can see from Figure 10.11, the code generated is not intended to run alone, but rather to be integrated into the main program listing as needed.

The result of this memory variable generation program is seen in Listing 10.5.

With this code it is a simple matter of stripping out the initialization section to create the memory variables (if needed), and including the replace segment if the user decides to save the changes made to the data table.

The dgREPORT code generator is the second program worth talking about. While the report code that is written is very basic and needs extra programming to make it do any type of sophisticated reporting, the program writes the screen using relative references. This feature can save you time in coding and, by itself, is more than worth the price of the program. As an example, I took the Employee Screen file, changed the type of report to dgREPORT, changed the report size in the footer and asked for relative referencing. Listing 10.6 is the code that was generated.

Most of the program will be stripped away, but the heart of it, the print commands are useable and the program is a big time saver.

What about the negatives of *dGENERATE*? First, the program will only work with one file. You can include fields from another file, but you will have to enter the field description in the footer yourself and no memory variables (if you have selected this option) will be be created for you. Second the program does not address the issue of multiple colors. You have to insert these statements in yourself or tear apart the program and re-assemble it if you are going to do complex color work. Third, the program relies on your editor. There are only a few editors that come equipped with a good capability to work with the extended character set. Most editors and word processing programs do a terrible job with this subject. Inserting graphics into your screens will therefore be a bit of a

Listing 10.4. *dGENERATE* Data Entry Program

```
* Program..: employee.dgp
* Author...: <name>
* Date.....: **/**/**
* Notice...: Copyright 1987, <name>, All Rights Reserved.
* Notes....:
*

undefined  = "***"


USE employee.dbf

m_lname    = Lname
m_fname    = Fname
m_mi       = Mi
m_staddl   = Staddl
m_stadd2   = Stadd2
m_city     = City
m_state    = State
m_zip      = Zip
m_htel     = Htel
m_ssn      = Ssn
m_married  = Married
m_depends  = Depends
m_cursal   = Cursal
m_raisedat = Raisedat
m_raisepct = Raisepct
m_jcode    = Jcode
m_depart   = Depart
m_superv   = Superv

* Entry algorithm

CLEAR

@  0, 0 SAY "dgENTRY"
@  2,25 SAY "EMPLOYEE DATA FILE"
@  3, 5 SAY "═══════════════════════════════════════" +;
           "═══════════════════════════════" "
@  5, 5 SAY "Last Name:"
```

```
@  5,16 GET m_lname
@  5,37 SAY "First Name:"
@  5,49 GET m_fname
@  5,66 SAY "MI:"
@  5,70 GET m_mi
@  7, 5 SAY "Street Address:"
@  7,21 GET m_staddl
@  8, 5 SAY "Street Address:"
@  8,21 GET m_stadd2
@ 10, 5 SAY "City:"
@ 10,11 GET m_city
@ 10,34 SAY "State:"
@ 10,41 GET m_state
@ 10,47 SAY "Zip Code:"
@ 10,57 GET m_zip
@ 12, 5 SAY "Home Telephone #:"
@ 12,23 GET m_htel
@ 12,40 SAY "Social Security #:"
@ 12,59 GET m_ssn
@ 14, 5 SAY "Married Y/N:"
@ 14,18 GET m_married PICTURE "Y"
@ 14,29 SAY "Number of Dependents:"
@ 14,51 GET m_depends
@ 16, 5 SAY "_____" +;
           "_____"
@ 18, 5 SAY "Current Salary:"
@ 18,21 GET m_cursal
@ 18,29 SAY "Date Last Raise:"
@ 18,46 GET m_raisedat
@ 18,58 SAY "Percent:"
@ 18,67 GET m_raisepct
@ 20, 5 SAY "Job Code :"
@ 20,16 GET m_jcode
@ 20,21 SAY "Department :"
@ 20,34 GET m_depart
@ 20,40 SAY "Supervisor:"
@ 20,52 GET m_superv
@ 21, 5 SAY "_____" +;
           "_____"

DO WHILE .T.
   @ 22,19 SAY "Press any key to edit, <S> to Save changes,"
   @ 23,18 SAY "or ENTER to return to menu without saving..."
   WAIT "" TO choice
```

```
      @ 22,19
      @ 23,18
      DO CASE
         CASE "" = choice
            RETURN
         CASE "S" = UPPER(choice)
            * Add replace statements here.
            RETURN
         OTHERWISE
            READ SAVE
      ENDCASE
   ENDDO (WHILE .T.)

USE

WAIT ""

* EOF: employee.dgp

***  End Data Entry Program Generated
```

_____

```
d G E N E R A T E  -  -  Generating Memvars  -  -  4:16:31 PM  -  -  01/22/87
==============================================================================
  1.  Memory variable names are generated from the file's field names.
      Only eight characters of the field name are significant in this
      operation: 'First_name' becomes 'm_first_na'.

  2.  Three sets of commands are generated using the memory variable
      names and field names from the database file.
        - The first set is composed of memory variable initialization
          statements from the file (memvar = Field).
        - The second set is composed of memory variable initialization
          statements from an expression (memvar = CTOD("  /  /  ")).
        - The third set is composed of REPLACE statements to transfer
          data from the memory variables to the file's fields
          (REPLACE Field WITH memvar).

  3.  This code is not intended to run as it stands.  It is to be
      incorporated in your program by reading it into your command file
      or procedure using your word processor.  Your program will probably
      use only some of this code, and the rest can be discarded.
==============================================================================
                    Press any key to continue...
```

Figure 10.11.   Memory Variable Generation Menu

Listing 10.5.   Memory Variable Program Segments Generated From Employee.DBF.

```
* Program..: employee.dgm
* Author...: <name>
* Date.....: **/**/**
* Notice...: Copyright 1987, <name>, All Rights Reserved.
* Notes....:
*

* Initialization commands from expressions.
m_city     = SPACE( 20)
m_depart   = SPACE(  4)
m_fname    = SPACE( 15)
m_htel     = SPACE( 10)
m_jcode    = SPACE(  3)
m_lname    = SPACE( 20)
m_mi       = SPACE(  1)
m_ssn      = SPACE(  9)
m_stadd1   = SPACE( 30)
m_stadd2   = SPACE( 30)
m_state    = SPACE(  2)
m_superv   = SPACE( 20)
m_zip      = SPACE(  5)
m_raisedat = CTOD("  /  /  ")
m_married  = .F.
m_cursal   = 000000
m_depends  = 00
m_raisepct = 00.0

* Initialization commands from fields.
m_city     = City
m_depart   = Depart
m_fname    = Fname
m_htel     = Htel
m_jcode    = Jcode
m_lname    = Lname
m_mi       = Mi
m_ssn      = Ssn
m_stadd1   = Stadd1
m_stadd2   = Stadd2
m_state    = State
```

```
m_superv    = Superv
m_zip       = Zip
m_raisedat  = Raisedat
m_married   = Married
m_cursal    = Cursal
m_depends   = Depends
m_raisepct  = Raisepct

* Replace commands.
REPLACE City        WITH m_city
REPLACE Depart      WITH m_depart
REPLACE Fname       WITH m_fname
REPLACE Htel        WITH m_htel
REPLACE Jcode       WITH m_jcode
REPLACE Lname       WITH m_lname
REPLACE Mi          WITH m_mi
REPLACE Ssn         WITH m_ssn
REPLACE Stadd1      WITH m_stadd1
REPLACE Stadd2      WITH m_stadd2
REPLACE State       WITH m_state
REPLACE Superv      WITH m_superv
REPLACE Zip         WITH m_zip
REPLACE Raisedat    WITH m_raisedat
REPLACE Married     WITH m_married
REPLACE Cursal      WITH m_cursal
REPLACE Depends     WITH m_depends
REPLACE Raisepct    WITH m_raisepct

* EOF: employee.dgm

*** End of Memory Variables Generated
```

---

problem. Fourth, there is no real-time interaction between *dGENERATE* and your data table. As an example, there is no information about the size of your entry fields and no space reserved for the fields on the screen. I found that in order to get an idea of what was going on I placed dashes after the GET designator (allowed as long as there are no spaces) to equal the length of the field that I was dealing with. Figure 10.12 shows the results of this effort.

Even with these complaints, *dGENERATE* is a great little program

Listing 10.6.   Report Code Generation From dGENERATE.

```
* Program..: employee.dgp
* Author...: <name>
* Date.....: 01/23/87
* Notice...: Copyright 1987, <name>, All Rights Reserved.
* Notes....:
*

undefined  = "***"


USE employee.dbf

m_lname    = Lname
m_fname    = Fname
m_mi       = Mi
m_staddl   = Staddl
m_stadd2   = Stadd2
m_city     = City
m_state    = State
m_zip      = Zip
m_htel     = Htel
m_ssn      = Ssn
m_married  = Married
m_depends  = Depends
m_cursal   = Cursal
m_raisedat = Raisedat
m_raisepct = Raisepct
m_jcode    = Jcode
m_depart   = Depart
m_superv   = Superv

* Report algorithm

* Prompt user to set up the printer or abort.

@ 12,23 SAY "Printing.  Please do not disturb..."

SET DEVICE TO PRINT

DO WHILE (.NOT. EOF()) .AND. "" < DBF()
```

```
@  0, 0 SAY ""
@ PROW()    , 0 SAY "dgREPORT"
@ PROW()+ 2,25 SAY "EMPLOYEE DATA FILE"
@ PROW()+ 1, 5 SAY "==================================" +;
                  "=========================="
@ PROW()+ 2, 5 SAY "Last Name:"
@ PROW()    ,16 SAY m_lname
@ PROW()    ,37 SAY "First Name:"
@ PROW()    ,49 SAY m_fname
@ PROW()    ,66 SAY "MI:"
@ PROW()    ,70 SAY m_mi
@ PROW()+ 2, 5 SAY "Street Address:"
@ PROW()    ,21 SAY m_staddl
@ PROW()+ 1, 5 SAY "Street Address:"
@ PROW()    ,21 SAY m_stadd2
@ PROW()+ 2, 5 SAY "City:"
@ PROW()    ,11 SAY m_city
@ PROW()    ,34 SAY "State:"
@ PROW()    ,41 SAY m_state
@ PROW()    ,47 SAY "Zip Code:"
@ PROW()    ,57 SAY m_zip
@ PROW()+ 2, 5 SAY "Home Telephone #:"
@ PROW()    ,23 SAY m_htel
@ PROW()    ,40 SAY "Social Security #:"
@ PROW()    ,59 SAY m_ssn
@ PROW()+ 2, 5 SAY "Married Y/N:"
@ PROW()    ,18 SAY m_married PICTURE "Y"
@ PROW()    ,29 SAY "Number of Dependents:"
@ PROW()    ,51 SAY m_depends
@ PROW()+ 2, 5 SAY "_____" +;
                  "_____"
@ PROW()+ 2, 5 SAY "Current Salary:"
@ PROW()    ,21 SAY m_cursal
@ PROW()    ,29 SAY "Date Last Raise:"
@ PROW()    ,46 SAY m_raisedat
@ PROW()    ,58 SAY "Percent:"
@ PROW()    ,67 SAY m_raisepct
@ PROW()+ 2, 5 SAY "Job Code :"
@ PROW()    ,16 SAY m_jcode
@ PROW()    ,21 SAY "Department :"
@ PROW()    ,34 SAY m_depart
@ PROW()    ,40 SAY "Supervisor:"
@ PROW()    ,52 SAY m_superv
@ PROW()+ 1, 5 SAY "_____" +;
                  "_____"
```

```
    SKIP
ENDDO

EJECT
SET DEVICE TO SCREEN
@ 12,23 SAY "  *** ***  Done Printing  *** ***  "
USE

WAIT ""
* EOF: employee.dgp

***  End Report Program Generated by dGENERATE
```

---

and is available at an attractive price. Mr. Rettig is to be congratulated and thanked for developing it for the *dBase* community.

SAYWHAT?! _____

SAYWHAT?! version 3.0 is a different type of program from the others reviewed in this book. The screens that the program generates are binary files that are called through the VIDPOP memory resident screen loader. Complicated screens load much faster than they do when programmed in *dBase* code. The VIDPOP loader also has a series of commands that allow you to load from file, load and save from memory, move and clear specified lines of the screen and to dump the screen to the printer. Screens are called from within *dBase III Plus* using a single line to call the file. GETS and SAYS then work just as they do in *dBase*.

SAYWHAT?! was designed to work with any computer language, using a single statement to call the screens. In certain languages (*dBase* being one of them) *SAYWHAT?!* also generates the statements necessary to read operator inputs (GETS and SAYS in *dBase*) or place information from within the program on the screen (SAYS in *dBase*). We will only deal with the program's abilities under *dBase* in this review.

SAYWHAT?!'s screen painter will take some getting used to. It is fully modal, with TEXT being one of the modes. Modes are invoked with a keyboard character ("T" for getting into text mode) and then either **Escape**d from or ended with some other keypress. Moving text,

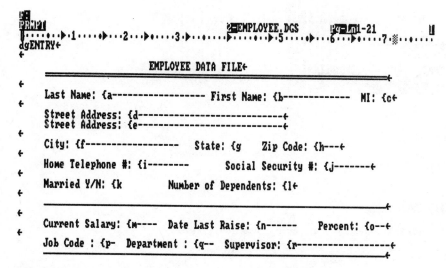

Figure 10.12.   Data Entry Screens with Field Length Identified

for instance, requires that you position the cursor over the first character in the block that you want to move, press "**M**", reposition your cursor over the last character in the blcok, press "**M**" again, move the block of text with the cursor to the appropriate location, and finally press **Escape** to terminate the move. The process requires more keystrokes than it should, and the combinations are not all entirely natural. *SAYWHAT?!* uses line zero of the screen: it is not available to the user at all. You are also limited to a total of 64 GETSon a single screen: the *dBase* limit is 128. While this most probably will not impact most applications, some screens full of number fields can easily use over 100 GETS. If this is going to happen to you, you will not be able to use this product.

SAYWHAT?! does not work directly with *dBase III Plus*. The program comes with a utility program that allows you to generate a screen image while in *dBase III Plus*, take a "snapshot" of it using a specially provided program, and then import that image into *SAYWHAT?!*. Figure 10.13 shows the result of this process when it was used on the EMPLOYEE data table.

The result of the import gives you the field names and their length to work with. Before using the information, several steps must be completed. First you must create your data fields. This can be done by positioning the cursor to the right of the imported field name and using the "autoget" mode, where *SAYWHAT?!* takes a guess at the desired name

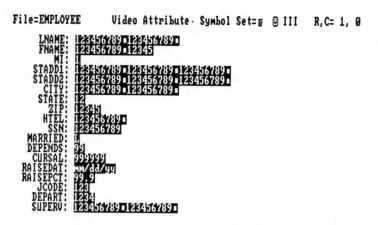

Figure 10.13. *SAYWHAT?!* Screen after Importing Data from *dBase*

from the information to the left of the cursor location. The result of this process is the "Propellers" (ASCII 21) that have appeared in the first column of the field length of each field in Figure 10.14. Next you must type in your fixed text as has been done in Figure 10.14.

Finally, the extraneous text must be deleted, and the field definitions moved to meet the fixed text. Figure 10.15 shows the results of this work.

Individual fields can then be marked and moved to the appropriate locations on the screen. I found the absence of a working cursor location indicator during the moves to be a real hindrance in this process and finally ended up putting marks on the screen and moving the appropriate field to that mark. This meant extra work, but it was necessary to accurately position the file. I also found that I was "dropped" into text mode if I started going through the move command sequence too fast. *SAYWHAT?!* "senses" the speed at which the operator hits keys and, if the rate is faster than a certain speed, automatically invokes the TEXT mode. There is no way to turn this off. I found that I had to consciously slow down while moving data in order to keep this from happening.

As you can see from Figure 10.16, *SAYWHAT?!* allows you to go in and change the field name associated with a specific propeller and add a PICTURE statement to it. It does not allow you to add a RANGE statement to your numeric fields. If you want to do this, you must go in and physically change the finished .RUN file that *SAYWHAT?!* generates.

When you have finished your work, you will have a screen that looks something like Figure 10.17.

```
File=EMPLOYEE      Video Attribute· Symbol Set=§   III   R,C=24,35
```

```
Last Name            LNAME:  §23456789·123456789·
First Name           FNAME:  §23456789·12345
MI                      MI:  §
Street Address       STADD1:  §23456789·123456789·123456789·
Street Address       STADD2:  §23456789·123456789·123456789·
City                  CITY:  §23456789·123456789·
State                STATE:  §2
Zip Code               ZIP:  §2345
Home Telephone #      HTEL:  §23456789·
Social Security #      SSN:  §23456789
Married Y/N        MARRIED:  §
Number of Dependents DEPENDS:  §9
Current Salary      CURSAL:  §99999
Date Last Raise    RAISEDAT:  §m/dd/yy
Percent            RAISEPCT:  §9.9
Job Code             JCODE:  §23
Department          DEPART:  §234
Supervisor           SUPERV:  §23456789·123456789·
```

Figure 10.14. *SAYWHAT?!* Screen in Process

```
File=EMPLOYEE      Video Attribute· Symbol Set=§   III   R,C=24,10
                        EMPLOYEE DATA FILE
```

```
Last Name: §23456789·123456789·
First Name: §23456789·12345
MI: §
Street Address: §23456789·123456789·123456789·
Street Address: §23456789·123456789·123456789·
City: §23456789·123456789·
State: §2
Zip Code: §2345
Home Telephone #: §23456789·
Social Security #: §23456789
Married Y/N: §
Number of Dependents: §9
Current Salary: §99999
Date Last Raise: §m/dd/yy
Percent: §9.9
Job Code: §23
Department: §234
Supervisor: §23456789·123456789·
```

Figure 10.15. *SAYWHAT?!* Screen Ready for Layout

When you save the screen, the program automatically generates three files for you. The screen image file, with its .SQZ extension, the GET file, with its .GET extension, and the execution file, with its .RUN extension.

```
GET VAR:<married   > PICTURE:"Y                    ■
                    EMPLOYEE DATA FILE
═══════════════════════════════════════════════════════════════

Last Name: §23456789■123456789■ First Name: §23456789■12345  MI: §

Street Address: §23456789■123456789■123456789■
Street Address: §23456789■123456789■123456789■

City: §23456789■123456789■   State: §2    Zip Code: §2345

Home Telephone #: §23456789■       Social Security #: §23456789

Married Y/N: §



Number of Dependents: §9
Current Salary: §99999
Date Last Raise: §w/dd/yy
Percent: §9.9
Job Code: §23
Department: §234
Supervisor: §23456789■123456789■
```

Figure 10.16.   Adding a Picture Clause to *SAYWHAT?!*


```
File=F:EMPLOYEE    Video Attribute· Symbol Set=▯    III   R,C=22,71
                    EMPLOYEE DATA FILE
═══════════════════════════════════════════════════════════════

Last Name: §23456789■12345678   First Name: §23456789■12345  MI: §

Street Address: §23456789■123456789■123456789■
Street Address: §23456789■123456789■123456789■

City: §23456789■123456789■   State: §2    Zip Code: §2345

Home Telephone #: §23456789■       Social Security #: §23456789

Married Y/N: §        Number of Dependents: §9
───────────────────────────────────────────────────────────────

Current Salary: §99999    Date Last Raise: §w/dd/yy   Percent: §9.9

Job Code: §23    Department: §234    Supervisor: §23456789■123456789■
───────────────────────────────────────────────────────────────
```

Figure 10.17.   Finished *SAYWHAT?!*

The RUN file (or parts of it) is what is used inside your *dBase III Plus* programs. The file generated for the employee screen is included as Listing 10.7.

There is less to this file than it seems. The line of code: ???

CHR(255) + CHR(255) + "EMPLOYEE/" calls the screen file and the GETs following that line of code fill for the propellers. All this could have been done without the use of *SAYWHAT?!* and with just a few more lines of code. It does not seem to be worthwhile to go through the entire process to end up with more files to handle and this type of code. As far as developing data entry screens, I would rather do it myself.

Given all the not so nice things that I have been saying about the product, why would you want to use *SAYWHAT?!* One application where the product would be of benefit would be in the situation where you have very complicated fixed text on your screen and very little else. *SAYWHAT?!* allows all this to go into the .SQZ file and paints it with a speed that *dBase* can only dream of. Multiple colors, boxes, extended ASCII characters (see Figure 10.18 for an example), lines and much more can be painted inside *SAYWHAT?!*, reduced to a single file, and then painted quickly. Creating this type of screen is what *SAYWHAT?!* is good for. Working with everyday data entry screens is not its forte.

ViewGen

ViewGen version 2.0 is both a complete application generator and a screen painter. Developed by Louis Castro, a long time employee of Ashton-Tate, and available for $125, it represents a significant step upwards both in terms of its screen painting capabilities, and in terms of the programs that it generates.

ViewGen is different from other screen painters in that it works both from the screen (the FORM view) and from an associated table (the TABLE view) with all the information used to build and back up the form. Screens can either be created from scratch, or can be developed from a named data table. If the latter is used you will end up with two starting views of your table, the FORM view (see Figure 10.19), and the TABLE view (see Figure 10.20).

The TABLE view gives the item number, the alias of the work area in which the data tables are located, the field name, type, width and number of decimals (if numeric), a starting label, the display color of the label, the row and column locations of the field, the display attribute for the field, and whether the label is to be placed on top of or beside the field. The alias allows you to set up and work with screens that call from more than one file. The program supports several other features that make this much easier to accomplish than it is with other screen generators.

Listing 10.7.   *SAYWHAT?!* .RUN File For Employee Screen

```
*** Full Screen:EMPLOYEE as of XX/XX/XX 11:03:54 ***
*** For dBASE III
* * * * * * * * * * * * * * * * * * * * * * * * * * * * * * * * * * *
* HEADER.DB    This is an optional file and may be modified to be anything  *
*              you want it to be.  If it exists it will be included in all   *
*    Erase     files created by SAYWHAT?!   It may even include commands     *
*    this      which you commonly include in your programs.   All non-       *
*    part.     commands must be appropriately commented out                  *
*              (ie: REM for basic or { } for pascal or * for dBase).         *
* * * * * * * * * * * * * * * * * * * * * * * * * * * * * * * * * * *
* Program.:                                                                  *
* Function:                                                                  *
* Author..: ---Your name here---                                            *
* Date....:                                                                  *
* Last Update:                                                               *
* Notice..: (C) Copyright 1986, ---Your name here---                        *
* * * * * * * * * * * * * * * * * * * * * * * * * * * * * * * * * * *
*
@ 0,0
?? CHR(255)+CHR(255)+"EMPLOYEE/"
SET COLOR TO  W/  ,  W/
@  5,16 GET lname
@  5,49 GET fname
@  5,70 GET mi
@  7,21 GET stadd1
@  8,21 GET stadd2
@ 10,11 GET city
@ 10,41 GET state
@ 10,57 GET zip
@ 12,23 GET htel
@ 12,59 GET ssn
@ 14,18 GET married PICTURE "Y"
@ 14,51 GET depends
@ 18,21 GET cursal
@ 18,47 GET raisedat
@ 18,67 GET raisepct
@ 20,15 GET jcode
@ 20,33 GET depart
@ 20,52 GET superv
READ
SET COLOR TO W/ , /W
RETURN

** End of EMPLOYEE Screen ***
```

File=EMPLOYEE   Video Attribute · Symbol Set=⌐   III   R,C= 2, 5

Figure 10.18.   Extended Graphics Capability of *SAYWHAT?!*

Figure 10.19.   Initial FORM View of Edit Screen in *ViewGen*

There is a second screen to the TABLE view, allowing the user to put in PICTURE and RANGE statements to aid in data entry. Included also are VALID sstatements (*Clipper*) and statements to initialize the field and perform other specialized functions. The second screen is included as Figure 10.21. There is one important difference between *ViewGen* and most other screen painters. While most other products look at fixed text and fields as two completely different elements, *ViewGen* does not. To *ViewGen* the fixed text that is associated with the field is its label and is part of that data element. The starting location of the element is the first letter of the fixed text (if you have opted to have the text and the field side by side). If you can get the length of the fixed text, the field position moves accordingly.

In the FORM view, *ViewGen* works like other screen painters. You can drag elements around the screen to change the way the screen looks. You can edit the fixed text as seen in Figure 10.22. As described above, when text is edited (shown at the bottom of the screen in Figure 10.22) the position of the field changes to accommodate the different length of the text.

The difference with *ViewGen* is that you can do the same thing by changing the information contained in the TABLE view of the screen. You can edit the label, change the location, and add information to the file just by editing the table. In Figure 10.23 the label "Date Last Raise:" is in the process of being edited.

Figure 10.24 shows you the completed TABLE view of the data entry screen.

F:EMPLOYEE.DBF   1:33 PM

#.	Als	Field	Typ	Wid	Dec	Label		Hue	Row	Col	Pag	(Fld)	(Atr)	Place
1.	A	Lname	C	20		[Lname	]	4	2	0	1	GET	112	SIDE
2.	A	Fname	C	15		[Fname	]	4	3	0	1	GET	112	SIDE
3.	A	Mi	C	1		[Mi	]	4	4	0	1	GET	112	SIDE
4.	A	Stadd1	C	30		[Stadd1	]	4	5	0	1	GET	112	SIDE
5.	A	Stadd2	C	30		[Stadd2	]	4	6	0	1	GET	112	SIDE
6.	A	City	C	20		[City	]	4	7	0	1	GET	112	SIDE
7.	A	State	C	2		[State	]	4	8	0	1	GET	112	SIDE
8.	A	Zip	C	5		[Zip	]	4	9	0	1	GET	112	SIDE
9.	A	Htel	C	10		[Htel	]	4	10	0	1	GET	112	SIDE
10.	A	Ssn	C	9		[Ssn	]	4	11	0	1	GET	112	SIDE
11.	A	Married	L	1		[Married	]	4	12	0	1	GET	112	SIDE
12.	A	Depends	N	2		[Depends	]	4	13	0	1	GET	112	SIDE
13.	A	Cursal	N	6		[Cursal	]	4	14	0	1	GET	112	SIDE
14.	A	Raisedat	D	8		[Raisedat	]	4	15	0	1	GET	112	SIDE
15.	A	Raisepct	N	4	1	[Raisepct	]	4	16	0	1	GET	112	SIDE
16.	A	Jcode	C	3		[Jcode	]	4	17	0	1	GET	112	SIDE
17.	A	Depart	C	4		[Depart	]	4	18	0	1	GET	112	SIDE
18.	A	Superv	C	20		[Superv	]	4	19	0	1	GET	112	SIDE

——Ins

FIELD: can be up to 10 alphanumeric characters and underscore

Figure 10.20.   Initial TABLE View of Edit Screen in *ViewGen*

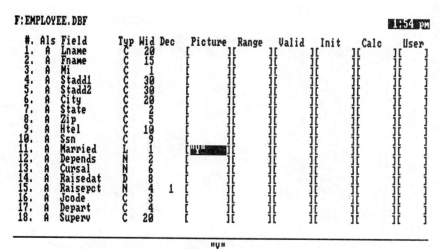

Figure 10.21.   View of Second TABLE Screen in *ViewGen*

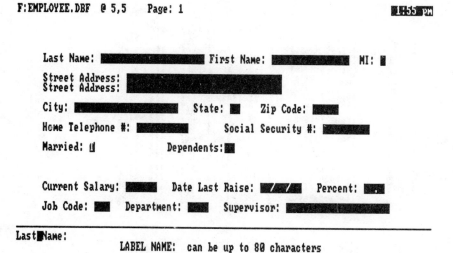

Figure 10.22.   *ViewGen* Editing of FORM View

Once the screen is finished to your satisfaction you have several options to choose from as far as programs are concerned. Figure 10.25 shows you the options that are available from the *GENERATE* menu.

F:EMPLOYEE.DBF   1:40 PM

#.	Als	Field	Typ	Wid	Dec	Label	Hue	Row	Col	Pag	(Fld)	(Atr)	Place
1.	A	Lname	C	20		[Last Name:]	7	2	0	1	GET	112	SIDE
2.	A	Fname	C	15		[First Name:]	7	3	0	1	GET	112	SIDE
3.	A	Mi	C	1		[MI:]	7	4	0	1	GET	112	SIDE
4.	A	Stadd1	C	30		[Street Addr]	7	5	0	1	GET	112	SIDE
5.	A	Stadd2	C	30		[Street Addr]	7	6	0	1	GET	112	SIDE
6.	A	City	C	20		[City:]	7	7	0	1	GET	112	SIDE
7.	A	State	C	2		[State:]	7	8	0	1	GET	112	SIDE
8.	A	Zip	C	5		[Zip Code:]	7	9	0	1	GET	112	SIDE
9.	A	Htel	C	10		[Home Teleph]	7	10	0	1	GET	112	SIDE
10.	A	Ssn	C	9		[Social Secu]	7	11	0	1	GET	112	SIDE
11.	A	Married	L	1		[Married:]	7	12	0	1	GET	112	SIDE
12.	A	Depends	N	2		[Dependents:]	7	13	0	1	GET	112	SIDE
13.	A	Cursal	N	6		[Current Sal]	7	14	0	1	GET	112	SIDE
14.	A	Raisedat	D	8		[Date Last R]	7	15	0	1	GET	112	SIDE
15.	A	Raisepct	N	4	1	[Raisepct]	7	16	0	1	GET	112	SIDE
16.	A	Jcode	C	3		[Jcode]	7	17	0	1	GET	112	SIDE
17.	A	Depart	C	4		[Depart]	7	18	0	1	GET	112	SIDE
18.	A	Superv	C	20		[Superv]	7	19	0	1	GET	112	SIDE

Date Last Raise: ■

LABEL NAME: can be up to 80 characters

Figure 10.23. *ViewGen* Editing of TABLE View   Screen

F:EMPLOYEE.DBF   1:43 PM

#.	Als	Field	Typ	Wid	Dec	Label	Hue	Row	Col	Pag	(Fld)	(Atr)	Place
1.	A	Lname	C	20		[Last Name:]	7	5	5	1	GET	112	SIDE
2.	A	Fname	C	15		[First Name:]	7	5	37	1	GET	112	SIDE
3.	A	Mi	C	1		[MI:]	7	5	66	1	GET	112	SIDE
4.	A	Stadd1	C	30		[Street Addr]	7	7	5	1	GET	112	SIDE
5.	A	Stadd2	C	30		[Street Addr]	7	8	5	1	GET	112	SIDE
6.	A	City	C	20		[City:]	7	10	5	1	GET	112	SIDE
7.	A	State	C	2		[State:]	7	10	34	1	GET	112	SIDE
8.	A	Zip	C	5		[Zip Code:]	7	10	47	1	GET	112	SIDE
9.	A	Htel	C	10		[Home Teleph]	7	12	5	1	GET	112	SIDE
10.	A	Ssn	C	9		[Social Secu]	7	12	40	1	GET	112	SIDE
11.	A	Married	L	1		[Married:]	7	14	5	1	GET	112	SIDE
12.	A	Depends	N	2		[Dependents:]	7	14	29	1	GET	112	SIDE
13.	A	Cursal	N	6		[Current Sal]	7	18	5	1	GET	112	SIDE
14.	A	Raisedat	D	8		[Date Last R]	7	18	30	1	GET	112	SIDE
15.	A	Raisepct	N	4	1	[Percent:]	7	18	58	1	GET	112	SIDE
16.	A	Jcode	C	3		[Job Code:]	7	20	5	1	GET	112	SIDE
17.	A	Depart	C	4		[Department:]	7	20	21	1	GET	112	SIDE
18.	A	Superv	C	20		[Supervisor:]	7	20	40	1	GET	112	SIDE

COL: number in the range 0..79

Figure 10.24. Completed TABLE View of Data Entry Screen

After making your choices, *ViewGen* will generate your program for
you. Listing 10.8 is the .FMT file that *ViewGen* generates.

There are several interesting things about this format file. First,

Listing 10.8. *ViewGen* Generated Format File

```
* Program.: EMPLOYEE.FMT
* Author..: Your Name
* Date....: xx/xx/xx
* Notice..: Copyright 1987, Your Company, All Rights Reserved
* Version.: dBASE III PLUS
* Notes...: Format file for EMPLOYEE.DBF
*
SET COLOR TO BU/N,N/W
@  0, 0 SAY "Record: " + SUBSTR( STR(RECNO()+1000000,7),2 )
SET COLOR TO W/N
@  5, 5 SAY "Last Name: "
@  3, 5 SAY;
 "===================================================="
@  2,26 SAY "EMPLOYEE DATA FILE"
@  5,37 SAY "First Name: "
@  5,66 SAY "MI: "
@  7, 5 SAY "Street Address: "
@  8, 5 SAY "Street Address: "
@ 10, 5 SAY "City: "
@ 10,34 SAY "State: "
@ 10,47 SAY "Zip Code: "
@ 12, 5 SAY "Home Telephone #: "
@ 12,40 SAY "Social Security #: "
@ 14, 5 SAY "Married: "
@ 14,29 SAY "Dependents:"
@ 16, 5 SAY;
 "_____"
@ 18, 5 SAY "Current Salary: "
@ 18,30 SAY "Date Last Raise: "
@ 18,58 SAY "Percent: "
@ 20, 5 SAY "Job Code: "
@ 20,21 SAY "Department: "
@ 20,40 SAY "Supervisor: "
@ 22, 5 SAY;
 "_____"
*
SET COLOR TO ,N/W
@  5,16 GET Lname
@  5,49 GET Fname
@  5,70 GET Mi
@  7,21 GET Stadd1
@  8,21 GET Stadd2
@ 10,11 GET City
@ 10,41 GET State
@ 10,57 GET Zip
@ 12,23 GET Htel
@ 12,59 GET Ssn
@ 14,14 GET Married      PICTURE "Y"
@ 14,40 GET Depends
@ 18,21 GET Cursal
```

```
@ 18,47 GET Raisedat
@ 18,67 GET Raisepct
@ 20,15 GET Jcode
@ 20,33 GET Depart
@ 20,52 GET Superv
SET COLOR TO
* EOF: EMPLOYEE.FMT
```

ViewGen puts in a SAY for the record number in the upper left hand corner of the screen. Second, the format file is generated item number by item number. In my file, the fixed text that shows up at the top of the screen was inserted after the fields were defined and placed. Notice that the double line and the text "EMPLOYEE DATA FILE" come after the fixed text of the first data element. Note also that all GETS are properly grouped after all the fixed text is painted on the screen.

If you were to select the second program option, REPORT, all the GETS would be converted to SAYS and all the elements would be re-ordered to move sequentially from left to right and from the top of the page to the bottom, as is necesary for proper printer operation. The row and column referencing, however, is absolute, and the program cannot deal with reports wider than 80 columns.

As mentioned earlier, it is beyond the scope of this book to deal with the programs that ViewGen develops for the complete system. Suffice it to say that they are complete, well thought out, well annotated, and tight in the code that they use. You have the option of working straight with the field variables, or working with memory variables instead. If you decide to work with memory variables, you can change the lead character in the configuration file. I was impressed with the code that was generated by *ViewGen*. If I were going to use the code, however, I would get rid of the BROWSE option, and completely re-do the opening menu. Code generation options are available for *dBase III, dBase III Developers Release, dBase III Plus, Clipper, dBIII Compiler* and *FoxBase +* .

ViewGen handles color by using the ASCII code for the colors. It would have been nice if Software Tools could have included a chart explaining what the numbers are and how to use them. If I have one complaint about *ViewGen* it is that the documentation that accompanies the product is to be kind, sparse. Several features are not completely documented and several are undocumented. An improvement in this area would be greatly appreciated.

Flash Code

Flash Code is a screen painter, an applications generator, and a little bit more. The Software Bottling Company of New York has provided a complete screen painter, database table generator, screen and applications program generator, and a window generator and popup module all for $150. Although the program has some aspects that you may not like, the total undertaking represents an interesting alternative approach to developing a complete application.

How does Flash Code work as a screen painter? For starters, it reserves the first and last line of the screen for itself, which you may find annoying. The Flash Code manual says that said *dBase* does not allow you to work with the first or last line of the screen. This just is not so. You can work with them, but you have to make sure that your environment is set properly to handle it. That Flash Code reserves these lines is a Flash Code problem, not a *dBase* problem. I would prefer that they call it like it is.

Some problems involve the editor. First, Flash Code does not import information from a *dBase III Plus* data table. It requires that you go through the entire definition process inside Flash Code. Too bad if you are working with data tables that are already defined: you will have to re-define them. Second, the field definition screen (see Figure 10.26) does not allow you to use the "Y" symbol for logical fields; it must be entered manually in the generated file. Third, there is no space left in the PICTURE definition field for literal text; this too must be manually entered into the finished program file. Fourth, RANGE data is supplied whether you need it or not. If you do not want to have it, you will have to go into the program file and get rid of it. Fifth, you have to manually press **F4** for each space that you have in a field. If you have a 30 character field, you have to hit the key 30 times to reserve the proper amount of space. After the space is reserved, you then have to go through the field definition screen (by backing up into the field with the left cursor key and pressing **F2**) to define what you have just reserved. Figure 10.27 shows you the completed Flash Code screen.

Flash Code is not the easiest program to paint with. Graphic characters, for instance, are accessed by going through the HELP screen (see Figure 10.28) and then pressing the space bar to have access to the graphics characters (see Figure 10.29). Once you have moved the cursor to the proper character, you can then go back to the screen. The selected characters is placed at the last cursor location. You can then paint with that character using Control-Cursor Key combinations. When you reach a corner of a box, you have to go back through the HELP screen to the

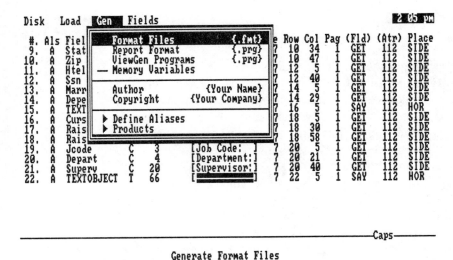

Figure 10.25. Program Generation Options

Figure 10.26. Flash Code Field Definition Screen

extended graphics screen, select the new character and finally go back to your work. There is no other way to draw boxes. While you can do whatever it is that you need to do, it takes more time and requires more work than it should.

Figure 10.30 shows you that Flash Code will generate programs

```
                    EMPLOYEE DATA FILE
_____

Last Name: ▪▪▪▪▪▪▪▪▪▪▪▪▪▪▪▪▪▪  First Name: ▪▪▪▪▪▪▪▪▪▪▪▪▪  MI: ▪
Street Address: ▪▪▪▪▪▪▪▪▪▪▪▪▪▪▪▪▪▪▪▪▪▪▪▪▪▪▪
Street Address: ▪▪▪▪▪▪▪▪▪▪▪▪▪▪▪▪▪▪▪▪▪▪▪▪▪▪▪

City: ▪▪▪▪▪▪▪▪▪▪▪▪▪▪▪▪▪▪   State: ▪▪   Zip Code: ▪▪▪▪▪
Home Telephone #: ▪▪▪▪▪▪▪▪▪▪    Social Security #: ▪▪▪▪▪▪▪▪▪
Married Y/N: ▪       Number of Dependents: ▪▪
_____

Current Salary: ▪▪▪▪▪▪  Date Last Raise: ▪▪/▪▪/▪▪  Percent: ▪▪.▪
Jobe Code: ▪▪▪  Department: ▪▪▪▪  Supervisor: ▪▪▪▪▪▪▪▪▪▪▪▪▪▪▪▪▪
_____

Lin= 22 Col= 71  Anchor= 0, PAINT OFF                Press F1 For Help
```

Figure 10.27.   Completed Flash Code Data Entry Screen

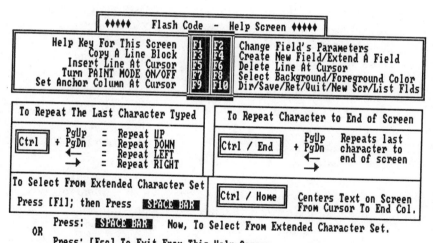

Figure 10.28.   Flash Code HELP Screen

linking more than one entry screen: Up to 10 can be included sequentially in a data entry program program *or* a complete application. Flash Code will generate standard *dBase III* code (not Plus) and will generate

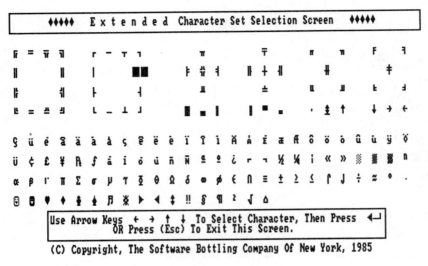

Figure 10.29.　Flash Code Graphics Selection Screen

a program that runs either directly from *dBase* or with Software Bottling Company's Flash-Up Windows (more about this later).

The program that Flash Code generates is shown in Listing 10.9.

There are several things to note in the Flash Code data entry program. First, it is set up for more than one data entry screen. If there were more than one, there would be separate case statements for each in both the section of the program displaying fixed text and the GETs section. Second, Flash Code works with memory variables preceded with an "X". This can be replaced with a different memory variable identifier (or eliminated to work with field variables) using a word processor. Note that all the variables are initialized at the top of the program. Note also that, at the end of the program, Flash Code provides optional sections for storing information from a data table and placing information held in memory variables in that table after the READ. Note also that, although the program is supposed to be complete, no code is present for dealing with ending an edit and invoking this replacement process.

Every field has its own PICTURE clause, even if that clause does nothing at all for any type of input. This is excess code because the fields have been initialized at the proper length (or information is stored to it from a data table, giving the field length). The code would be cleaner if these extraneous PICTURE statements were left off.

Finally, as Flash Code does not pay any attention to *dBase* in the generation process, the program cannot pay any attention to multiple

Listing 10.9.   Flash Code Data Entry Program.

```
*  -- EMPLOYEE.PRG
*  -- Procedures Generated By FlashCode V1.00 on 01/28/1987 - 11:9:51
*  -- (C) Copyright 1985, The Software Bottling Company Of New York
*  -- This Program may not be used without the above Copyright Notice
*
*
* -- Screen Input Program For EMPLOYEE --
*
CLEAR
SET TALK OFF
SET ECHO OFF
@ 24,0 SAY "Initializing Variables"
* -- F:EMPLOYEE
PUBLIC Xlname,Xfname,Xmi,Xstadd1,Xstadd2,Xcity,Xstate,Xzip,Xhtel,Xssn,Xmarried
PUBLIC Xdepends,Xcursal,Xraisedat,Xraisepct,Xjcode,Xdepart,Xsuperv
Xlname = SPACE(20)
Xfname = SPACE(15)
Xmi = SPACE(1)
Xstadd1 = SPACE(30)
Xstadd2 = SPACE(30)
Xcity = SPACE(20)
Xstate = SPACE(2)
Xzip = SPACE(5)
Xhtel = SPACE(10)
Xssn = SPACE(9)
Xmarried = .Y.
Xdepends = 0
Xcursal = 0
Xraisedat = CTOD("  /  /  ")
Xraisepct = 0.0
Xjcode = SPACE(3)
Xdepart = SPACE(4)
Xsuperv = SPACE(20)
@ 24,0
ScrnNumFL = 1
MaxScrnFL = 1

DO WHILE .T.
  * -- DISPLAY SCREEN --
  DO CASE
  CASE ScrnNumFL=1
    * -- Screen Display F:EMPLOYEE.SCR
    SET COLOR TO W+/ ,W+/
    CLEAR
@ 2,26 SAY "EMPLOYEE DATA FILE"
@ 3,5 SAY "═══════════════════════════════════════════════════════════════════"
@ 5,5 SAY "Last Name:"
@ 5,37 SAY "First Name:"
@ 5,66 SAY "MI:"
@ 7,5 SAY "Street Address:"
```

```
@ 8,5 SAY "Street Address:"
@ 10,5 SAY "City:"
@ 10,34 SAY "State:        Zip Code:"
@ 12,5 SAY "Home Telephone #:"
@ 12,40 SAY "Social Security #:"
@ 14,5 SAY "Married Y/N:"
@ 14,29 SAY "Number of Dependents:"
@ 16,5 SAY; "—————————————————————————————————— "
"
@ 18,5 SAY "Current Salary:"
@ 18,30 SAY "Date Last Raise:   /  /      Percent:    ."
@ 20,5 SAY "Jobe Code:     Department:        Supervisor:"
@ 22,5 SAY;"—————————————————————————————————————— "
SET COLOR TO W+/ , /W
  ENDCASE
  @ 0,0 SAY "SCREEN #"+STR(ScrnNumFL,2)
  * -- Do Calculations For All Fields --

  * -- Get Data Input --
  @ 24,0 SAY "Enter or Re-Enter Information"
  DO CASE
  * -- From Screen F:EMPLOYEE --
  CASE ScrnNumFL=1
    SET COLOR TO W+/ ,W+/
    @ 5,16 GET Xlname PICT "XXXXXXXXXXXXXXXXXXXX"
    @ 5,49 GET Xfname PICT "XXXXXXXXXXXXXXX"
    @ 5,70 GET Xmi PICT "X"
    @ 7,21 GET Xstadd1 PICT "XXXXXXXXXXXXXXXXXXXXXXXXXXXXXX"
    @ 8,21 GET Xstadd2 PICT "XXXXXXXXXXXXXXXXXXXXXXXXXXXXXX"
    @ 10,11 GET Xcity PICT "XXXXXXXXXXXXXXXXXXX"
    @ 10,41 GET Xstate PICT "XX"
    @ 10,57 GET Xzip PICT "XXXXX"
    @ 12,23 GET Xhtel PICT "XXXXXXXXXX"
    @ 12,59 GET Xssn PICT "XXXXXXXXX"
    @ 14,18 GET Xmarried
    @ 14,51 GET Xdepends PICT "99" RANGE 0,99
    @ 18,21 GET Xcursal PICT "999999" RANGE 0,999999
    @ 18,47 GET Xraisedat
    @ 18,67 GET Xraisepct PICT "99.9" RANGE 0.0,99.9
    @ 20,16 GET Xjcode PICT "XXX"
    @ 20,33 GET Xdepart PICT "XXXX"
    @ 20,52 GET Xsuperv PICT "XXXXXXXXXXXXXXXXXXXX"
  ENDCASE
  READ
  SET COLOR TO 15/0, 0/7

  @ 24,0 SAY "Edit Calculations OR Press 'PgDn' To Exit."
  * -- Re-Do Calculations For All Fields and Re-Display --
  DO CASE
  ENDCASE
  READ
  SET COLOR TO 15/0, 0/7

  @ 24,0
  @ 23,80 CLEAR
  WAIT
```

```
    ScrnNumFL = ScrnNumFL+1
    IF ScrnNumFL > MaxScrnFL
      ScrnNumFL = 1
    ENDIF
ENDDO

*****************************************************************************
*     The following section is provided by FlashCode for use in programs with  *
*  a .DBF file.  It is not needed in the "Screen Only" program but is helpfull  *
*  nevertheless.                                                                *
*****************************************************************************

* -- RETRIEVE data from a file section --
* -- From Screen F:EMPLOYEE --
Xlname = lname
Xfname = fname
Xmi = mi
Xstadd1 = stadd1
Xstadd2 = stadd2
Xcity = city
Xstate = state
Xzip = zip
Xhtel = htel
Xssn = ssn
Xmarried = married
Xdepends = depends
Xcursal = cursal
Xraisedat = raisedat
Xraisepct = raisepct
Xjcode = jcode
Xdepart = depart
Xsuperv = superv

* -- REPLACE data in a file section --
* -- From Screen F:EMPLOYEE --
    REPLACE lname WITH Xlname,fname WITH Xfname,mi WITH Xmi
    REPLACE stadd1 WITH Xstadd1,stadd2 WITH Xstadd2,city WITH Xcity
    REPLACE state WITH Xstate,zip WITH Xzip,htel WITH Xhtel,ssn WITH Xssn
    REPLACE married WITH Xmarried,depends WITH Xdepends,cursal WITH Xcursal
    REPLACE raisedat WITH Xraisedat,raisepct WITH Xraisepct,jcode WITH Xjcode
    REPLACE depart WITH Xdepart,superv WITH Xsuperv

*** End Data Entry Program
```

data tables. There is no provision in the product to handle this common occurrence. You will have to go in and modify the code to handle this situation after the program has been generated.

Flash Code will also generate a complete application for you from your data entry screen. It is beyond the scope of this review to evaluate it

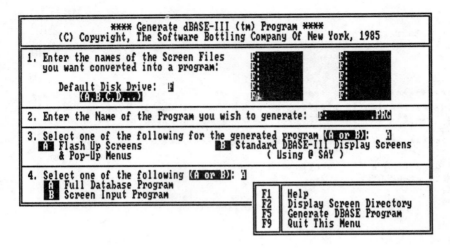

Figure 10.30.   Flash Code Program Generation Menu

in its entirety, but the Opening Menu and the Look Up Record Menu (Figures 10-31 and 10-32 respectively) will give you an indication of how the program is structured. The program is complete, but requires substantial programming work to change if you do not like the way that it is put together.

The Software Bottling Company of New York provides the capability of "flashing-up" menus and HELP screens using their Flash-Up module. One version of the program comes with Flash Code, and a more complete version, which will run with a wide variety of software products including *dBase*. The product can create menus that pop up, HELP screens that appear at the touch of a key and disappear at the touch of another. Working with it is easy and operation is swift.

The stand-alone product is available for $90 for one copy, $60 each if you purchase five copies, and $31 each in quantities of over a thousand. The volume prices are significant because you must purchase a complete copy of the product even for runtime distribution.

UI Programmer

Before going any further, I have to say that I reviewed the pre-release version of the product. The version that I reviewed is, I am assured, substantially the same as the distribution product that is being prepared for

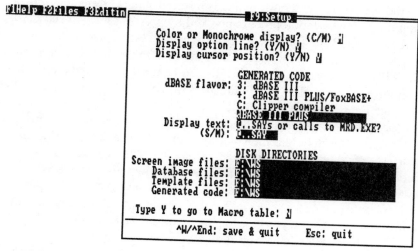

Figure 10.31. UI Programmer Setup Screen

market. It is not my habit to evaluate pre-release products but I have to make an exception here because UI Programmer represents a significant enough product innovation that it is worthwhile including it in these reviews.

UI Programmer, which as of this date is still to be officially released, is a product of WallSoft, the makers of dFLOW and The Documenter, two excellent productivity aids for *dBase* programmers. The UI Programmer is a screen painter, a code generator, and a memory resident screen painting program. The memory resident screen program, MRD was discussed at the end of Chapter 4, so it will not be covered here. Comments will be limited to the program's screen painting and program generating capabilities.

As a screen painter, UI Programmer is excellent. Figure 10.31 shows you that the UI Programmer can be set up to generate programs using *dBase III*, *dBase III Plus*, and *Clipper* commands. Other options can be modified to accommodate the desires of the specific system and user. Figure 10.32 shows the Macro table, where the user can either customize the editor's navigation keys (shown) or can program keyboard macros to accomplish complicated keystroke sequences in a single command.

Working with UI Programmer is intuitive, with the program giving you substantial information as you go along. Fixed text is simply typed on the screen and field information is inserted at the current cursor location through a selection process invoked by pressing **F4**. All activity is screen oriented and follows a logical sequence. After placing the cursor where you want the first character of the field to be placed, you invoke the FIELDS option by pressing **F4**. You then select the data table that you wish to work with (see Figure 10.33). You are then presented with the data fields that are available from that table (see Figure 10.34) and, by moving the cursor to the desired location and pressing the carriage return, the chosen field is then placed on the screen at the specified location, (see Figure 10.35) with its length indicated by the shaded box and the field name (or as much of it as can be shown inside the box) indicating the field that is at that location.

Should you desire to create a field, memory variable, or change the definition of the field, you can do it by invoking the Revise Field Definition option of the Fields Menu shown in Figure 10.36.

This simple function of UI Programmer makes it very powerful. You can include information from more than one data table, you can mix field with memory variables, you can define PICTUREs, RANGEs, and even *Clipper* VALID clauses in this operation.

Figures 10.37 and 10.38 and 10.39 give you some indication of the support for basic editing, drawing with graphic characters, and creating and moving boxes on the screen that UI Programmer provides.

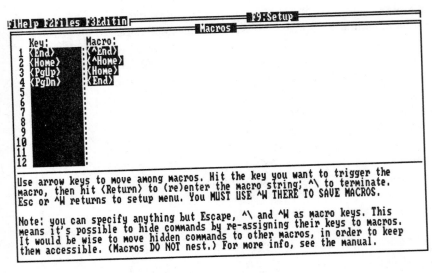

Figure 10.32. UI Programmer Keyboard Macro Screen

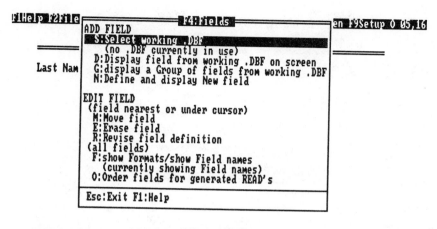

Figure 10.33. UI Programmer Choose Data Table Option Screen

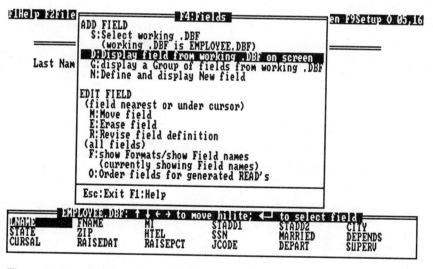

Figure 10.34. UI Programmer Choose Field Option Screen

UI Programmer also supports the complete use of color. Choosing your colors is a matter of invoking the proper menu choice, and going to the color selection chart. As you change the color selection, the results show up in a box so you can see what the results will look like, Figure 10.39 and 10.40 detail the selection process used by the program.

F1Help F2Files F3Editing F4Fields F5Boxes F6Menus F7Colors F8Gen F9Setup I 05,16

EMPLOYEE DATA FILE

Last Name: LNAME

Figure 10.35.   UI Programmer Working Screen with Field Inserted

F1Help F2Files F3Editing F4Fields F5Boxes F6Menus F7Colors F8Gen F9Setup O 05,16

EMPLOYEE DATA FILE

Last Name: LNAME
```
════════════════════ FIELD DEFINITION ══════════════════════
 Name: LNAME                  Type: C  Length: 20  Dec:  0

 Field or Memory variable(F/M)?: F
    If field variable, what .DBF?: EMPLOYEE.DBF
       If field var, what alias?: EMPLOYEE
          Display only (Y/N)?: N

 Picture clause (no quotes):

12345678901234567890123456789012345678901234567890123456789012345678
        1         2         3         4         5         6

 Validation expression (Clipper) or procedure name (dBASE/FoxBASE+):

   (^W/^End when done, Esc to abort)
```

Figure 10.36.   UI Programmer Revise Field Definition Screen

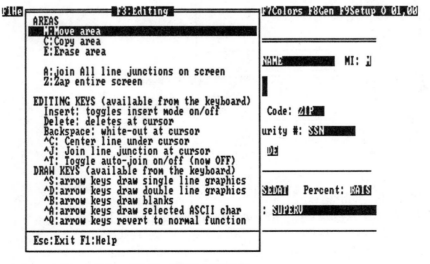

```
F1He ┌─────────── F3:Editing ─────────── F7Colors F8Gen F9Setup O 01,00
     │ AREAS
     │ M:Move area
     │ C:Copy area
     │ E:Erase area
     │                                   NAME        MI: J
     │ A:join All line junctions on screen
     │ Z:Zap entire screen
     │
     │ EDITING KEYS (available from the keyboard)
     │  Insert: toggles insert mode on/off     Code: ZIP
     │  Delete: deletes at cursor
     │  Backspace: white-out at cursor    urity #: SSN
     │  ^C: Center line under cursor
     │  ^J: Join line junction at cursor   DE
     │  ^T: Toggle auto-join on/off (now OFF)
     │ DRAW KEYS (available from the keyboard)
     │  ^S:arrow keys draw single line graphics
     │  ^D:arrow keys draw double line graphics  SEDAT  Percent: RATE
     │  ^B:arrow keys draw blanks
     │  ^A:arrow keys draw selected ASCII char  : SUPERV
     │  ^Q:arrow keys revert to normal function
     │
     │ Esc:Exit F1:Help
     └───────────────────────────────────
```

Figure 10.37.   Editing Aids for UI Programmer

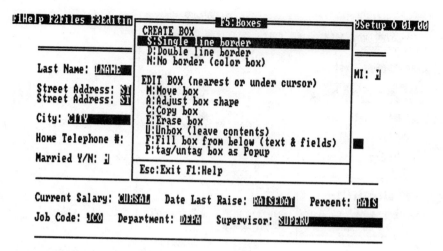

Figure 10.38. Box Design Aids for UI Programmer

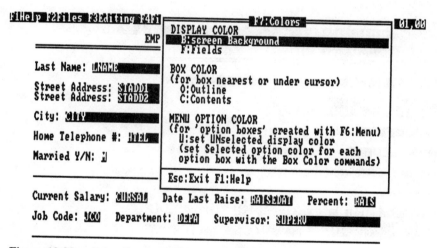

Figure 10.39. Color Command Screen for UI Programmer

Figure 10.41 shows the finished UI Programmer screen, ready for program generation.

It is at this point that UI Programmer becomes more than just a screen painter. When you request program generator from UI Programmer you are presented with a menu template list. Figure 10.42 lists the options that are available to you.

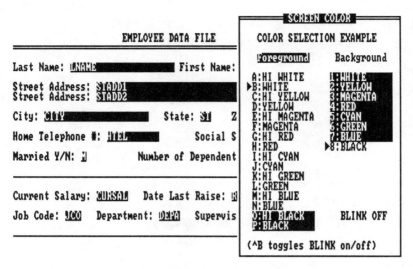

Figure 10.40.   Color Selection Chart for UI Programmer

F1Help F2Files F3Editing F4Fields F5Boxes F6Menus F7Colors F8Gen F9Setup O 22,71

                    EMPLOYEE DATA FILE

Last Name: LNAME   First Name: FNAME   MI: M

Street Address: STADD1
Street Address: STADD2

City: CITY   State: ST   Zip Code: ZIP

Home Telephone #: HTEL   Social Security #: SSN

Married Y/N: M   Number of Dependents: DE

Current Salary: CURSAL   Date Last Raise: RAISEDAT   Percent: RAIS

Job Code: JCO   Department: DEPA   Supervisor: SUPERU

Figure 10.41.   Finished UI Programmer Screen

Here we have requested the basic display program. UI Programmer reads the instructions from the program and generates the *dBase III Plus* code required. Listing 10.10 is the screen code that the program generates.

The template that was used to generate this code consists of fixed text, which can either be comments or *dBase* code, and commands about

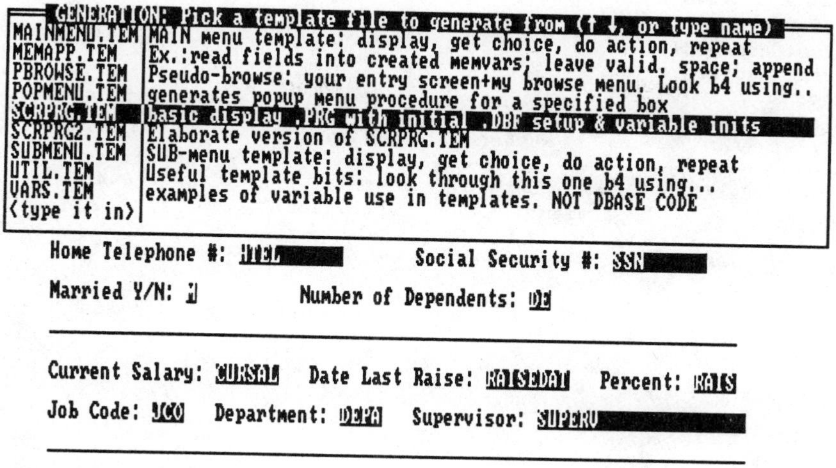

```
GENERATION: Pick a template file to generate from (↑ ↓, or type name)
MAINMENU.TEM  MAIN menu template: display, get choice, do action, repeat
MEMAPP.TEM    Ex.:read fields into created memvars; leave valid. space; append
PBROWSE.TEM   Pseudo-browse: your entry screen+my browse menu. Look b4 using..
POPMENU.TEM   generates popup menu procedure for a specified box
SCRPRG.TEM    basic display .PRG with initial .DBF setup & variable inits
SCRPRG2.TEM   Elaborate version of SCRPRG.TEM
SUBMENU.TEM   SUB-menu template: display, get choice, do action, repeat
UTIL.TEM      Useful template bits: look through this one b4 using...
VARS.TEM      examples of variable use in templates. NOT DBASE CODE
<type it in>
```

Home Telephone #: HTEL   Social Security #: SSN

Married Y/N: J   Number of Dependents: DE

Current Salary: CURSAL   Date Last Raise: RAISEDAT   Percent: RAIS

Job Code: JCO   Department: DEPA   Supervisor: SUPERV

Figure 10.42.   UI Programmer

Listing 10.10.   UI Programmer Generated Edit Screen Code

```
***
*** F:\WS\EMPLOYEE.PRG : screen display, dbf & memvar inits, read
*** Generated 11:06:18 January 29, 1987 from template SCRPRG.tem
*** Author: XXXXXXXXXXXXXXXX
*** (C) copyright 1986 Hyperthyroid Mania Inc.
***

*** set up environment
SET TALK OFF
SET STATUS OFF
SET SCOREBOARD OFF


*** Initialize .DBF's and work areas
SELECT 1
USE EMPLOYEE ALIAS EMPLOYEE


*** Display fixed text
SET COLOR TO W/N
CLEAR
@ 02,26 SAY "EMPLOYEE DATA FILE"
@ 03,05 SAY;
```

```
"═══════════════════════════════════════════════════════"
@ 05,05 SAY "Last Name:                    First Name:                MI:"
@ 07,05 SAY "Street Address:"
@ 08,05 SAY "Street Address:"
@ 10,05 SAY "City:                    State:      Zip Code:"
@ 12,05 SAY "Home Telephone #:              Social Security #:"
@ 14,05 SAY "Married Y/N:          Number of Dependents:"
@ 16,05 SAY "═══════════════════════════════════════════════════════"
@ 18,05 SAY "Current Salary:        Date Last Raise:          Percent:"
@ 20,05 SAY "Job Code:      Department:      Supervisor:"
@ 22,05 SAY;
"═══════════════════════════════════════════════════════"


*** Says



*** Gets
SET COLOR TO W/N, N/W

@ 05,16 GET LNAME
@ 05,49 GET FNAME
@ 05,70 GET MI
@ 07,21 GET STADD1
@ 08,21 GET STADD2
@ 10,11 GET CITY
@ 10,41 GET STATE
@ 10,57 GET ZIP
@ 12,23 GET HTEL
@ 12,59 GET SSN
@ 14,18 GET MARRIED PICTURE "Y"
@ 14,51 GET DEPENDS
@ 18,21 GET CURSAL
@ 18,47 GET RAISEDAT
@ 18,67 GET RAISEPCT
@ 20,15 GET JCODE
@ 20,33 GET DEPART
@ 20,52 GET SUPERV

READ

*** End of Edit program.
```

what to do with the information that is presented the generator in the screen file. The template used to generate this simple program is shown in Listing 10.11.

The template is an ASCII file that is open to anyone wishing to modify it. Additional comments can be added, and additional _dBase_ commands can be inserted wherever desired to directly modify the outcome of

Listing 10.11.   UI Programmer Screen Program Template

```
<<title basic display .PRG with initial .DBF setup & variable inits>>

***
*** {file}.PRG : screen display, dbf & memvar inits, read
*** Generated {time} {date} from template SCRPRG.tem
*** Author: XXXXXXXXXXXXXXXXX
*** (C) copyright 1986 Hyperthyroid Mania Inc.
***

<<if DB3>>
*** set up environment
SET TALK OFF
<<endif>>
<<if DB3PLUS>>
*** set up environment
SET TALK OFF
SET STATUS OFF
SET SCOREBOARD OFF
<<endif>>

<<if MRD>>
*** NOTE: MRD.exe must be in memory before dBASE is run!!
*** load MRD command processor
load MRDCMD.bin
*** load screen image file (.SIF) for this screen
call MRDCMD with "l {file}"
<<endif>>

<<if dbfs>>
*** Initialize .DBF's and work areas
{init all dbfs}
<<endif>>

<<if memvars>>
*** Initialize memory variables
{init all memvars}
<<endif>>

*** Display fixed text
{display text}

*** Says
{say all variables}

*** Gets
{get all variables}
READ
P


*** End Screen Generation Template
```

---

program generation. The commands used in UI Programmer templates, in effect, constitute a programming language themselves. They can be as simple as the one shown here or complicated enough to do an entire program module in a single pass. The reference manual for the template language (not the reference manual for UI Programmer) is 165 pages long.

The exciting thing about UI Programmer's capability to generate custom programs is that a serious programming professional can set up his or her own templates and apply them to specific screens to generate a personal style of code. Anyone working long hours on programs will appreciate this. The other exciting thing is that templates, once perfected, are then available for those with less need and less experience as finished products that will generate a specific type of system or program.

UI Programmer does a lot more than just edit and create screens. Templates for traditional and bounce bar menus are included in the program, as is the capability of completely designing a menu system including trigger actions for each of the menu choices. Figure 10.43 shows you some of the support that is given to this function.

UI Programmer also comes with a "Movie" recording capability. If you desire, you can link screens and commands together into a large command macro to give an animated display of program execution. This function works well for product demos at computer shows but its real value is for demonstrating system prototypes to clients. All screen work can be linked together and shown to the client *before* the first line of code is generated. This time saver alone is worth the price of the product.

UI Programmer will retail for $195 when it hits the streets. It will require 290K of free memory and will work best with a color monitor.

QUICKCODE PLUS

QUICKCODE PLUS is the updated applications generator from Fox & Geller. To call the product a screen painter would be unfair. It is intended to be much more than that and it is. It is a full featured applications generator, producing up to 41 different program modules, depending on the needs of the specific situation. It will also develop menus, lists, link files, create conditional branching, set up index files and create reports. With all this capability, it seems a shame to evaluate only the screen painting capabilities of the product.

QUICKCODE PLUS's screen painter will do virtually everything that you need. It can even handle multiple page data entry forms. The user interface for the product has been improved substantially from the

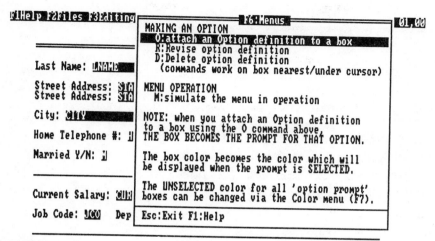

Figure 10.43. Menu Generation Support of UI Programmer

old product, making it much easier to use. QUICKCODE PLUS uses a 1-2-3-like menu structure on the top two lines of the screen. Unlike 1-2-3, the menu disappears when you are in the editor, but can be called back at any time that it is needed. QUICKCODE PLUS comes with a full installation program that not only allows you to change the default parameters of the editor (see Figure 10.44), but also to customize both the printer installation (Figure 10.45) *and* the print characteristics of each of the color combinations (Figure 10.46).

The printer information goes far beyond the basic capabilities of *dBase III Plus* and reminds the user that he or she is dealing with more than just a screen painter.

QUICKCODE PLUS allows you to go in and change the screen size parameters of the editor (see Figure 10.44) to values other than 24 lines by 80 columns. Unfortunately, neither the top margin nor the left margin can be set to zero to conform with the *dBase III Plus* screen description. You will constantly have to make the subtractions if absolute screen position is needed when you are developing your screens.

The menu system has an intuitive feel to it that makes using the product quite easy. Most management tasks can be handled simply by moving the cursor along the menu and reading the prompt that shows up below it.

Once you have invoked the FORM editor; fixed text, lines, and

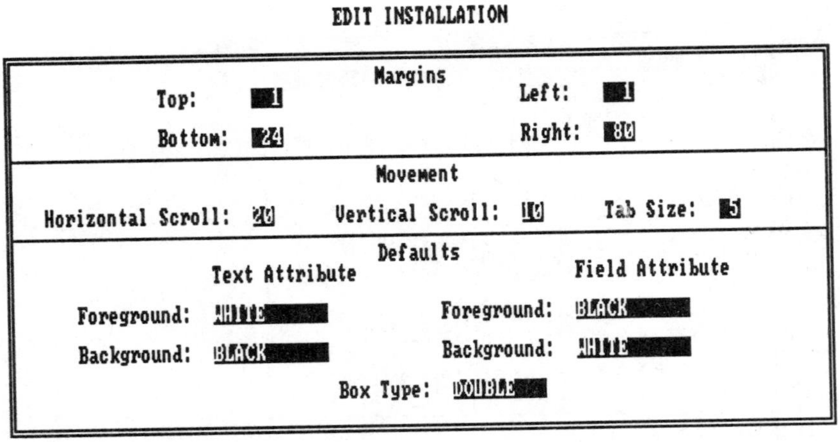

EDIT INSTALLATION

Figure 10.44. QUICKCODE PLUS Editor Installation Screen

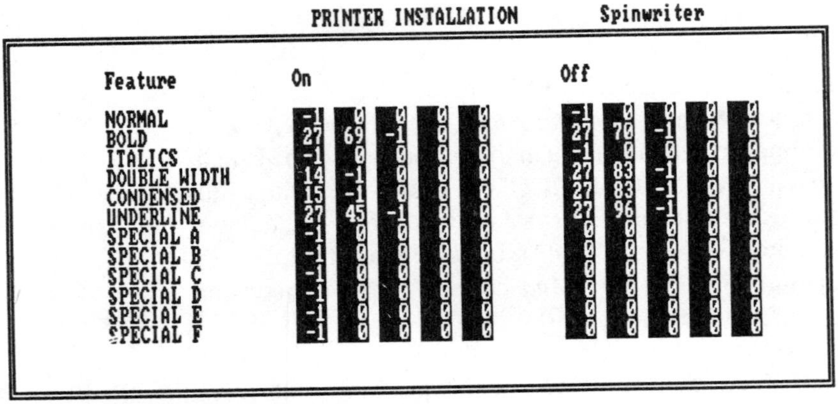

Figure 10.45. QUICKCODE PLUS Printer Customizing Screen

boxes can be entered anywhere on the screen. Fields are retrieved from the active data table by placing the cursor on the starting location of the field, pressing **F5**, signifying that you want to retrieve the field (not the default), selecting the proper field from the menu or typing it in (See Figure 10.47) and pressing the carriage return to place that field on the marked location. If desired, you can go into the field definition table by placing the cursor in the appropriate field and striking **F2** again. Figure 10.48 shows the Field definition table. A full range of customizing

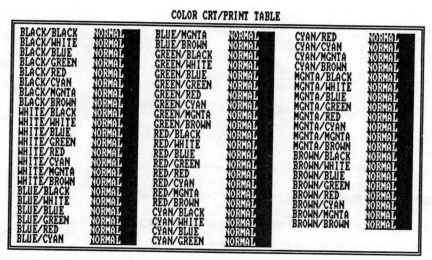

Figure 10.46. QUICKCODE PLUS Color/Print Table

Figure 10.47. QUICKCODE PLUS Field Selection Process

options are available to the user, including the capability of computer values for the field and adding validation in the form of lookups to specified lists.

```
Field:    LNAME          From Database:    EMPLOYEE
┌─────────────────────────────────────────────────────────────┐
│                                                               │
│      Type       Length        Decimals      Field Source     │
│   [Character]    [20]           [0]             [DBF]         │
│                                                               │
├─────────────────────────────────────────────────────────────┤
│   Picture                                                     │
│ [XXXXXXXXXXXXXXXXXXXXX]                                        │
│                                                               │
│      Print Attribute      Field Display      Protected        │
│        [NORMAL]              [YES]              [NO]           │
│                                                               │
├─────────────────────────────────────────────────────────────┤
│   Computation                                                 │
│                                                               │
├─────────────────────────────────────────────────────────────┤
│   Validation                                                  │
│                                                               │
└─────────────────────────────────────────────────────────────┘
```

Figure 10.48. QUICKCODE PLUS Field Definition Sheet

Boxes are handled through a Box Creation option that allows you to size boxes on the screen. The only irritation here is that, in order to draw both single and double line boxes, you must go back to the editor installation screen (see Figure 10.44) and physically change the installation parameter. This is a strange and inconvenient way of handling this process, but you *can* have both types of boxes on the same screen.

Graphics characters are also handled in a unique and somewhat cumbersome fashion. Pressing **ALT** + **F** − **6** changes the assignments of the keyboard keys from their normal alphanumeric assignments into extended graphics assignments. There are several different selections and you must toggle through them to the one that you want. To get back to alpha characters, you must continue to move through these selections until you come back to the normal selection. The character assignments are seen by pressing the HELP key (**F1**). Figure 10.49 illustrates the line drawing selections from the extended character set. The only problem is that you have to go back and forth between the sheet and the editor if you are going to use several of these characters. It works, but I did not find it a natural process.

The finished screen, ready for QUICKCODE PLUS screen generation can be seen in Figure 10.50. Note that as much of the field names as can be shown in the filed space is placed on the screen to aid the developer.

At this point, you are ready to generate your screen program.

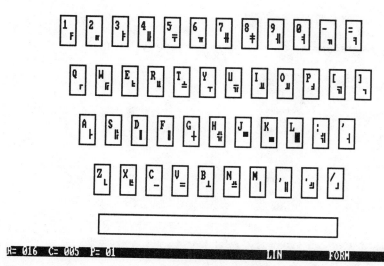

Figure 10.49. Extended Graphics Selection HELP Screen

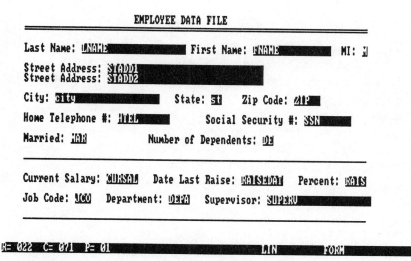

Figure 10.50. Finished Screen Design in QUICKCODE PLUS

Generate your screen program you say? Take your choice. Figure 10.51 shows you the program options that are available to you as a QUICK-CODE PLUS user.

Note that not one of the options says anything about a screen program

PROGRAM GENERATION OPTIONS

```
┌──────────────────────────────────────────────────────────────────┐
│  PROGRAM    FORMAT      PROGRAM   FORMAT      PROGRAM    FORMAT     │
│  Add        PRG         Index     *****       Recalc     *****      │
│  Browse     PRG         Key       *****       Replace    *****      │
│  Calculate  *****       Labels    *****       Report     PRG        │
│  Commands   *****       Link      *****       Say        *****      │
│  DBF        PRG         Lookup    *****       Setup      *****      │
│  DBM        *****       Memory    *****       Size       *****      │
│  Defaults   *****       Menu      *****       Sort       *****      │
│  Edit       PRG         On        *****       Stop       *****      │
│  Error      *****       Output    PRG         Test       *****      │
│  Field      *****       Page      *****       Top        *****      │
│  File       *****       PRN       PRG         Transfer   *****      │
│  Filter     *****       Print     *****       Update     *****      │
│  Get        *****       Put       *****       Utility    *****      │
│  Help       PRG         Query     PRG         Validate   *****      │
└──────────────────────────────────────────────────────────────────┘
```

PRG= A .PRG File; PROCEDURE= A Procedure within .PRC File; *****= Don't Generate

Figure 10.51.   QUICKCODE PLUS Program Generation Menu

or a format file. Quite surprisingly, QUICKCODE PLUS does not have this option. A screen program has to be built from pieces of at least two of the generated programs: one to paint the screen and one for the GETs. Listing 10.12 shows the two programs that contain this information. If you wanted to get a format file or a simple screen entry portion of a larger program, you would have to do some work to get rid of the extraneous pieces that QUICKCODE PLUS generated for you. In fairness, QUICK-CODE PLUS is much more than a simple screen painter/code generator, but it would have been better if they had included an option to generate this simple piece of code for you.

QUICKCODE PLUS is a powerful applications generator. The code that is generated by the product is powerful and well constructed. If you have need of this type of program and need a screen generator as well, it may be worth spending the $295 that the product costs. If you have the time and experience you can even take the code templates that they provide and make modifications to them to suit your own needs. If you are only looking for the screen editor, you will find that you have purchased more than you need, spent more money than was necessary and ended up with a program that is not as flexible or easy to use as some of the other, cheaper alternatives.

Listing 10.12. QUICKCODE PLUS Screen Programs

```
* --- emp_onq
* c COPYRIGHT 1986 Fox & Geller, Inc.  All Rights Reserved
* --- Paints titles & borders on the screen
ucodeq="ActMsg"
CLEAR
@ 1,25 SAY "EMPLOYEE DATA FILE"
@ 2,4 SAY "==================================================="
@ 4,4 SAY "Last Name:"
@ 4,36 SAY "First Name:"
@ 4,65 SAY "MI:"
@ 6,4 SAY "Street Address:"
@ 7,4 SAY "Street Address:"
@ 9,4 SAY "City:"
@ 9,33 SAY "State:"
@ 9,46 SAY "Zip Code:"
@ 11,4 SAY "Home Telephone #:"
@ 11,39 SAY "Social Security #:"
@ 13,4 SAY "Married Y/N:"
@ 13,28 SAY "Number of Dependents:"
@ 15,4 SAY "------------------------------------------------"
@ 17,4 SAY "Current Salary:"
@ 17,29 SAY "Date Last Raise:"
@ 17,57 SAY "Percent:"
@ 19,4 SAY "Job Code:"
@ 19,20 SAY "Department:"
@ 19,39 SAY "Supervisor:"
@ 21,4 SAY "------------------------------------------------"
DO emp_utlq
RETURN         && End emp_onq

*** END OF FIRST PROGRAM

*** START OF SECOND PROGRAM
* --- emp_getq
* c COPYRIGHT 1986 Fox & Geller, Inc.  All Rights Reserved
* --- Gets input for a form
SET EXACT ON
bitmapq="."
IF pgchangeq
   DO emp_onq
ENDIF
* --- Say all fields
DO emp_sayq
* --- Get data from user
fq=1       && current field number
fminq=1       && first field number
fmaxq=1       && last field number
readdoneq=.F.
DO WHILE .T.
```

```
IF fq=1
   @ 4,15 GET mllname PICT 'XXXXXXXXXXXXXXXXXXX'
   @ 4,48 GET mlfname PICT 'XXXXXXXXXXXXXX'
   @ 4,69 GET mlmi PICT 'X'
   @ 6,20 GET mlstadd1 PICT 'XXXXXXXXXXXXXXXXXXXXXXXXXXXX'
   @ 7,20 GET mlstadd2 PICT 'XXXXXXXXXXXXXXXXXXXXXXXXXXXX'
   @ 9,10 GET mlcity PICT 'XXXXXXXXXXXXXXXXXX'
   @ 9,40 GET mlstate PICT 'XX'
   @ 9,56 GET mlzip PICT 'XXXXX'
   @ 11,22 GET mlhtel PICT 'XXXXXXXXXX'
   @ 11,58 GET mlssn PICT 'XXXXXXXXX'
   @ 13,17 GET mlmarried PICT 'Y'
   @ 13,50 GET mldepends PICT '99'
   @ 17,20 GET mlcursal PICT '999999'
   @ 17,46 GET mlraisedat PICT '@D'
   @ 17,66 GET mlraisepct PICT '99.9'
   @ 19,14 GET mljcode PICT 'XXX'
   @ 19,32 GET mldepart PICT 'XXXX'
   @ 19,51 GET mlsuperv PICT 'XXXXXXXXXXXXXXXXXX'
   READ
   kq=READKEY()
   DO CASE
      CASE (kq=15 .OR. kq=271)        && [Return]
         fq=-1
         readdoneq=.F.
         updatedq=IIF(kq=271 .OR. updatedq,.T.,.F.)
      OTHERWISE
         readdoneq=.T.
         DO emp_keyq
   ENDCASE
ENDIF
IF fq < 0
   EXIT
ENDIF
ENDDO
SET EXACT OFF
RETURN

*** END OF SECOND PROGRAM
```

Two New Packages

Just as I was finishing up the work on this book, two new software products hit the market that substantially improve *dBase III Plus*. It was already too late to go back and re-work the book to include these products in their appropriate places, but the products were too good not to mention. This appendix was included to give you, the reader, a brief synopsis of the products and what they can do. The first product is

The dBase Programmer's Utilities, published by Ashton-Tate and available from them for $89.95. The second product is *Tom Rettig's Library*, published by Tom Rettig Associates. The product is available for $99.95.

The *dBase* Programmer's Utilities

The dBase Programmer's Utilities consists of two sets of programs. The first set is the binary programs, with a .BIN file extension. They are designed to be used from within *dBase III Plus* (or the Developer's Release). These programs are first LOADed into RAM and then CALLed from within *dBase*. The *dBase* limit of 16 .BIN files is in effect. The second set is the object code files with a .OBJ extension. These files are the same as the assembly programs, use the same syntax, but have been modified to run with *Clipper* in the same way other *Clipper* program extensions run. You can run these utilities either from within *dBase*, or from *Clipper*. This represents a first for Ashton-Tate and is a welcome change of attitude.

    The dBase Programmer's Utilities is divided into three different sections, with different types of programs in each. The first section contains the modules that are for use inside *dBase III Plus* (or *Clipper*). The second set is *dBase* related DOS programs. The third set contains a collection of DOS programs that have nothing to do with *dBase* but are useful not only in the *dBase* environment, but also when working with the computer generally.

dBase Assembly Language Programs

A total of 15 different .BIN programs are provided with *The dBase Programmer's Utilities*. Depending on the environment that you are programming for, some will be more useful than others but, in general, all the programs are useful and worth having. Alphabetically they are:

    ADDFILES: This program allows you to extend the *dBase* limit of open files from 15 to 20. Depending on the complexity of your system and how you handle files, you may come up against the *dBase* 15 open files limit. If you have, you know that it can present a programming problem as you struggle to re-work your program structure and the number of open files and indexes to stay within this file limit. This program will allow you another five open files which should resolve these difficult situations. The *dBase* limit of ten open data files is still in effect, and this module does not work with *Clipper*.

BELL: This program allows you to change the bell tone and duration from the single tone that you get with CHR(7). You pass both the duration and frequency (in cycles per second) as parameters to this CALL. This will allow you to program several different tone messages into your applications which will provide the user with more information than a single tone can. Used with prudence, this can add immeasurably to the user interface.

BRIGHT/FADE: These two programs set the *entire* screen including color selections (as it is presented at the moment of the call) to either high or low intensity. Once changed to either BRIGHT or FADE, the individual differences in intensity are lost. The FADE works well to "throw" the entire screen into the background for new information written in a popup box, but only if you are prepared to re-write (or get rid of) the screens after the popup box is no longer needed.

CFILL: This program will fill the whole screen or a specified portion of it with a screen attribute instantly. The program writes directly to the screen buffer and does not affect the text that is on the screen at the time the comand is issued. Screen writing commands issued after CFILL has been CALLed will write over the area in the *dBase* set colors.

CHAR: This program is the same as CFILL except that a specific character is specified and, unlike CFILL, all data that was on the screen in the specified CHAR area will be overwritten.

CURSOR1 & CURSOR2: These two programs control the shape of the cursor on the screen. CURSOR1 allows you to specify the size and screen location (within the specific screen block) of the cursor. CURSOR2 allows you to turn the cursor off, or choose between a normal (line) or a block cursor.

DELAY: This program allows you to set a specific delay (measured in seconds) into your program. The routine works in seconds and is independent of computer clock speed. The old delay routine (a DO WHILE loop) used to delay a lot less on a PC AT than it did on a regular PC. This routine solves that problem.

MENUBAR: Ashton-Tate has their own version of the bounce bar menu. This one is different from the others in that the program simply moves a "light bar" over text that is defined prior to invoking the menu program. The defined text must be situated properly in a uniform manner on the screen and parameters indicating the number of choices, the number of columns, the space between each choice (horizontally) and the width of the light bar (as well as other information) must be passed to the menu program. The program returns the choice (selected either by hitting the carriage return or the **Escape** key) and the key that was used to select the choice. It appears that you must have each row of choices on adjacent lines. Empty lines are not handled by the program.

PPORT: This program allows you to select a parallel port, test for printer status, initialize an Epson printer or write directly to the device hooked up to the parallel port. Of all these options, the Status option is the most useful. It will tell you whether the printer is busy or not, whether it is selected, or out of paper. This makes testing for printer on-line much easier and more flexible than described in Chapter 6.

PROTECT: This program allows the developer to lock access to a *dBase* data table. The header is changed when PROTECT is in effect so that a person with a copy of *dBase* cannot open the file. The file must first be unlocked using the PROTECT call. The protection that this gives is better than nothing, but less than total: what is required to unlock the file is simply a copy of the program PROTECT.

SAVESCR: Ashton-Tate did something about *dBase III Plus*'s problem of saving screens. This program allows you to save and recall up to five screens. The screens can only be saved from the screen, they cannot be pre-loaded from disk files.

SOUNDEX: This program gives you the SOUNDEX code of character strings. (See Chapter 8 for a discussion of this subject.)

SPORT: SPORT is like PPORT except that the program will allow you to read information from the serial port as well as write to it.

DOS Programs for *dBase*

The dBase Programmer's Utilities includes three .EXE programs for use with *dBase* programs. DPROTECT.EXE is functionally the same as

PROTECT except that is works from DOS instead of within *dBase*. DXREF.EXE analyzes a specific *dBase III* program to check for simple errors in the program, a list of programs that are called by that program, a code listing with indentation, and cross reference tables for both symbols and programs. The last program included in this section is the DREPAIR.EXE program that may repair damaged *dBase III* files and recover some or all the lost records. The best protection (as stated in *The dBase Programmer's Utilities* as well as in this book) is to close files only to get information out of them or back into them. If however, you do have a damaged file, this program may be worth the price of the whole *The dBase Programmer's Utilities* package.

DOS Programs

There are 17 different DOS programs included with *The dBase Programmer's Utilities*. While they all appear to be useful, they do not have anything directly to do with *dBase*. Some appear to be very powerful and some may be dangerous at the same time. There is one interesting program, RM, that erases specified files and specified directories in one pass according to specified parameters. Used properly, this program will save you time and effort when you purge your hard disk. Used with less than total caution, it can wipe all data from your FAT and give you a day's work recovering files with Peter Norton's Utilities. As these programs really do not have anything directly to do with *dBase*, I will not comment on them here.

Tom Rettig's Library

Tom Rettig's Library approaches *dBase III* in a different manner: the main program, TRLIB.EXE is called from DOS and it, in turn calls *dBase*. The functions that are available within the library are then directly accessible from within *dBase*. The program requires about 90K of additional memory. Depending on your specific needs you may need even more memory than this (if you anticipate saving mulitple screens). The library contains 135 different functions that you can either add to the *dBase* language as procedures or by CALLing the appropriate .BIN file. The Library also contains five different stand-alone utilities that can be executed either from the DOS prompt or RUN from within *dBase*. Included with the programs is all the source code for the functions.

Those with the need (or interest) can go in and modify the source code for a specific purpose. Help is available from Tom Rettig Associates on a fee basis for specific modification requests. Help is available directly from the company for any functions included in the library either by telephone or by mail. The Library is also available for *Clipper* so the same functions can be included in compiled programs as well. The *Clipper* Library is sold separately for the same price of $99.95.

It is beyond the scope of this review to go into detail on each function, but there are many that may be of significant value to you in different environments. The ones that I consider to be more interesting will be mentioned by name.

The Library is broken down into 14 different areas. These areas and some of the interesting programs in each are:

BUSINESS: Included are several depreciation functions, a yield function, economic order quantity and a function to change a numeric string (Dollars and Cents) into a written out chracter string (Seventeen Dollars and Sixty-five Cents).

CHARACTER: Included are extensions of the AT( ) function, a centering and a capitalization function, a character count function, encryption and decryption of strings, right and left justification, and several other functions. Of real interest is a function called WRAP( ) which returns the value of the last blank space before a given line width. This function will allow you to do word wrapping of a long character string onto multiple lines without having to use the MEMO field and the SET MEMOWIDTH TO command.

DATABASE: Functions include a count of the number of fields, header size, index size calculation, a SOUNDEX routine and a street name index function that will index on the street name instead of the street number.

DATE: Date functions include several useful tools for working with Quarters, weeks (including weekend and weekday functions),months, and even one to see if the year in question is a leap year.

DEBUGGING: Two functions are included to help with debugging.

DISK: Functions are available to give you information on the current drive and directory, whether the drive is fixed, and whether the drive is a valid and operational drive.

LOGICAL: Two functions are included that determine if two different logical variables are either the same or different.

NUMERIC: Functions abound for converting numbers to different bases (including binary) logs (to various bases) exponentiation, roots, factorials, and other functions such as INFINITY( ) and MANTISSA( ) (for uses too daring to be put on paper).

PRINTER: Printer functions include ISPRINTER( ) (see Chapter 6 for *Clipper* explanation of this function) a function to swap parallel ports, a Top Of Form function and a printer screen function.

SCREEN: Screen functions in the library include a program to give you the current screen attribute, a scroll function that allows you to scroll only a portion of the screen, to functions to call from and save screens to disk, and a program to turn the cursor on and off.

Beyond these specific screen programs there are PEEK and POKE functions for a single character, a character string, a specific byte, an integer, an eight-byte floating-point, and entire screens to a specific memory address. The memory for these functions is reserved originally from the "Heap" that is set up when TRLIB.EXE is invoked. 4K bytes is set up as a default, but more may be specified (if your computer has the memory available). Specific memory addresses are set up using the ALLO-CATE( ) functions (see system functions) and then desired information is written to and read from these addresses. These functions appear to be quite flexible, but also appear to be ones whose use requires a certain degree of caution.

SYSTEM: The System function includes the allocation function mentioned above, plus functions to release memory allocated, change file attributes, read, write, or determine the size of a file, execute a ROM BIOS interrupt, and others. The manual also states that care should be taken when using these functions.

TIME: Time functions include a whole set of time conversion functions to change one form of time to others.

The stand-alone utilities included in Tom Rettig's Library include a bitstrip program that removes the high order bits from word processing files like WordStar, a memory reservation program, a CHKDSK-type memory checking program, a change file attribute program, and a program to find out the index key of an index file.

Tom Rettig's Library provides a vast extension to the *dBase III Plus* language. Several of the programs are extremely useful in that they save a tremendous amount of coding. I am looking forward to really getting in and working with the code. I suspect that I will be pleasantly surprised at some of the things that will become possible.

Index

User Interface Listings Available on Disk

If you like the programs in this book and find that you have use for them, you can send for the listings on diskette and avoid the problems of typing them in yourself and then having to correct them. All the listings and updates to both the listings and the reviews are available for $25.00 directly from Performance Dynamics Associates.

Send the order form below, specifying the disk size that you desire and a check or money order for $25.00 to the address listed. Please allow four to six weeks for delivery. No telephone orders or COD's please.

New York State residents must add 8.25% sales tax.

Send to: Performance Dynamics Associates
　　　　　306 Madison Ave., Suite 1420
　　　　　New York, NY 10165

　　　　　　　Attn: Disk Offer

Name: _____

Address: _____

City:　　　　　　　　　State:　　　　　Zip:

_____　　_____　　_____

Disk Size: 5-1/4": _____　　3-1/2": _____